Margins of the Market

THE CALIFORNIA WORLD HISTORY LIBRARY

Edited by Edmund Burke III, Kenneth Pomeranz, and Patricia Seed

Margins of the Market

TRAFFICKING AND CAPITALISM
ACROSS THE ARABIAN SEA

Johan Mathew

UNIVERSITY OF CALIFORNIA PRESS

University of California Press, one of the most distinguished university presses in the United States, enriches lives around the world by advancing scholarship in the humanities, social sciences, and natural sciences. Its activities are supported by the UC Press Foundation and by philanthropic contributions from individuals and institutions. For more information, visit www.ucpress.edu.

University of California Press
Oakland, California

Library of Congress Cataloging-in-Publication Data

Names: Mathew, Johan, author.
Title: Margins of the market : trafficking and capitalism across the Arabian
    Sea / Johan Mathew.
Description: Oakland, California : University of California Press, [2016] |
    Includes bibliographical references and index.
Identifiers: LCCN 2015046018 | ISBN 9780520288546 (cloth : alk. paper) |
    ISBN 9780520288553 (pbk. : alk. paper)
Subjects: LCSH: Smuggling—Arabian Sea. | Capitalism—Arabian
    Sea—History—19th century. | Capitalism—Arabian Sea—History—20th
    century. | Free trade—Arabian Sea—History—19th century. | Free trade—
    Arabian Sea—History—20th century. | Human smuggling—Arabian
    Sea. | Slave trade—Arabian Sea—History.
Classification: LCC HJ7033.5.Z5 M37 2016 | DDC 364.1/336091824—dc23
LC record available at http://lccn.loc.gov/2015046018

Manufactured in the United States of America

25 24 23 22 21 20 19 18 17 16
10 9 8 7 6 5 4 3 2 1

In keeping with a commitment to support environmentally responsible and sustainable printing practices, UC Press has printed this book on Natures Natural, a fiber that contains 30% post-consumer waste and meets the minimum requirements of ANSI/NISO Z39.48–1992 (R 1997) (*Permanence of Paper*).

To Mom and Dad

CONTENTS

ILLUSTRATIONS

MAPS

FIGURES

ACKNOWLEDGMENTS

A book that examines maritime trade and transnational merchants requires its own global diaspora of scholars, librarians, archivists, businesspeople, friends, and family. People across the globe have helped me in this endeavor, and it is impossible to adequately thank all of them for their contributions. For lack of space or knowledge, many I have relied upon remain unnamed, but please do not let my silence be mistaken for ingratitude. Others have made a special impact on me and on this book, so while it is poor recompense I would like to recognize and express my profound gratitude to them here.

This book depends on the merchant families that are at the heart of this history. First, Vimal Purecha has been exceedingly generous with his time, his hospitality, and his family history. Umesh Khimji, Usha Khimji, and their entire family were similarly open with their homes and memories. Shawqi Sultan, Redha Bhacker, Rajiv Ahuja, and Mohan Jashanmal all granted me important insights into the lives of merchants in the Gulf. Though I never had the pleasure of meeting him, Abdullah al-Ṭābūr's collection of merchant letters kept at the Jumʿa al-Mājid Library were an indispensable source of access to the lives of Khaleeji merchants.

Next, I'd like to thank both the institutions and the staffs of archives and libraries across the world. I began this work at Harvard's Widener Library and ended it at the University of Massachusetts's DuBois Library; both library systems and particularly their interlibrary loans were indispensable. In my research, I relied on the tireless assistance of myriad people at the British Library, particularly the staff of the Asian and African Studies Reading Room, the National Archives of the United Kingdom, the Guildhall Library, the Caird Library of the National Maritime Museum, the Middle East Centre Archive at St. Anthony's College, Oxford University, and the

Faculty of Middle East and Asian Studies, the Kings College Archive Centre, and the University Library at Cambridge University. In India, I am very much indebted to the staff at the Maharashtra State Archives, the National Archives of India, and the Mumbai University Library. I also thank the Center for Documentation and Research in Abu Dhabi and the Jumʿa al-Mājid Library in Dubai for their help. The staff at the Zanzibar National Archives were particularly helpful, and I must thank Seif and Omar for their enthusiasm and gracious hospitality. I'd also like to thank Judi Palmer for her efforts to help me secure the cover image for this book. I would especially like to express my appreciation to HSBC, the Standard Chartered Bank, and the P&O Heritage Collection for giving me permission to use their archives and those of their predecessors.

This book began as a dissertation at Harvard University, and it could not have been completed without the generous financial and institutional support provided by the History Department, the South Asia Initiative, the Asia Center, and the Weatherhead Center. I would particularly like to acknowledge generous funding from the Foreign Language and Area Studies Program, the John Clive Fellowship, the Merit/Term Time Fellowship, and the Harvard Academy for International and Area Studies. The dissertation was turned into a book manuscript while I was at the University of Massachusetts, Amherst. I thank the university and especially the departments of history and economics at UMass for their financial support, especially in allowing me to take research leave in just my second year on the job. Last, but certainly not least, I want to express my deep gratitude to the Inter-Asia Program of the Social Science Research Council for granting me their Postdoctoral Fellowship for Transregional Research. This book would not have existed without the generosity of all these institutions.

It has been a privilege to publish with the University of California Press. Niels Hooper, Bradley Depew, Jessica Moll, and Ryan Furtkamp have made the process smooth and painless. Elisabeth Magnus cleaned up my confused prose and Alexander Trotter created the wonderful index. Ritu Birla and John Willis read this as ultimately not very anonymous reviewers; their comments, suggestions, and critiques were deeply insightful and untied Gordian knots that I had been struggling with for years. I was fortunate to have three presses agree to review the manuscript simultaneously, and though I did not end up working with them I want to acknowledge the generous efforts of Lucy Rhymer at Cambridge University Press and Susan Ferber at Oxford University Press. Two more anonymous reviewers for Cambridge University Press and one anonymous reviewer at Oxford University Press gave similarly insightful and incisive comments for which I am immensely appreciative. Chapter 3 is a revised version of an article that appeared in *Slavery and Abolition* (vol. 33, no. 1, March 2012, pp. 139–56) under the title "Trafficking Labor: Abolition and the Exchange of Labor across the Arabian Sea, 1861–1947." I would like to thank the Taylor & Francis Group and the editors of *Slavery and Abolition* for generously agreeing to permit this revised publication, and the anonymous reviewers for their suggestions. This book is infinitely better as a result of this wide variety of editorial and reviewer feedback.

In writing a book one relies on the guidance and mentoring of many scholars. First, I have to thank my dissertation adviser, Roger Owen. Through many years and many permutations of this project he was always conscientious and attentive and helped me to move ever "onwards." Sugata Bose was always a skilled guide to the world of South Asian history, presiding over a movable feast of fine wine, delectable food, and stimulating intellectual debates. Engseng Ho has expanded my networks of scholarly interlocutors, prodded me to more rigorous analysis, and pushed me to plumb the conceptual depths of capitalism. Various chapters and sections of this book have been presented at a number of conferences and workshops, where I have received invaluable feedback. It would bore the reader to tears if I listed all of these events here, but a few participants and organizers deserve special mention: Gwyn Campbell, Prasenjit Duara, Katie Eagleton, Jeffrey Fear, Nelida Fuccaro, Arang Keshavarzian, Elizabeth Koll, Andrew Liu, Noora Lori, Matt Maclean, Nawaz Mody, Prasannan Parthasarathi, and Steven Serels. Extra gratitude goes to Laleh Khalili and David Ludden, who willingly read the entire manuscript, just as I was finishing the whole process. These scholars are responsible for many of the insights and contributions of this book, but I alone take responsibility for its failings.

From graduate school, through archives, classrooms, and various other locations, I have been fortunate to find numerous fellow travelers. At Harvard, Misha Akulov, Tariq Ali, Jesse Howell, Kuba Kabala, John Mathew, Sreemati Mitter, Ricardo Salazar, Henry Shapiro, Aleksander Sopov, Gitanjali Surendran, Heidi and Michael Tworek, and Jeremy Yellen all distracted me from what I should have been doing. Research can be an isolating experience, where one communes only with dead bureaucrats and archive-inhabiting insects, but I was fortunate to have friends and family everywhere I went. On the road, I was lucky to share archival dust and many a libation with Fahad Bishara, Rohit De, Jatin Dua, Derek Elliot, Chhaya

Goswami, Fanar Haddad, Shekhar Krishnan, Simon Layton, Pedro Machado, and Dodie McDow. My diasporic family is at the core of this whole endeavor, but particular parts of it literally provided a home away from home. I am grateful to Nalini Mama, Sunny Uncle, Nithya and Sandhya, Vinay, Anina and Vianne, Susan Auntie and Aby Uncle, Rebecca Auntie, Brian and Anu Kochamma, Suzie Kochamma and Joey Chayan, Rekha Auntie, Geo Uncle, Reuben, and Rahael.

At the Five Colleges I have benefited from the food, wine, and conversations with Nusrat Chowdhury, Kavita Datla, Pinky Hota, Yael Rice, Dwaipayan Sen, Uditi Sen, and Krupa Shandilya. It has been my distinct pleasure to work with and learn from Laura Doyle, Mwangi wa Githinji, Jocelyn Almeida-Beveridge, and Annette Lienau as part of the World Studies Interdisciplinary Project. The UMass history department has been a wonderful scholarly home, and Joye Bowman, Anne Broadbridge, Julio Capo, Richard Chu, Sarah Cornell, Jose Angel Hernandez, Jennifer Heuer, John Higginson, Jason Moralee, Brian Ogilvie, Jon Olsen, Sam Redman, Emily Redman, Heidi Scott, Priyanka Srivastava, and Mary Wilson have been exemplary colleagues. Michael Ash, Gerald Friedman, Carol Heim, Leonce Ndikumana, and Vamsi Vakulabharanum have shown me the light of heterodox economics. My participation in these many scholarly worlds in the Pioneer Valley has profoundly enriched this book.

No one has had a greater role in this book than Julie Stephens. At every step from conceptualization, to research, to writing, to researching again and rewriting, she has been my most cogent critic and reassuring supporter. Julie has endured this book through its darkest depths and enjoyed the never-quite compensating highs. Her devoted companionship despite my crankiness was the only reason this work could ever come to fruition. Along the way we went from strangers to partners in crime; I am still not sure how I got so lucky.

Finally, there is my family, who has suffered me the longest. It is embarrassing to think how my brother, Vikram, was the firm anchor who counseled me even as his own life was tested by far more significant challenges. My father and mother, Varkey and Miriam John Mathew, were a source of constant concern, support, and love despite my often obscure problems and impenetrable silences. They shared with me the long diasporic history of my family stretching from Kerala back to first-century Syria. Then they carted me along from Bombay to Riyadh to New York and now to Hong Kong. By sheer accumulation of air miles they have laid down the tracks that led me to these pages. So it is to my parents that I dedicate this book.

NOTE ON TERMS AND TRANSLITERATION

In this book, I have assumed that the reader is not familiar with the many languages used around the Arabian Sea. Wherever they exist, I use common English spellings for words in languages other than English. When there is a direct citation from a source text, I use the transliterations in the source text. For Arabic and Persian terms and phrases that I transliterate myself I have used the *International Journal of Middle East Studies* system. Transliterations from Gujarati, Urdu/Hindi, Swahili, and so on are largely from the texts themselves. Place-names are transliterated as they would have been in the historical period (e.g., Kutch instead of Kachchh and Bombay instead of Mumbai). Given the controversy over the naming of the Arabian/Persian Gulf, I have chosen to use the generic term *the Gulf* except when quoting or referring directly to the archival sources. As will become clear in chapter 4, it would be a hopeless task to attempt to provide even a rough contemporary value for the currencies used around the Arabian Sea in this period.

Introduction

Capital cannot abide a limit.[1] The incessant drive for profit pushes business-men and corporations to overcome all barriers to growth. Taxes are mini-mized, regulations are circumvented, and borders are turned into endless frontiers for expansion. According to this logic, smuggling is the ultimate form of free trade.[2] No less an authority than Adam Smith absolved smug-glers of their crimes, stating: "The smuggler is a person who, though no doubt blamable for violating the laws of his country, is frequently incapable of violating those of natural justice."[3]

Smuggling in various forms occurs thousands of times each day at border crossings, train stations, container ports, and airports across the world. These crimes are so pervasive as to make them a rather mundane part of our exis-tence. The global economy is riddled with the impacts of undocumented transactions, from neglecting to report your earnings from tips to your bank's neglecting to report that it was manipulating interest rates. Furthermore, it seems that every day we hear new revelations concerning the misdeeds of corporations, politicians, and ordinary individuals. Yet even as we are perfectly aware of these activities, we continue to assume that illicit trade occupies a shadowy and sinister world totally separate from our own.

If our global economy is rampant with illicit activity, should we conclude that trafficking is the perfection of free trade? Or does trafficking cross some fundamental limit, making trafficking the perversion of free trade? Or is it somehow both simultaneously? Despite Smith's endorsement of smuggling, some types of illicit trade do seem to violate natural justice. Certain traffics frighten and disgust us; they bring into question not merely the wisdom of certain laws but whole systems of morality. Traffics in children, biological weapons, or terrorist financing seem to be not so much a natural extension of free markets as something that undermines the existential bases of capitalism itself. Trafficking, then, is trade that transgresses the conceptual limits of capitalism. Adam Smith, Karl Marx, and many others have argued that concepts like free labor or private property rights are basic requirements of capitalist political economy. Trades that subvert these concepts of free labor or property rights violate the fundamental boundaries of free markets. However, while we can define these capitalist concepts in theory, it is far more difficult to enforce them in the real world. In practice, government bureaucrats are responsible for defining and policing these limits of capitalism. Moreover, traders are constantly engaged in traffics that bend and break these conceptual limits. In this sense, capitalism is not the same thing across space and time; it diverges from theory as traders and bureaucrats contest the boundaries of the free market. This book argues that this contestation over the boundaries of the market is constitutive of capitalism itself.

Scholars have traced how capital vanquishes the limits erected by political systems, human cultures, and the natural world. Yet if capital cannot abide these external limitations, it must constantly struggle with the boundaries that are integral to capitalist exchange. These conceptual boundaries are the framework of free markets: they turn slaves into labor, guns into property and coins into capital.[4] This book examines these transformations by tracing the entangled histories of trafficking and capitalism in the Arabian Sea. I explore how these practices were once the same and how they became different over the course of the late nineteenth and early twentieth centuries. But to trace these limits and frameworks we must first abandon our conventional assumptions about space and time and try to see the world a little more like a trafficker.

SPACE AND TIME

The ocean seems largely insignificant to modern life. While an ever increasing number of commodities cross the oceans, ever fewer human beings are needed to move these massive cargoes from port to port. Previous generations knew the salt and spray, the waves and winds, the turbulence and monotony of maritime travel. The sea is all but vanished today, little more than something to look at from the window seat of your airplane. Maps paint the sea a homogeneous blue, a vacant space between continents. Yet this space looks rather different from the perspective of the trafficker or anyone looking to evade political authority. Traffickers pay close attention to the winds and waves. To them, the sea is not an empty space that must be crossed as quickly as possible but rather a space of overlapping connections and hidden opportunities. To understand the Arabian Sea from the perspective of the trafficker we must not look from the "God's eye view" of the latest satellite images but from the more constrained but mobile view of a sailor from the deck of a ship.[5] There is perhaps no better place to find this perspective than in the writings of the ancients.

The *Periplus of the Erythraean Sea* is a pithy, unvarnished sailing manual written by an Alexandrine merchant around the first century of the Common Era. The *Periplus* is not a map. It does not provide a simple visual representation or precise measurements of distance. Nor does it give a synchronic image of a fixed space. Rather, we are given a tour through a dense and complex trading network: an immense diversity of languages, cultures, polities, and of course trading goods. The Erythraean (Red) Sea is not a clearly defined geographic entity; indeed, what we now think of as the Red Sea occupies only the first few paragraphs of the text. Most of the *Periplus* describes ports down the Swahili coast, across southern Arabia and India, and as far east as China. It describes a *littoral,* which refers to the stretches of coast that outline a body of water, rather than bounding a landmass.[6] The *Periplus* is not a dispassionate account; it does not abstract objective scientific truths about geography. Rather, the author teaches the reader how best to experience and engage a heterogeneous network that is tied together by the predictable alternation of the monsoon winds. The *Periplus* is an itinerary through a maritime world, replete with advice on when to travel, what to buy, and who to avoid.[7]

This book engages with the Arabian Sea in a similar manner. You will not find in the following pages a sweeping grand narrative of the Arabian Sea as a geological, environmental, and social entity. Many historians of the Indian Ocean world have tried to find the structural contours of the ocean and to trace the shared cultures that unified this maritime world.[8] However, this is not a history *of* the Arabian Sea as a coherent unit of space but multiple entangled histories of trafficking and capitalism *in* the Arabian Sea.[9] The Arabian Sea depicted here is consequently a network of traffics: it was an uneven, crowded, and dynamic environment full of dangers and opportunities. While there are (hopefully useful) maps in the following pages, the accompanying text should unsettle the synchronic and simplified representations they produce. Merchants crossed the Arabian Sea in complex and shifting itineraries that cannot be reduced to lines on a map. It was precisely by being unpredictable, flexible, and antisystemic that traffics could flourish in a world of increasingly powerful states.

While there were shared customs around the coasts of the Arabian Sea, the trade that really connected these populations was premised on difference. Only with different goods and diverse skills can we barter, truck, and exchange. The littoral was incredibly diverse, and travels across the sea were as generative of differences as they were of unities.[10] Three major world regions meet in this body of water, and while this led to intermixing and cosmopolitanism it also led to xenophobia and violence. The Arabian Sea is such a unique space to study because it was shaped both by enormous heterogeneity and by dense connectivity. As a result, the Arabian Sea brings into relief those exchanges that have been occluded by narratives of capitalism and empire. European capital and empires appear to have severed these waters into separate territories. Yet these empires were ill equipped to monitor, much less control, the traffics that rode these waves. The space of the Arabian Sea is easy on travelers, profitable for traders, and exasperating for bureaucracies, and as a result it is particularly conducive to a study of trafficking. We will follow these traffickers to stitch together a picture of the networks that subverted and connected colonial markets.

The heterogeneity of the Arabian Sea also leaves us with another problem: the dimension of time. A homogeneous space makes it possible to tell a linear narrative, whereas the Arabian Sea confounds any attempt to find a linear or progressive history. The chronology of events in each port is divergent, as is the history of each commodity or diaspora. They are interdependent but do not march to the same tune. Trafficking, in particular, confounds the desire for a smooth narrative. The opportunistic quality of traffics lends a simultaneously erratic and repetitive rhythm to the events recounted here. New laws were met with new methods of evasion, which elicited even stronger laws and more ingenious evasions. The cycle then repeated itself ad nauseum. The reader may experience a little seasickness as the ensuing narrative jumps from one port to another or back and forth in time. However, discontinuities and reversals are reflective of the rhythms of trafficking. This syncopated tempo was one of the mechanisms by which traffickers subverted the seamless narrative of a transition to capitalism.[11] Ultimately, there was a slow but perceptible change over time in which empires and capitalism entrenched themselves in the Arabian Sea, but this transformation was iterative, sporadic, and deeply contingent.

The short century from the 1860s to the 1950s is often associated with the transition to capitalism in Asia and Africa. So it is a particularly appropriate period to study how capitalism was manifested through the progressive elision of trafficking. These decades also marked the only period in the history of the Arabian Sea that one political entity was clearly dominant. From the sixteenth century onward, the Portuguese, Ottoman, Mughal, Safavid, and Omani Empires struggled for dominance. Only in the 1860s did the British Empire break up Omani power and comfortably dominate these waters. Britain did have to accommodate German and French colonies, Qajar and Ethiopian imperial influence, and the autonomy of various petty sheikhs and nawabs around the littoral. Nevertheless, only the British Navy sought to patrol the high seas and could exercise its influence along the entire littoral. Whereas other polities tended to turn a blind eye to trafficking, the British Empire consistently worked to monitor, identify, and suppress trafficking. This lasted until the 1960s, when Cold War competition provided massive incentives to smuggling on both sides and little interest in regulation.

Moreover, the British Empire brought with it a political economy that started to transform the common usage of the word *trafficking*. While *trafficking* has been used in English from the sixteenth century, it had the wider meaning of any exchange of goods or movement of people through a particular space. Only by the late nineteenth century did trafficking start to signify a trade that exceeded the moral bounds of the market.[12] While states have probably suppressed smuggling from time immemorial, trafficking is tied to the ideology of free trade. It became essential to prevent traffics in slaves, weapons, and currency, precisely when free trade was most comprehensively embraced. I use the term *trafficking* in this sense, referring not simply to smuggling but to trades that undermined the foundations of capitalism. Britain's "empire of free trade" was thus the prime mover in defining and segregating trafficking from free trade. The imperial apogee of the late nineteenth and early twentieth centuries heralded the "first wave" of modern globalization and supposedly completed the integration of Asia and Africa into the Europe-centered world system.[13] Yet by straddling different empires, trafficking networks were well placed to exploit the gaps and contradictions between imperial regulation and economic life. The period from the 1860s to the 1950s was when trafficking in the Arabian Sea became an existential threat to free trade, and consequently it is the ideal period to examine their entangled histories.

FRAMING THE FREE MARKET

During the early nineteenth century, trade in the Arabian Sea was diverse and disparate. It involved monopolistic trading companies, empires, diasporas, pirates, and slaves. It was a world in which various different groups exercised power but no single state was sovereign. This was trade that operated without regulation, at least in our contemporary understanding of the term. Of course violence, monopolies, and customs all presented obstacles and constraints on exchange.[14] Merchant networks overcame these difficulties by organizing their exchange through family ties, personal networks, and religious law.[15] The British East India Company imposed monopolies and violence as a powerful state in South Asia and as a trading company operating through different diasporic agents.[16] But by 1858 the last vestiges of the East India Company were disbanded and the mercantilist policies with which it was associated were sloughed off.

If the East India Company of the mid-nineteenth century maintained only the veneer of a trading enterprise, the British Raj had no truck with trading. Rather, the British Empire was the protector and police of trade. In the middle of the nineteenth century, it was infamous for enforcing free trade policies through gunboat diplomacy. There were plenty of British gunboats in the Arabian Sea, but they were not forcing rulers to open their borders to trade or reduce tariff barriers. In fact, rulers along the Arabian Sea littoral were generally open to foreign trade and had relatively low tariffs. British gunboats were in the Arabian Sea to find contraband and regulate traders. Thus in the Arabian Sea free trade ideology was actually implemented through intervention in markets and the abolition of certain trades.

British officials justified this hypocrisy by insisting that certain trades were beyond the pale. The liberal dilemma was how to limit freedom when it impinged on the freedoms of other market participants and free trade where it breached the boundaries of the market itself. What particularly elicited the repression of British authorities was trading in arms, slaves, and gold. These three trades corresponded to three key concepts in political economy. For Adam Smith, land, labor and capital were the basic factors of production.[17] For Karl Marx, land, labor, and capital were the trinity of secrets that undergirded social production under capitalism.[18] For Karl Polanyi, land, labor, and capital were the fictitious commodities through which the market was disembedded from society.[19] In the trading world of the Arabian Sea, I would like to suggest that these three commodities are again central, though they appear in a different form.

On terra firma, the history of capitalism has been traced as the incorporation of land, labor, and capital into the market, but a maritime perspective inverts this history. What we witness in the Arabian Sea is less an effort to produce free labor, private property, and interest-bearing capital, and more an effort to decommodify human beings, violence, and money. This was a maritime world in which landed property did not exist, factories could not function, and governments could not assert territorial sovereignty. The sheer immensity of the sea, the fierce power of its waves, and the opacity of its waters made the sea impossible to control. Bureaucratic techniques could not organize this space, and the market could not bring order to those who crossed it.[20] The Arabian Sea was a space of trade and exchange but not a space of production and consumption. The work of framing the market on land was consequently inverted in the Arabian Sea.

It is most obvious that abolishing the slave trade was the inverse of producing wage labor as a commodity. Somewhat more confusing is the necessity of decommodifying money. In the Arabian Sea, different monies competed with each other and fluctuated wildly. Yet in classical political economy money needed a stable value so that it could function as a standard of price for other commodities. The international gold standard was consequently an effort to decommodify monies by affixing their values to the price of gold. Only when money itself was a stable standard of value could capital become a commodity to be priced by the market. Most obscure perhaps is the relationship between weapons and property. Landed property is absent from the sea, but there were vast quantities of private property in the form of commodities moving across the waves. The key concern for property owners was to secure possession of this property against the private violence wielded by pirates. The elimination of piracy was the basic requirement for security of private property. Firearms, though, were simultaneously property and violence. So it was through the regulation of firearms that officials had to complete the process of securing property rights by decommodifying violence.

Following the work of Michel Callon, we might then call these problematic commodities *intermediaries*. Callon describes intermediaries as those objects, people, or ideas that both frame and overflow a market. He persuasively argues that the act of framing always implies an overflowing: a wider context that is being pushed out of view. With a little reflection, it becomes obvious that a picture frame is an intermediary because it simultaneously closes off and connects the picture inside the frame to the world outside the frame.[21] This book argues that human bodies, firearms, and coins are the key intermediaries that both frame and overflow the free market. Wage labor, private property, and capital are within the market, while slavery, violence, and counterfeits are outside the market.

For many social theorists, markets are constantly expanding and the imperative of capitalists (and neoclassical economists) is to bring ever more of the social world into the calculative domain of the market. What the trading world of the Arabian Sea reveals to us is something quite different: here the *expulsion* of certain trades was the foundational work of free market capitalism. I'd like to refer to this process as *framing out*. *Framing out* suggests that the process of expulsion was just as integral to the emergence of the free market as processes of enframing. *Framing out* is not quite the same as *overflowing*, which connotes an unintentional excess or the inevitable slippages in economists' efforts to enframe the market. Instead, it connotes a concerted effort on the part of bureaucracies to push certain practices outside the calculations of markets.

As it occurred in the Arabian Sea, framing out involved three intertwined processes: division, elision, and suppression. Those commodities, transactions, and practices that undermined the foundational assumptions of capitalism had to be identified and divided off from those that could be incorporated within the free market. This was not a simple or straightforward process. As you will see in the following chapters, it was exceedingly difficult to distinguish between a slave and an adopted child, a sporting rifle and a military rifle, or a genuine and a counterfeit coin. Customs authorities were constantly struggling to discern who was following the regulations and who was subverting them. The division of the licit from the illicit was thus imprecise and arbitrary.

Once these illicit trades were identified, they needed to be elided from the marketplace. Contraband frequently flowed through exactly the same physical spaces as licit commodities. Indeed, the same object might be licit in some hands and illicit in others. Nevertheless, illicit transactions had to become invisible to the operation of the market. Colonial authorities were obviously aware of illicit activities, but this knowledge was siphoned into the domain of crime and policing. The market could appear free and self-regulating precisely because bureaucracies concerned with the economy were walled off from bureaucracies concerned with law and order. Finally, colonial bureaucracies recorded, calculated, and published statistics as if licit and illicit trade occupied distinct worlds. In this way, illicit transactions were elided from free markets.

Last, but not least, empires and navies employed substantial force to suppress these illicit trades. Naval cruisers, police officers, and customs agents were all deployed to capture and punish merchants who subverted trading regulations. The armed forces of different states confiscated contraband, imposed fines, imprisoned traffickers, engaged in pitched battles with traders, and sank ships with their cargo and crew on board. Colonial authorities invested time, resources, and manpower to eradicate trafficking networks, yet it was a never-ending process. The traffics that could not be eradicated were subject to forms of coercion and violence that placed them beyond the pale of trade. The institutions that were supposed to structure market transactions were in fact responsible for segregating and harassing trade that did not conform to capitalist models.

Division, elision, and suppression were not distinct or sequential processes but were inseparable. Moreover, these processes powerfully shaped what was occurring within the frame of the market. In his genealogy of governmentalities, Michel Foucault suggests that modern, liberal governmentality takes this form. He argues that as the freedom of the market became the central aim of governance, government policies turned to managing civil society in order to produce free markets.[22] To put it a different way, by determining what was pushed outside the frame of the market and what happened there, bureaucracies could shape a particular kind of freedom within the market. Thus framing out is not just the overflow of efforts to integrate the world into the market but the structuring of market freedoms through intensive interventions at the margins of the market.

The concept of framing out highlights the visual and descriptive aspects of political economy. But it does not presume that these descriptions are linguistic or quantitative representations separate from physical reality. Michel Callon's discussion of framing/overflowing is part of a wider range of scholarly debates over the "performativity of economics." For Callon and others, economics is a description of reality that intervenes in that reality: it arranges and organizes the world in such a way that its descriptions are validated. However, there remains considerable dispute over the extent to which "economists make markets" and the conditions under which this might occur.[23] This scholarship, then, does not present a critique of economics as a discipline so much as a critique of its claims to be a purely descriptive science. These scholars are primarily concerned with tracing how economic models and concepts shape the world we live in.

This book builds on these notions of performativity, yet "economics" does not quite capture the ideas presented here. Economics as a positivistic science largely emerges in the second half of the twentieth century along with the neoclassical consensus.[24] In the nineteenth century, however, it would be almost tautological to suggest that political economy was trying to shape the world. The writings of Smith and Ricardo were examinations of human society explicitly developed to promote certain policies and reshape the state's relationship with the market. By the late nineteenth century, economists took a step back from this prescriptive mode and focused more on detailed quantitative studies of markets. Yet this new emphasis on quantitative measures intervened in markets in a more subtle way. Customs houses, statistical officers, and revenue collectors demanded new information from traders and in new formats. While trade statistics had been collected for centuries, in the late nineteenth century statistical categories and statistical analysis gained greater influence over trading practice and the determination of state policies.[25] Economists continued to follow diverse methodologies, but the increasing availability of statistics and the success of econometric analysis would eventually lead in the middle of the twentieth century to the neoclassical consensus and a unified conception of "the economy" as an object of study.[26]

Consequently, in the period before we can speak of economics as a unified discipline, we need some alternative term to label the new concepts that were starting to pervade the trading world of the Arabian Sea. I employ the term *capitalism* despite the fact that it is so freighted with meaning and can be so multivalent as to preclude any analytical value. Capitalism means something different to Marxist scholars, world systems theorists, liberal social theorists, and others. I find compelling the critique that capitalism is somehow omnipresent and yet everywhere limited and uneven, or that it explains everything and consequently nothing.[27] Yet what if, instead of insisting that capitalism describes a bounded and comprehensive economic system, we utilize the term to refer to a performative set of ideas? Capitalism in this sense need not be internally coherent or analytically precise but rather indicates a loose set of ideas concerning free labor, property rights, monetized exchange, and competitive markets. To the extent that these ideas were adopted by government officials, were utilized in markets, and shaped trading practice across the world, we might consider them performative. Performativity also suggests that there are always exceptions and slippages, so these categories are maintained only through constant repetition and reiteration.[28] In this sense, capitalism was performative in the trading world of the Arabian Sea in the late nineteenth and early twentieth centuries.

Within the Arabian Sea we witness, not the perfect implementation of political-economic theories, but a far messier performance of these ideas filtered through the heuristics and preoccupations of colonial officials. These officials imbibed the ideas of classical and marginalist political economy in an often vague and haphazard way. Their understanding of monetary theory or marginal utility was often simplistic and imprecise; nevertheless, they were responsible for implementing regulations based on these ideas. Colonial bureaucrats were supposedly recording transparent knowledge about market prices, but they had to intervene in each transaction to elicit information about buyers, sellers, prices, and conditions. Customs officials extracted information from traders and translated complex trading relationships into simple and standardized market transactions. These transactions were then quantified, aggregated, and calculated to produce market prices that were not otherwise visible and market forces that were not otherwise operative. This information was then publicized as representing market conditions that traders should act upon. These practices of perceiving and representing the market thus shaped how traders interacted with colonial states and with each other.

The transformations detailed in the following pages involve the increasing penetration and hegemony of capitalist categories, yet this process never reaches completion. Among colonial officials and in their documentation, capitalist concepts became hegemonic, and they could dismiss the diversity of economic life as aberrations and anachronisms that would inevitably be integrated into the capitalist system.[29] These officials characterized slavery, piracy, and commodity monies as anachronistic holdovers, and economists began to see the family firm and barter arrangements as the vestiges of a precapitalist world. This periodization of trading practices was part of the performance of capitalism that this book seeks to unveil. In framing out diverse exchange relations as illicit and anachronistic we can see the constant iterative work that naturalized the categories and temporalities of capitalism.

CONTRIVANCE AND ARBITRAGE

Yet this was not a simple or uncontested process; the performativity of capitalist categories required the cooperation of multiple parties with varied incentives. Most importantly, the measurement of exchange relied on the truthfulness of traders as well as their inclination to translate their practices into the conventions of commercial statistics. Merchant networks recognized the importance of these measurements and quickly learned how to represent their transactions *as if* they operated within the rules of the market. These contrived forms of compliance were pervasive. Merchants complied with the letter of the law or documented their transactions as conventional exchanges. But they also subverted the intentions of the law or concealed practices that strayed from the standard documentary formats. Long before any social scientist, these merchants recognized and exploited the performativity of economic concepts in their trading world.

My use of the term *contrivance* builds on the theoretical frameworks developed by Michel de Certeau. De Certeau's theorization of "tactics" reveals the dispersed and clandestine creativity of individuals caught up in structures of discipline and suggests that their methods of "using the system" are central to understanding everyday life.[30] His exposition allows us to see how the strategies deployed by systems were entangled in the tactics improvised by those caught within these systems. The process of *framing out* that I have outlined so far was constantly interrupted and redirected by the traffics that were ostensibly expunged from the market. Traffickers bent frameworks, blurred borders, and expanded loopholes, thus affecting the structure of the free market. As many others have argued, power is relational, and those subjected to capital are constantly working to engage, co-opt, and domesticate it.[31]

These ways of "using" the system have been around for millennia, long before the disciplinary frameworks of colonialism. Scholars have studied the early controversies over *ḥiyal* (ruses or maneuvers) in the development of Islamic law. *Ḥiyal* refers to legal contrivances that allowed merchants to circumvent some of the constraints of the *Sharia*. While there was some dispute over the morality of these contrivances, they were generally condoned in juridical practice.[32] This highlights the fact that loopholes are often the most frequently utilized clauses in legislation. It is precisely by occupying the margins of categories that businesses squeeze out their competitive edge. Laws structured trade across the Arabian Sea, but merchants determined which spaces within the law were most heavily utilized. This feedback loop, in which regulations produce circumventions that are in turn incorporated into legal structures, is crucial to the history of capitalism across the Arabian Sea.[33]

Trafficking networks were particularly attuned to the loopholes in law and the hidden margins of conceptual categories because they operated across multiple jurisdictions. It was precisely the movement of merchants across territories that rendered slightly different framings of the market visible. Capitalist markets were defined by the bureaucracies that governed them and the territories that they encompassed. The British Empire may have dominated the Arabian Sea, but it directly administered a comparatively small portion of its coastline. Different political economies influenced policies in independent states like Ethiopia and Muscat, as well as in colonies like Portuguese Goa and French Djibouti. Moreover, there were substantial variations in colonial rule between British colonies like India and Somaliland and between territories administered by British officials, like Aden, and those administered by subordinate princes, like Kutch. So trafficking networks were able to identify and exploit subtle differences in documentary regimes or the implementation of regulations.

Traffickers were engaged, not in equal exchanges within a market, but in exchanges that profited from the differences between markets. In a word, trafficking networks were engaged in *arbitrage*. Arbitrage takes advantage of a difference in price for the same good in different markets.[34] Trading networks across the Arabian Sea were acutely aware of opportunities for arbitrage arising from differences in climate, season, culture, and urbanization. In the nineteenth and twentieth centuries they were increasingly attuned to differences in regulation, forms of documentation, statistics, and economic calculation. Trafficking networks selected which regulations to follow and filled out documentation to take maximum advantage of the variations in enforcement around the Arabian Sea littoral.

In economic theory, arbitrage is supposed to be evanescent because market participants quickly move to buy where prices are low and sell where prices are high. This should cause cheap markets to become more expensive as demand rises and expensive markets to become cheaper as supply increases, resulting in equalized prices. However, arbitrageurs in the Arabian Sea did not seem to bring about the same price coordination. Differences persisted, and diasporic merchants tended to see these differences as a resource to be cultivated and sustained.[35] The equalizing exchanges of free markets were performed for the benefit of colonial officials even as they were overdetermined by power differentials. Merchants documented their commodities at local market prices and then secretly bought below or sold above those prices. Markets around the Arabian Sea did not integrate because trafficking networks produced documentation that satisfied regulators without fully revealing the details of their transactions.[36] Competition was evaded because prices were hidden. Capitalist ideology framed transactions within its categories, but merchants also arranged their business to exploit the ambiguities in those categories.

The contrivances and arbitrage of trafficking networks were documented as licit transactions that were aggregated and analyzed as part of the free market. The transformation of diasporic exchanges into free trade was the result of merchant networks adapting to new regimes of documentation. But as these measures became important indicators of the progress of colonized societies, the fiscal rectitude of colonial governments, or the success of British trade, they also became compromised. Scholars have noted that the more a statistical measure becomes used for decision making, the greater the incentives are to subvert that measurement and the more likely it is that the measurement will distort the very processes it is supposed to measure.[37] To put it simply: people learn how to game the system. Merchants were anxious to have their transactions sanctioned by the British Empire and consequently arranged their transactions to exploit the ambiguities in regulatory categories. The free markets that emerged across the Arabian Sea were consequently framed both by the categories of capitalism and by the manipulations of trafficking networks.

It is worth noting that trafficking networks were not engaged in heroic resistance and are not necessarily something to celebrate. These merchants were not fighting the system or defending their way of life against the onslaught of colonialism or capitalism. Theirs was a form of accommodation and acceptance, but one that manipulated these new forms of trade and regulation to their own advantage. These merchants were exploiting peasants, enslaving children, and profiting from violence, but they were also subverting colonial governments and usurping capitalist profits. Contrivance and arbitrage are not something to celebrate, but they are nevertheless vital to understanding the history of capitalism and colonialism.

SOUNDS OF SILENCE

A merchant approached the eminent jurist Abdullah al-Sālimī and asked him whether it was correct for a foreign ruler to prohibit the export of goods or money from his country. Al-Sālimī was a Muslim jurist of the Ibāḍi tradition in Oman, so he explored this question as the ethical problem of addressing difficulties arising outside the scope of one's knowledge. Al-Sālimī opined that one could not know the needs of absent others, so it was correct for a person to prohibit the export of goods to another country if there was a real need for them in his own. He took the opposite stance in the case of wealth, because it was through the expenditure of money that scarcities were alleviated. In support of this opinion, he quoted a passage from the Quran stating that the poor had a right to the money of the wealthy.[38] Al-Sālimī thus parsed Islamic law to argue that in both cases the needs of one's countrymen took precedence over the needs of absent others.

This is a rather remarkable entry in the fatwa collection of Imam al-Sālimī. We are given wonderful insights into his legal reasoning and notions of political economy. We see a certain privileging of the local and an understanding of money as legally distinct from other trading goods. But al-Sālimī's fatwa opens up more questions than it answers. It is written in the abstract language characteristic of fatwa collections, so the specific circumstances of this merchant and his motivations are concealed from the reader.[39] There are tantalizing hints where al-Sālimī states that the prohibitor need not actually be from the country where he prohibits the export of goods. Could the merchant be asking about British officials in India? The fatwa uses the ambiguous phrase "the administrator of his money/wealth" (*mutaṣarrif bi mālihi*), which leaves open whether this is a wealthy merchant holding onto his capital or an official protecting a national currency. Does the discussion of absent others indicate the argument that a more pressing need in another country might override this prohibition? Indeed, is this merchant seeking sanction in the *Sharia* to smuggle goods against a foreign legal prohibition?

This study, like Imam al-Sālimī, is afflicted with the problem of the absent and unknown. We are trying to follow people who wanted to be inconspicuous and transactions that were designed to be opaque. Even businessmen engaged in perfectly legitimate activities did not generate or preserve detailed records because these would only proliferate the possibilities for lawsuits. So it would seem that there would be barely any trace of trafficking in the historical record. I found, quite to the contrary, that if you just look in the wrong places, trafficking has generated some of the most richly detailed records on economic life. It is merely necessary to read silence not as absence but as an indication of particular kinds of commercial and documentary practice. The letter that suggests continuing the conversation in person and away from prying eyes, the reliable evidence of a shipment that somehow disappears into thin air, the suspicious silhouette on a vessel that cannot be searched: none of these provide incontrovertible proof of illicit activity. However, they are silences that speak to patterns of concealment, evasiveness, and subversion of documentary regimes. Indeed, while they do not *prove* anything, they nonetheless indicate the success of trafficking. Silences and slippages in documentation are poor evidence in a courtroom, but they speak volumes.[40]

Historians of smuggling invariably apologize for the erratic nature of their archives, and economic historians more generally bemoan the lack of consistent quantitative data. Economists of smuggling, though, have long read the gaps in quantitative data as quantifiable evidence of smuggling.[41] While one might disagree with their conclusions, there is merit in the impulse to read into these silences. I came to this topic precisely because I was looking for a cultural archive of exchange in the Indian Ocean but found only quantitative data in colonial economic records. Only when desperation pushed me to look beyond these bureaucratic boundaries, did I stumble upon the prolific records of trade that exceeded the frame of the market. Police surveillance, court transcripts, and regulatory memoranda produced detailed, almost ethnographic accounts of trafficking. This highlights the extent to which the colonial archive is strategically silent.[42] The bounty of quantitative documentation renders invisible the sociocultural relationships that ordered transactions and accentuates the aggregate forces of market competition. The bounty of qualitative documentation on trafficking conceals the impact and extent of trafficking within the market. The silences of the colonial archive speak most eloquently to the framing out of the free market.

Records produced by imperial businesses provide another perspective on this process. Business records reveal the extent to which white skins and posh accents concealed far more diverse and complex methods of profit making. On the one hand, these firms relied heavily on government contracts, monopolies, and regulation to maintain their position as capitalists. On the other hand, colonial businesses depended on diasporic merchants to access local consumers. Personnel files, petitions, letters, and contracts reveal how the operations of reputable colonial firms were underwritten by "Asiatic" business practices. Far from disciplining local merchants to the superior efficiencies of capitalist production, colonial businesses profited by putting a capitalist face on imperial patronage and diasporic arbitrage.

One might then assume that vernacular documents provide an authentic voice for colonized populations. However, vernacular sources are usually the product of social and administrative elites. Like al-Sālimī's fatwa collection, these records tend to offer competing normative structures rather than firsthand accounts of trade. The practical interests of sailors and traders are at best objects of conjecture. In most cases the written Arabic of legal documents has little connection to the colloquial and hybridized Arabic spoken by Arab sailors and merchants, much less the Swahili, Kutchi, and Iranian spoken by residents of the Arabian Sea littoral. At best these other languages are preserved in marginalia and a few stray letters, but more often their dialects and pidgins were an effective mode of keeping information secret. We can never know the mentalité of traffickers in the Arabian Sea, but that is no excuse to ignore their actions.

The correspondence of merchant families provides a view from below, but these documents are directed upwards toward courts and political authorities. Studies of merchant correspondence strongly suggest that merchants preserved certain documents precisely because they might be useful in a courtroom.[43] Deeds, contracts, and letters were preserved in the hope of collecting debts and enforcing commitments when other forms of coercion were not available. The documents maintained in family collections are consequently the product of a certain form of self-censorship: they omitted activities that might draw the attention of authorities. Ironically, the only uncensored access we have to merchant practice is the result of government censorship: a few scraps of correspondence captured from ships or extracted from telegraph operators. Merchants tried to keep their information secret, and they were incentivized to preserve information only when they derived benefits from such an effort. Thus even merchant letters and accounts cannot be taken as authentic representations of mercantile practice.

Even when nothing untoward was occurring, these traders had little desire to record, much less preserve, documentation of their activities. When I asked the descendant of the preeminent merchant of nineteenth-century Muscat whether his family maintained old account books, he explained that every Diwali (the Hindu New Year) his ancestors would transfer any outstanding debts and credits into a new accounts ledger. Then they would travel out to sea and in a little ceremony would throw the previous year's ledgers into the water, allowing the waves to wash away both the victories and the hardships of the preceding months.[44] When I first heard this, my heart broke. Like most historians, I lamented the loss of precious traces of the past. But in the following years, as this issue of absent documentation has repeatedly resurfaced, I've come to see this practice with more equanimity. It represents the fact that these merchants preserved what they wanted of the past. They succeeded in silencing the histories that they had no use for, whether because these were compromising or simply because they did not wish to be tied to the past. We cannot access an exhaustive and objective picture of this past, but in reading the tactics of silence and the strategies of archiving we might get a glimpse of a more entangled history.

The concern for objective documentation is largely the preserve of courts, bureaucracies, and of course historians. The silence of subaltern voices has become an enduring frustration and tragedy for cultural historians. Since it is clear that we cannot access the "authentic" voice of these populations, it may be worth considering that the failure of the historian might also reflect the success of the subaltern in evading documentation.[45] This book consequently seeks to make a virtue out of a failing: it attempts to trace the tactics of sailors and traders by paying close attention to the silences in different forms of documentation and triangulating between them. Transactions were performed for certain audiences, and documents were carefully curated to produce strategic silences. So, just as merchants in the Arabian Sea sought out slippages and ambiguities in colonial regulation, we might arbitrage across archives to gain a mobile perspective on trafficking networks. In paying attention to silences and shuttling between archives, we might—to paraphrase Donald Rumsfeld— turn unknown unknowns into known unknowns.[46]

MARGINS OF THE MARKET

Examining the shadowy world of trafficking is consequently an attempt to understand the history of the market but from its margins. Margins are relevant to this study in three distinct but interrelated senses. The first chapter of this book engages with spatial margins: the borders and coastlines that mark the limit and the commencement of a particular territorial market. These geographic boundaries were essential to the freedom of markets because they were the sites where duties were collected, contraband was confiscated, and trade was carefully documented. This regulation at the coastline formed a sort of exoskeleton for colonial markets: both defining external limits and providing structural support for the exchanges inside. By acting at the limit of their territorial power, colonial governments could adopt laissez-faire policies within their markets. This chapter therefore examines the steamship lines and dhow (littoral sailing vessels) traffics that connected the coasts of the Arabian Sea. It traces how these different ships were monitored, regulated, and channeled into particular routes. The chapter reveals how steamship lines came to represent a model of free trade in which distance could be reduced to price and the sea was an empty space between markets. However, there were also competing and complementary traffics of dhows that subverted this vision of free trade. Dhow networks revealed the extent to which the sea was a vast and occluded frontier and free markets were both penetrated and produced by illicit traffics.

The middle three chapters examine the margins of the conceptual market: those exchanges that occurred in the dark corners of the marketplace. The concept of the free market evokes a space of exchange characterized by equality, competition, and fungible commodities. But many types of exchange do not conform to this model of the market, including gift exchange, ritual exchange, charity, marriage, theft, and fraud. They cannot be quantified as market exchanges, and thus they are marginal to the concept of the free market as envisioned by classical political economy. These exchanges were not marginal in that they were unimportant but rather in that they reveal precisely how porous the boundaries of the market really were.

In the Arabian Sea, three physical objects were particularly transgressive of the boundaries between market and nonmarket exchange: bodies, weapons, and coins. Human beings were buyers and sellers in the market, yet they were also exchanged in marriage and adoption. Human labor was exchanged as a commodity in the free market, but human bodies were contraband. The human body thus occupied different roles, was divided many ways, and was exchanged in different forums. Weapons traversed similarly marginal zones of the market. Guns used for sport or the protection of private property were perfectly acceptable commodities, but they also helped usurp property rights through theft and extortion. Weapons used to secure borders were outside the market but essential to preserving the security of private property within the market. Lastly, bullion was exchanged in free markets and was among the first commodities to have a global market price, yet as the basis of monetary standards gold and silver had to be rigorously controlled. However, gold and silver denominated as charity both escaped the control of monetary authorities and subverted their efforts to maintain stable currencies. Bodies, weapons, and coins were thus intermediary objects that transgressed the limits and spanned the margins of the conceptual market.

The final chapter of this book examines a type of margin that comes into existence only in the 1860s: quantified marginal utility as a measure of value. The marginalist revolution in economics introduced the notion that it was utility at the margin (the final unit produced or the usefulness provided when buying one more unit) that determined value. Market price was a quantified expression of this value because it coordinated marginal utility with marginal cost. However, in marginalist economics price was a publicly known quantity, while in the trading world of the Arabian Sea it was a carefully protected piece of intelligence. This chapter unpacks how marginal utility was performed in the trading world of the Arabian Sea by standardizing weights and qualities, demanding documentation, and enforcing market prices on merchant networks. While trade statistics had been collected for decades, equilibrium market price now became the measure of "real value." These market prices were then enrolled in the determination of tariffs, the production of macroeconomic indicators, and the organization of colonial development. By the same token, merchant networks exploited the ambiguities of invoices, scales, and categories to shift market prices in their favor. Real value was not just the product of market-determined prices but a contentious interaction between merchant networks and customs bureaucracies.

The margins of the market are consequently a much-neglected yet constitutive part of the history of capitalism. They are not necessarily representative of the larger trajectories of economic history, but they expose the mechanisms that undergird the expansion of capitalist forms of exchange and the hegemony of capitalist categories of political economy. Trafficking networks did not resist changing structures of exchange but manipulated and subverted them through contrived compliance and astute arbitrage. Ultimately, this book demonstrates how capitalism in the Arabian Sea was framed both by colonial states that formatted trade according to capitalist categories and by trafficking networks that arbitraged across the margins of these markets.

ONE

Commoditizing Transport

Hain baghla ḍāqit bi daqaliha

What *baghla* ever straightened on account of its own mast?

OMANI PROVERB

DHOWS IN THE ARABIAN SEA are the very image of the romantic Orient: sails billowing in the wind, half–naked brown men climbing up a raking mast, and perhaps some whitewashed Saracenic architecture in the background. Photographs of dhows intimate a world on the verge of extinction: they capitalize on nostalgia and the charm of anachronism. Yet it is not altogether clear what a dhow is: dhows belong to that category of "You know it when you see it." Contemporary scholars and the British administrators that preceded them have struggled to identify the unifying aspects of this diverse group of vessels. The name *dhow* was already widely in use and was a commonly understood referent, but colonial officials and historians wracked their brains to define this ambiguous category.[1] Lateen sails, raked masts, teak hulls, and nail-less construction were all suggested as the defining characteristic of dhows, yet invariably some vessel that was widely considered a dhow proved to be an exception. Yet maybe officials were going about the problem in the wrong way: perhaps it was precisely this feeling of nostalgia and romanticism that defined the category of the dhow. I'd suggest that dhows were defined not by the physical qualities of the vessel's construction but by the way that European observers interacted with these vessels as a picturesque anachronism. Dhows cannot be understood as a clearly defined class of ships extracted and abstracted from the networks and environments in which they operated.

Dhow captains, known as *nākhudā*s, and dhow crews were of course too busy sailing and trading to concern themselves with such categorical quandaries. These sailors referred to their ships as *baghla*s, *sambuk*s, *boom*s, *pattimar*s, *machwa*s, and so on. European officials in the Indian Ocean could not make these fine distinctions, but they could easily distinguish dhows as a category from the steamships that they were invariably traveling upon. Floating alongside a steamship, dhows appeared small, insignificant, and doomed to obsolescence. I do not want to suggest that dhows were actually anachronisms; rather, the category of the *dhow* made sense only when these vessels were placed in an anachronistic relationship with the "modern" European steamship.

Yet over the course of the nineteenth and twentieth centuries, this seeming anachronism persisted and even thrived in the waters of the Arabian Sea. Strangely enough, it was because of this anachronistic quality that dhows were able to thrive. Colonial regulators saw dhows as a relic of traditional transportation and consequently as insignificant components of the modern world of trade. This colonial neglect allowed dhows to carry goods and make profits in places and trades that regulators deemed insignificant. They served ports and populations that steamship lines were incapable of reaching. Steamships could benefit from economies of scale by servicing trunk routes, but they relied on the feeder routes of dhows to obtain and distribute goods from major entrepôts to smaller anchorages. It appeared as if steamships existed in a separate time from dhows, but the image of modernity symbolized by the steamship was contingent on obscured and often illicit dhow traffics. It is essential to understand dhows and steamships not as isolated and abstract vessels but as interdependent components of a complex network of people, goods, and vessels that connected the Arabian Sea littoral.

The epigraph to this chapter points us to this fact. The *baghla,* a type of dhow, had a particularly precarious appearance, with a tall slanting mast and lateen sail that made it seem to be on the verge of falling over. One scholar called this lateen sail "the most dangerous rig ever devised by the wit of man."[2] Yet in the hands of an experienced *nākhudā* and a capable crew, and directed in the right relationship to the winds and currents, this ungainly vehicle became quite elegant and efficient. On its own the *baghla* listed, but in concert with people, wind, and cargo it sailed straight and true. Both colonial officials and more recent scholars have tended to focus on the ancient technologies and material qualities of dhows, divorced from these wider networks and contexts. Dhows as abstracted vessels did not change very much between the eighteenth century and the second half of the twentieth. Yet the goods that dhows carried, the routes they plied, and the networks in which they operated were transformed to accommodate steamship lines and circumvent colonial regulations. These changing networks were both invisible and integral to the steamship lines that crossed the Arabian Sea.

Dhows became invisible because the British Empire imposed new ways of seeing and conceiving of the Arabian Sea. New techniques of scientific cartography elided long porous coastlines and dense littoral traffics. Dhows inhabited a littoral world: one in which the sea was the center and the shore was marginal. Colonial maps reversed this order, conceiving of the world as centered on territorial states and enclosed markets. Coastlines were carefully demarcated and territories were clearly indicated by different colors. The sea was just the empty space left over, a vast barren frontier or margin between bounded territories. The littoral perspective of dhows was cartographically effaced and commercially marginalized. Colonial maps depicted coastlines that were closed except at specific ports where customs officials could closely monitor, control, and tax the flow of commodities. However, this vision of free markets was made possible only by the framing out of dhows that frequented foreign enclaves, neglected harbors, and hidden coves. The coastline and the port were thus the limit of the market where governments could intervene to preserve freedom within the market. The littoral was a geographic margin but continued to be a hive of activity that was sidelined only in the geographic imaginations of colonial officials.

The vast expanse of the sea was consequently a marginal space par excellence, a no-man's-land between territorial states. The Arabian Sea was a space of freedom but also a potentially chaotic space haunted by pirates, sharks, typhoons, and reefs. Steamship lines effaced this tortuous terrain and worked to make the sea a barren, flat expanse between territorial markets. Steamers turned the vicissitudes of crossing the Arabian Sea into a straight line connecting one market to another. Where dhows traveled only with the monsoon and charged variable fares, steamships covered these distances in roughly the same time, year round and for the same price. Steamships were "liners" because they formed a constant line of connection that instantiated the lines drawn on modern maps. Trade across the sea was broken down into increments of nautical miles, and the price of transportation was calibrated to this objective measure of distance. Transportation consequently became a commodity that had a calculable price incorporated into abstract, free market exchange. Steamer lines dominated the formal market by framing out the volatilities of the maritime environment; dhows thrived in informal trade by capitalizing on the volatilities of space, season, and social life.

Just beneath the pacific image of stately ships effortlessly crossing the sea was the chaotic reality of dhows darting into hidden coves, passengers smuggling goods through customs, and bureaucrats frantically managing the confusion of people at dockside. Imperial subsidies, discriminatory regulations, and the contrivances of dhows were responsible for funneling trade into orderly steamship lines. Only with these essential support networks could steamships profit from economies of scale in cargo and passenger traffic. Colonial officials dismissed dhow trade as peddling: a small-scale, irrational, and obsolete form of commerce. Scholars of the early modern Indian Ocean have rightly contested this characterization, but there may be something worth rescuing in the term *peddling*.[3] By the late nineteenth century, when European steamships dominated large-scale transport, dhows survived by operating in niche markets. Dhow traffics could be characterized as peddling in that they were more nimble, responsive, and elastic than the rigid and encumbered bureaucracies of steamship lines. Peddling need not be irrational or archaic but rather can be a creative response to changing conditions of trade and geography. Dhow captains were not the vanguard of the capitalist bourgeoisie, but they were sharp traders who used their mobility to exploit information asymmetries, market imperfections, and arbitrage opportunities. Only by framing out dhows and peddling could steamship lines form the hegemonic image of transportation in the Arabian Sea.

This chapter will consequently trace how the global network of steamship lines was dependent on dhow traffics peddling their wares on the monsoon winds. We will begin by tracing the itineraries of dhows, how they navigated through the Arabian Sea, and how they circumvented new orderings of space developed for steam travel. Then we will examine how the British Empire strove to bring dhows under the Union Jack and how dhow traffics evaded British jurisdiction. The chapter will subsequently investigate the regulations and fixed capital investments in port infrastructures that connected dhow traffics to global steamship lines. Last, we will turn to the rebates, cartels, and anticompetitive business practices that made steamship lines profitable. Colonial governments intervened extensively in the spatial margins of the market, regulating commodity flows across the sea and through ports to produce free markets within the coastline. From the bow of a steamship liner, the sea appeared as a flat homogeneous expanse between bounded free markets. The geopolitical map of the Arabian Sea showed clearly defined borders and precisely calculated distances, but this image was both undermined and undergirded by marginal dhow traffics.

Dhows exhibited an improbable resilience to the onslaught of the latest European technologies and suspicious bureaucrats.[4] The persistence of dhows was not a consequence of any particular mechanical advantage or of a cultural resistance to innovations. Rather, dhows thrived in a world of steamships precisely because they adapted their networks to the changing world around them. *Nākhudā*s were canny operators who adapted their business to the routes where they were protected from the competition of steamship lines and the spaces where they were protected from the invasive attentions of colonial bureaucrats. Dhow traffics evolved and rerouted so that these vessels continued to be the preferred method of transportation for a particular niche of goods and people crossing the Arabian Sea.

The slipperiness of the term *dhow* proved to be a frustration to regulators and a boon to trafficking networks. In 1889–90, European diplomats, ostensibly concerned with the slave trade, came together in Brussels and tried to define and regulate these sailing craft. The General Act of the Brussels Conference established definitions that would be repeated in a number of colonial regulations throughout the Arabian Sea. British authorities in East Africa, Aden, and India copied this language wholesale and incorporated it into colonial law.[5] The Brussels Conference divided ships on the Arabian Sea into three categories: fishing boats, trading dhows, and steamships.[6] The Brussels Conference enforced the least amount of regulation on fishing boats. It required only that these vessels carry a license specifying basic information about the vessel, its crew, and the waters in which it was permitted to sail.[7] Since these vessels were not expected to engage in international trade, the delegates at the Brussels Conference presumed that that they could not be used for smuggling or slave trading. However, naval officers had long suspected that pearling and fishing vessels were being used to carry slaves on a small scale.[8] Pearling boats in particular could be at sea for months and had many opportunities to sneak across territorial waters.[9] Moreover, the Straits of Hormuz, the channel between Zanzibar and German Tanganyika, and the Bab el-Mandeb all posed a threat because of the short distance between different jurisdictions. Traffickers frequently took advantage of fishing boats to move illicit goods and people across these short stretches of the sea.[10] The category of fishing boats was too vague to regulate and thus provided an opening for trafficking.

Under the Brussels Conference regulations, one step above fishing boats were trading dhows. Since it was impossible to define dhows by any physical characteristic, European diplomats took recourse to indigeneity as a rule of thumb. Article 31 of the General Act defined a "native vessel" in the following way:

1. It shall present the outward appearance of native build or rigging.
2. It shall be manned by a crew of whom the captain and the majority of the seamen belong by origin to one of the countries on the coast of the Indian Ocean, the Red Sea, or the Persian Gulf.[11]

The definition was rather circular: a "native vessel" was a vessel that appeared to be "native" and whose crew was native to the Indian Ocean littoral. Though this definition was awkward, the General Act attempted to regulate this diffuse category of vessels to prevent trafficking.[12] Unsurprisingly, officials quickly discovered dhows that escaped the definition of a native vessel, and European ships that tried to fall under dhow regulations.

The accurate measurement of dhows was far more difficult in practice than legislators imagined. The volume of Arab dhows was calculated by a vernacular metric of the number of date packages they could carry.[13] European tonnage was of course originally derived from a similar measurement of the number of casks (or tuns) of wine that a ship could hold. Over the nineteenth century, tons had been standardized, abstracted, and then applied as a neutral scientific standard to all ships under European authority. Port authorities tried to use the latest European techniques of calculating the tonnage of vessels, but these methods provided unwieldy and inaccurate measurements for dhows.[14] Moreover, builders began to construct dhows precisely to subvert these new techniques of measurement. The parts of a vessel that were measured by shipping authorities would conform to the specified requirements, but other parts of the hull would be expanded to allow larger volumes than these measurements calculated. *Nākhudā*s also had their vessels inspected and afterwards erected temporary constructions on deck to exceed the intended provisions.[15] Dhows were thus contrived to both comply with tonnage regulations and subvert their intentions.

Dhows were further required to be legible by having a name and tonnage painted in Latin characters with black ink on their hull and sail.[16] Yet dhows in the Arabian Sea did not have stable names and often seemed to carry no name at all.[17] When these vessels did have a name it was usually one of about a dozen names that were considered auspicious. Officials could barely keep track of the innumerable vessels just named *Fath al-Khair*.[18] Names painted on vessels were therefore so generic that they were of little use as a means of identification. Dhows were known not as a particular vessel but as the vessel of a particular *nākhudā,* and *nākhudās* identified each other through intimate knowledge of the idiosyncratic ways that they sailed.[19] This embedded knowledge could not be transcribed into bureaucratic documentation, so the effort to name and measure dhows was doomed to frustration. Regulations thus failed to make ships identifiable or volumes commensurable.

Colonial authorities imagined that each vessel on the ocean was a single isolated individual and attempted to govern these vessels as such. *Nākhudās,* however, acted in concert and sailed in fleets for both social and commercial reasons.[20] *Nākhudās* and crews from the same ports and communities would trade and sail together, so social life was not limited to shipmates but involved a broader seafaring population.[21] These convoys were also a practical method of obstructing naval patrols. One boat in a convoy courted arrest with a relatively insignificant amount of illicit cargo. This would tie up British cruisers, allowing the remainder of the convoy to travel unimpeded.[22] What made dhows conducive to trafficking was not merely their particular designs but also communal methods of sailing that allowed dhow traffics to remain illegible to regulators.

Regulations tried to limit dhow routes to the constrained vision of colonial authorities. Colonial authorities, however, missed facets of what sustained dhow traffics, and *nākhudās* capitalized on these oversights by orienting their traffics into opaque spaces. The sea was a fundamentally different space to these sailors than it was to the bureaucrats who monitored them or the steamship captains against whom they competed. This is amply exhibited in the maps that *nākhudās* used. Steamship captains and colonial officials used modern, "scientific" maps rendered from the ostensible "God's eye view." In contrast is a map used by a Kutchi pilot in the Red Sea and Gulf of Aden (figure 1). The most careful depictions are of islands near the shore and seemingly cartoonish drawings of hills and buildings onshore. The lines on the map do not indicate precise representations of distance but a directional bearing and a number of *zams* (the distance a ship would normally cover in the course of a three-hour watch). The most striking facet of this map from the perspective of scientific cartography is that the Bab al-Mandeb, which turns at an almost ninety-degree angle from the Red Sea to the Gulf of Aden, is here represented as a straight passage. This seems strange only because we are trained to read maps in a particular way. A *nākhudā* using this map would

FIGURE 1. Kutchi pilot's map of the Bab al-Mandeb, ca. 1835. The Royal Geographical Society: Asia S.4, "A Native Indian Chart of the Coast of Arabia and the Red Sea," given to Alexander Burnes ca. 1835. Reproduced with the kind permission of the Royal Geographical Society (with IBG).

have found it perfectly intuitive.[23] It represents how these spaces appear if you were actually on the deck of a dhow and highlights those landmarks that would help you orient yourself and circumvent obstacles.

To a sailor who knew how to read it, this is a far more practical guide than any "scientific" map. On board a ship sailing through the Bab al-Mandeb you would not need to be reminded that the coast turns a corner. That would be both obvious and unnecessary information. We might think of this as the sort of map you might encounter on the GPS device in your car: a map that directs you through space rather than an abstract map that objectifies and standardizes space. Moreover, this kind of map provides the kind of practical information that cannot be represented from above. It reveals hidden itineraries which would allow a *nākhudā* to circumvent regulations formulated from the abstract perspective of a colonial map. Whereas the British Empire was developing strategies of regulation and development from the abstract perspective of scientific cartography, *nākhudā*s took advan-

tage of their mobile perspectives to short-circuit colonial framings of free trade.

In particular, the pilot's map above depicts, not a single line between two points, but multiple options for sailing through the sea. *Nākhudā*s were anxious to maintain the flexibility necessary for their traffics. Registration at a British port could confer many advantages, including British protection at foreign ports, limited liability under the Indian Merchant Shipping Act, and greater ease in the sale of one's ship. Yet these advantages were outweighed by the fact that one's itinerary would be subject to greater amounts of paperwork. Until they were forced to, the majority of dhow owners in the port of Aden declined to register their dhows. This allowed them to avoid the hassles of having their registration verified every time they entered port, keeping logs of their ports of call, and paying to renew their registration every year.[24] *Nākhudā*s often wished to make unscheduled stops at ports or to buy or sell goods at markets where they happened to find good prices. Registration would prevent them from changing their itineraries and seizing the best opportunities for arbitrage. Registration did not simply record existing methods of trade; it fundamentally altered how trade was organized.

Over time, port authorities began to recognize that merely encouraging *nākhudā*s to register their vessels was not working. Dhow owners and *nākhudā*s happily declined the privileges of registered status.[25] By World War II, the increasing stakes of smuggling led officials to require that all trading dhows be registered.[26] Yet this registration was also subverted with relative ease. A class of brokers emerged in Bombay to handle the bureaucratic paperwork for registration. For a fee, these brokers produced false or misleading documentation that would pass muster with port authorities. The paperwork was in perfect order, but the information was contrived to veil the true owners or itineraries of vessels.[27] As long as the papers appeared to be in order, regulators could do little to detect false information. This easy conflation of paperwork and actual surveillance was frequently exploited by merchants to evade regulation. The routes of documentary circulation indicated a competitive market, while dhows and their cargoes flowed along very different itineraries.

Naval patrols also had to confront the fact that while steamers were faster and unfettered by winds they could not exploit these advantages to capture dhows. On the open sea, a steamship could easily overtake a dhow, but dhows sailed in sight of the coastline and maintained contact with other dhows as well as informants in various ports. Operating within this wider network, dhows were more aware of naval steamers than the steamers were aware of any particular dhow. Steamers were easy to see, so a dhow could take measures to avoid capture well before the steamer arrived in the vicinity.[28] Since dhow crews loaded and unloaded their ships and were paid as a share of the journey's profits, there was little likelihood that a crew member would leak information about illicit cargoes.[29] Dhows and land-based informants signaled to each other about the presence of British men-of-war though flashing lamps and bonfires. These signals were inscrutable to naval officers and effective in preventing capture.[30] Dhows therefore effectively neutralized the advantages of steam engines by operating in a network with land-based accomplices. This larger network permitted dhows to comply with regulatory demands even as they evaded surveillance.

Personal networks that stretched across the ocean not only were helpful for smuggling but also were the very foundation of dhow trading. *Nākhudā*s derived their profits by nimbly seizing upon opportunities for arbitrage in whatever form they might appear. Dispersed networks of family and friends provided information on where opportunities were, but they also provided a safety net in case these opportunities fell through. Friends and family provided additional loans, extended terms of credit, and renegotiated agreements when adverse conditions threatened both a business and a social bond.[31] Risk was thus dispersed across personal networks, as well as across various commodities and businesses. *Nākhudās* tended not to specialize in a commodity or invest in economies of scale; rather, they carried diverse cargoes including passengers and contraband on every trip. The larger merchants who backed *nākhudās* generally spread their capital among many different vessels and cargoes, as well as pearling voyages, date crops, and other enterprises.[32] From large merchants down to petty sailors, risks were mitigated by a diversified commercial portfolio, backstopped by a broad personal network.

Dhow traffics were constituted this way partly because insurance was a deeply fraught concept in Islamic jurisprudence.[33] The uncertainty at the heart of insurance seemed to run afoul of Islamic restrictions on gambling, speculation, and other moral hazards of engaging in highly risky endeavors. So Muslim shippers rarely purchased insurance, and even if they wanted to it was difficult to find, was expensive, and increased tariff valuations.[34] Instead, they split up their cargoes, used smaller vessels, and did not take big gambles on their businesses. The exception seemed to be dhows owned and managed by Hindus. These were often the largest dhows on the sea, operated as purely freight-carrying businesses, and so purchased insurance.[35] For these firms, the regulation of insurance would shape their trading practice and even their ships. Insurance premiums varied by the type of vessel and the types of technology on board. Colonial regulations demanded that ships carry beacons, wireless radios, safety equipment, and load lines largely to appease the concerns of insurers.[36] Indeed, the very definition of illegal trade was often delineated by courts adjudicating insurance claims.[37] Insurance allowed shipping firms to take larger risks but also forced them into a more rigid, regulated, and heavily documented mode of trade.

Without the regulatory demands of colonial bureaucracies, dhow traffics could operate at a substantial advantage among the price-sensitive consumers of the Arabian Sea littoral. Arab, African, and Indian shippers preferred dhows because they were cheap, involved minimal regulation, and were flexibly operated. Dhows were slower and less reliable, but for many merchants this was preferable to the higher costs, capital requirements, rigidities, planning, and visibility demanded in transportation by steamships. Cowasjee Dinshaw and Brothers was a prominent Indian firm that ran a steamship line servicing the Gulf of Aden and the Red Sea. During World War I, this shipping line did very well because fears of smuggling had led the British government to forbid dhow traffics. After World War I, the firm complained that local shippers turned to steamships only when dhows were not available. So when trade was slack, smaller steamship companies like Cowasjee Dinshaw could not compete.[38] Over small distances, where dhows and steamships competed on an even playing field, dhows operated at an advantage. At this scale, only colonial regulations allowed steamships to out-compete dhow traffics.

These bureaucratic demands forced dhow traffics to interact with ports and other vessels in ways that frustrated existing modes of interaction between dhows at sea. This is most visible in the way that ships used lights for communication. The dhows of the Arabian Sea did not utilize electric lights for illumination or signaling. Dhows kept watch by starlight and were generally capable of navigation and quick maneuvers in semidarkness when necessary.[39] Collisions between dhows were relatively rare, and those that occurred were less destructive, because all ships were sailing along the same currents and winds.[40] But new international safety conventions in the early twentieth century mandated the use of lights to prevent collisions at sea. Ships of more than 150 tons were required to maintain two white lights on their masts, a stern light (which faced the back of the vessel), a daytime signal, and a horn.[41] These rules were all intended to prevent collisions, but they grated against the established practices among dhows in the Arabian Sea.

*Nākhudā*s were reluctant to keep their lamps lit during the night for a number of reasons. First, lamps were an additional cost, both in their initial purchase and in their nightly operation. Given the slim margins and uncertainties of dhow travel, *nākhudās* were loath to take on this heavy fixed cost. What *nākhudās* often did was keep one lamp available but light it only when another ship was sighted on the horizon.[42] The lamps also had a number of negative consequences for dhows. They scared away many fish while attracting swordfish that rammed the hull of the dhow. Lamps also disturbed the crew and passengers who slept on deck.[43] For all these reasons *nākhudās* and dhow crews did not use lights or used them only sparingly. But while this created little danger from other sailing vessels, the growing numbers of steamships were a mortal threat to inattentive dhow crews.

In the early twentieth century, there were repeated collisions between steamships and dhows, usually with the latter suffering the majority of damages and taking the blame. Collisions between vessels were adjudicated by vice admiralty courts. Case after case came before these courts, and while some decisions granted compensation to dhow owners, the majority concluded that the dhow was to blame and thus deserved no compensation. Steamship captains were usually British, so they obtained the benefit of the doubt from British judges. Around the turn of the twentieth century, these collisions were also blamed on *nākhudā*s because they did not carry lights.[44] However, by the middle of the century *nākhudā*s had learned to sail more effectively around steamships, light their lamps at the right moment, and testify more successfully in court.[45] Initially, dhows did not adapt to the presence of steamships and maritime regulations and paid dearly for it. Over time, *nākhudā*s accommodated steamships on their sea-lanes and learned how to operate within and around these regulatory structures. These collisions were a physical manifestation of the confrontation between the two networks of trade operating in the Arabian Sea. Colonial regulations constructed a world in which transportation had to be organized through bureaucratic rules; dhow traffics could not ignore these rules, but they could adapt to them.

Steamships and their accompanying bureaucracy did not just alter dhow traffics, they reformatted the sea itself. Steamers interacted with the sea through a number of technical and scientific devices that allowed them to navigate through treacherous littorals and changing shorelines. Steamship captains relied on charts, compasses, wireless radios, beacons, and other devices that were standardized across the British Empire. Captains, mates, and engineers had to learn these technologies and signals in order to obtain certificates of competency to run their steamships. In the nineteenth century, the British Navy surveyed and mapped the waters of the Arabian Sea and the Gulf. Over the first half of the twentieth century, the British India Steam Navigation Company set up lights and buoys along the coasts of the Arabian Peninsula.[46] These devices altered the sea itself and how ships interacted with it. While *nākhudā*s navigated these waters through embodied knowledge gained from years of sailing experience, the standardization of lights, signals, and buoys across the globe enabled any trained British captain to sail those seas without any prior experience.

Maritime infrastructures formatted the sea, rendering it navigable to steamship captains and legible to officials. Colonial officials particularly attempted to regulate dhows by defining and categorizing them. Regulators hoped that by applying different levels of surveillance to different categories of vessels they might efficiently monitor trade. Merchants quickly recognized that they could manipulate these categories or find amenable categories within this system to facilitate their informal traffics. Colonial regulations tried to isolate dhows and make them interact with the sea through bureaucratic channels. *Nākhudā*s instead relied on flexible personal networks to evade surveillance and confound regulation. By continuing to view the sea through their own mobile perspectives, *nākhudā*s were able to thrive in the routes obscured to the panoptic ambitions of the colonial state.

FLAGS AND JURISDICTION

At the beginning of the nineteenth century, many Arab dhows would have flown a plain red flag at the top of their masts. How exactly this practice began and what it meant to Arab merchants and sailors is not very clear. While Islamic history has a long tradition of white, black, and green banners, the red piece of cloth on Arab ships does not seem to have followed in this tradition of caliphal insignia. It is unlikely that it indicated a particular political allegiance, since it was used by sailors who pledged allegiance to different sheikhs and sultans. Yet one of the key provisions of the maritime truce imposed on the Gulf sheikhs in 1820 was the requirement to place "Britain's white border of peace" around the red Arab ensign.[47] This modification of the flag captures how the physical appearance of ships came to be tied to the political ambitions of the British Empire and its notions of maritime sovereignty. The lengths to which Arab *nākhudā*s went to avoid pinning this symbol of colonial subjugation to their masts equally indicates how those ambitions were frustrated.

By the second half of the nineteenth century, the main concern of the Royal Navy on the waters of the Arabian Sea was the slave trade. British cruisers spread out along the Swahili Coast and the coast of South Arabia, lying in wait for dhows that might be carrying slaves. Dhows flying the red Arab flag or British Union Jack were stopped and searched. Yet British cruisers could not search ships carrying the flags of its European rivals, as this would be a breach of their sovereignty. European maritime law suggested that the sea was free and open to all, but each ship was an island of colonial sovereignty.[48] The Portuguese and Spanish crowns condoned the slave trade late into the nineteenth century, so British officers could not search these ships without provoking a diplomatic incident. Traders running slaves within the

Arabian Sea were drawn to the flags of Portugal or Spain in order to evade the scrutiny of the Royal Navy.[49] This concern over slave dhows would prompt the regulations on seaborne trade enshrined in the previously mentioned General Act of the Brussels Conference.

The Brussels Conference coordinated the efforts of European powers and reinforced the power of British officers to stop and seize dhows suspected of engaging in the slave trade. The Brussels Conference affirmed a European consensus against the slave trade and presumed that officials were monitoring dhows permitted to fly their flags. But most of the dhows traversing the Arabian Sea were not registered by any of these states and flew the plain red flag or no flag at all. The increasing attentions of the Royal Navy created a tremendous nuisance for Arab dhows even on unobjectionable trading voyages. The political agent in Zanzibar highlighted an instance where "the same Arab vessel, engaged in a perfectly legitimate voyage, has been exposed to visit and search six times in succession in passing up the coast of the Island of Zanzibar, that is, she was searched every 10 miles, and on each occasion compelled to stop her voyage and lower her sail, perhaps at a critical spot between dangerous reefs."[50] It is indicative of the extent of the problem that even British officials acknowledged that it amounted to harassment. The Brussels convention had made a ship's flag a key component of maritime commerce, but the Arab flag became little more than a provocation to British cruisers.

If the red Arab flag was an invitation for harassment, *nākhudās* quickly realized that the French flag was a license to traffic. When the Brussels Conference act was sent to France for ratification, the French legislature exempted the articles regarding the monitoring and seizure of dhows.[51] Consequently, British cruisers in the Arabian Sea could only verify that a ship had valid French papers, and if it did the ship was shielded from any further inspection. The French Empire in the Arabian Sea was effectively limited to the colony of Djibouti at the mouth of the Red Sea. France had a smaller presence in terms of land area or coastline than the Portuguese, the Germans, or the Italians, but the French interest in chastening British power was much larger. Thus French officials were only too happy to issue the French tricolor to Arab dhow owners. These officials received a small fee, gained additional property holders and additional trade for their ports—and acquired a means to contest the dominance of the British Empire. As a result, British officials repeatedly complained that their efforts were being undermined by dhows that had obtained French protection.[52] Their frustrations were further exacerbated by a number of *nākhudās* who flew the French flag without even obtaining permission. On encountering such vessels, British cruisers had to send these dhows to a French port for judgment.[53] Of course, what most galled British officers was witnessing dhows with fully legitimate papers and full cargos of contraband go on to their destinations without any consequences.[54] So for all the fanfare of the Brussels Conference, its major impact was to move dhows under the French flag.

Dhow owners understood that keeping their French papers in full order resulted in immunity from search, so they continued to bring their dhows under French protection by various means. Perhaps the easiest method was to obtain authorization from the French consul in Aden. *Nākhudās* could claim to be residents of one of the French colonies, and the consul in Aden allegedly issued papers without verifying the information. French officials, like British ones, were frequently the only official and possibly the only European in a port. They were often merchants who handled consular business on the side, so they had little time to double-check statements. These officials were entirely dependent on African and Asian subordinates and found it simply impossible to rigorously implement many regulations. *Nākhudās* frequently registered passengers with the French consulate and then carried slaves in their place, often many more than their passenger allowance. Though they were less scrupulously detailed in British records, British agents and vice-consuls were often guilty of similar negligence. Thus the detailed and time-consuming regulations established by the Brussels Conference were only weakly implemented.[55]

British complaints ultimately embarrassed French authorities, who agreed to tighten up their oversight and issue papers only where such information could be verified.[56] Yet even this was not a great hardship for dhow owners who were regular visitors in French ports in Djibouti, Madagascar, and the Comoros Islands. Dhow owners bought a small plot of land or a house in these colonies or placed the vessels under the nominal ownership of relatives who were resident in these colonies. With this small investment they could receive complete official papers for even armed dhows with large crews, making both arms and slave trading easy to conceal from British cruisers.[57] For a well-networked population of dhow owners, surmounting the bureaucratic hurdles of obtaining immunity from search by British cruisers was a simple task.

The contentions between British and French officials died down after the Anglo-French Entente of 1907, and until the First World War the system of granting flags became well established. After the war, however, the newly assertive nationalism of Reza Shah Pahlavi upset the balance of the Brussels

Conference. Reza Shah had consolidated his rule within Iran in the first half of the 1920s and by the end of the decade was expanding the operations of the Iranian Navy in the Gulf. Iranian government vessels seized Arab dhows in the Gulf that ventured too close to the disputed islands of Tunb and Abu Musa. This caused a number of incidents with the British Navy, which claimed to protect the sheikhdoms of the Arab side of the Gulf as well as to preserve maritime peace. Britain complained to the Iranian authorities and was occasionally able to repossess goods for Arab *nākhudās*.[58] In the 1930s and 1940s concerns arose again over the endemic problem of smuggling. Kuwait and Dubai, in particular, had emerged as important centers for the redistribution of restricted goods. They had low taxes and minimal regulation and evolved as important centers for the interregional trade in tea, silk, and weapons.[59] Reza Shah was a modernizing ruler anxious to seal his borders and quickly develop the Iranian economy. High tariff barriers were key to these plans, but Iran's proximity to the Arab Gulf states made these tariffs virtually impossible to enforce. The Gulf had long been a space of exchange and interaction between Arabs, Iranians, and Indians, and its coasts were filled with diasporic traders and sailors from other shores. Iran and Britain increasingly tried to police these waters in the interwar years, but the Arab and Iranian traders of the Gulf exploited the gaps and overlaps between their jurisdictions.

Dhow building had long been centered on the Arab coast, and Iranian merchants had purchased their ships from builders in Oman and Kuwait for centuries. The Pahlavi government, hoping to encourage shipbuilding in Iran, forbade the registration of Arab-built dhows in Iran. But the result was the opposite of what the government had intended. Iranian merchants and *nākhudās* registered their vessels in Kuwait, even though their itineraries, owners, and crews were all Iranian.[60] This not only preserved Arab dominance in shipbuilding but also helped Iranian *nākhudās* to circumvent Iranian shipping regulations. Pahlavi Iran, along with Iraq and later India and Pakistan, all asserted the authority to control their shipping and coastal waters. They absorbed from colonial governments the desire to seal their borders and bring the open seas into the system of interstate control. The Gulf sheikhs' desire to attract trade consistently undermined these neatly delineated spheres.

Beginning at the turn of the twentieth century, international law and particularly the British Navy began to require that all vessels in international waters had to be regulated by a recognized state. While the waters of the

Arabian Sea were open to all ships, the ships themselves were subject to the jurisdiction of particular states. Thus the first component of control over shipping in the Arabian Sea involved planting a flag atop every ship that left shore. The Brussels Conference had placed the entire Arabian Sea under a single system of international law, but the fractured implementation of these regulations opened up substantial room for *nākhudā*s to evade these regulations. *Nākhudā*s knew that the right flag meant they could act with impunity either because regulatory authorities were uninterested or because those who were interested had no authority. While dhows increasingly flew one flag or another, they easily navigated the interstices of international maritime regulation.

PORTS AND NODES

If flags were an ineffective device for imposing regulation, perhaps dhows networks could be regulated at ports? Controlling the nodes of Arabian Sea trading networks was indeed an essential component of shipping regulation. Yet dhows were only minimally constrained in where they could unload their cargoes. They were generally smaller vessels and could be beached with relative ease. Consequently, a dhow port was defined less by an infrastructure of docks than by a sheltered harbor where traders could anchor their vessels. Steamships required a very different type of port. Where dhow networks were an intricate web of connections between many smaller anchorages, steamships required a smaller number of ports handling a large volume of trade. Regulation concentrated steamship lines in ports like Bombay but also prompted the development of Sur as an informal and illicit mirror of Bombay. This section outlines how colonial policies fostered the thicker links between steamship ports and how this network was embedded in and undermined by a thinner but more pervasive dhow network. Free trade in the Arabian Sea involved ports like Bombay working in tandem with ports like Sur.

One of the main issues facing early shipping lines as well as European navies was the problem of coal. Coal power liberated shipping from the fickleness of the wind, making possible year-round shipping and predictable journey times. Coal made possible frequent and regular connections between major ports and hence instantiated the shipping lines drawn on colonial maps. Coal was consequently central to the process of commoditizing distance that unfolded in the Arabian Sea during this period. Even as coal liberated shipping in certain ways it constrained it in others. Little coal could be obtained near the Arabian Sea, so British shipping was dependent on the importation of clean-burning Welsh coal.[61] Especially early in the development of steam navigation, frequent stops were required to refill holds with coal for the inefficient engines that powered these vessels onward. Port Said, Aden, Mombasa, and Bombay all developed as vital coal depots for the operation of British naval and merchant marine vessels. These coaling depots became essential components of Britain's naval dominance of the Arabian Sea and evolved as key nodes for the regulation of trade and the projection of imperial power.

Coal depots were only the first requirement of steamships. Over time these liners required the reimagining of harbors to accommodate the demands of a modern port. Steamships had difficulty navigating reefs and shallow water, so deep-water harbors were dredged and purpose-built docks were constructed to facilitate the unloading of cargo. Such ports were few and far between in the Arabian Sea because they required large investments and high operational costs. Ports in this new sense were initially limited to a few colonial metropolises like Bombay, Aden, and Mombasa. On the other hand, a harbor where a ship anchored and unloaded its cargo into smaller boats was deemed merely an anchorage.[62] Anchorages were far less efficient at loading and unloading cargo and delayed the time that a ship had to stay in port. While steamship lines converged in efficient modern ports, anchorages were still frequented by dhows. Yet colonial ports never serviced only steamships; they always included docks and anchorages for dhows. In Aden, Steamer Point unsurprisingly served steamships, but Ma'alla Wharf served dhows. In Bombay, steamers used Victoria, Princes, and Mazagaon docks while dhows landed in the dhow *bandar*s further up the harbor.[63] Muscat harbor served steamships, but dhows used the adjacent harbor of Muttrah. These ports were key points of linkage between increasingly distinct networks of trade.

Colonial officials assumed that dhow *bandar*s were inherently suspicious and thus required more surveillance. In Aden, dhows were permitted to enter the port only during daylight hours when customs officials could easily keep track of them. Dhows leaving the port had to obtain clearances from the port officer, the port health officer, the police inspector, and the wharf manager.[64] Dhow *bandar*s were subject to this oppressive surveillance precisely because these were the points where the large trade of steamships met the inscrutable traffics of the Arabian Sea. Steamship lines depended on these smaller capillary traffics to distribute and collect goods for their larger trunk routes. So the link from *bandar* to dock was simultaneously necessary and nerve-racking for bureaucrats who could not accurately monitor which goods were going where. Unable to effectively surveil their coastlines, colonial authorities attempted to regulate dhow traffics through documentation beginning during the First World War. Dhows had to carry port clearances for each port where they stopped, and port authorities could then restrict where commodities were sent. Port officers were required to maintain lists of the vessels that had been cleared and the ports to which they were headed.[65] These records made it possible to collect statistics and measure the extent of trade with different countries. This system of port clearances, colonial officials hoped, would control dhows by making their movements transparent.

As surveillance within British harbors increased, innumerable methods were developed to circumvent it. Perhaps the most brazen was the loading or landing of cargo just outside the bounds of a harbor. Small ships could launch from beaches a few meters down the coast and meet up with ships that had already received full port clearances. Just outside the harbor the larger trading vessels could accept or dispose of illicit cargo with little fear of prosecution.[66] Secluded coves far from trading hubs were similarly utilized (after all, there is some basis for the tourist cliché of the "smuggler's cove"). Colonial authorities tried to contain this trafficking by ever more coercive restrictions. Blockades were often imposed to suppress illicit trades or simply to punish recalcitrant populations.[67] Somali or Arab tribes that attacked British shipping or carried slaves were blockaded. Where British regulation was resisted, starvation through blockade could achieve pacification.[68] Trafficking itineraries exposed the blind spots in surveillance and forced authorities to redouble their efforts to harden territorial boundaries and consolidate trade through approved ports.

Blockades became particularly expansive during the First World War. After an attack on a British naval vessel in 1915, ports on the Arab coast of the Red Sea were blockaded to prevent supplies from getting to Ottoman forces. The imperial administration decided that all vessels entering the Red Sea would be required to stop at the naval station at Kamaran Island. This measure failed to control illicit trading, and consequently the entire dhow trade of the Red Sea was limited to five preapproved dhows.[69] *Nākhudā*s operating from the protectorates of British Aden and Somaliland were bankrupted by these provisions. One official stated: "Almost all the dhows of Arabia, Aden included, are ruined by being laid up in accordance with dhow restriction orders."[70] These restrictions were ostensibly organized to monitor trade between allied or at least neutral parties, but the exigencies of war justified the virtual abolition of dhows.

Blockades could be effected only temporarily against small areas of coastline, so another important component of these wartime restrictions was a system of bonds to secure legitimate trade. This system required that a vessel which desired to leave port had to provide customs officials with a bond equivalent to the value of the entire cargo of the vessel. If the vessel sailed to the approved destination and sold its full cargo, it would receive a certificate from an official at the port of sale that could be brought back to the home port to redeem the bond.[71] This bond system was continued in a modified form during the interwar period in order to prevent smuggling of highly taxed commodities like sugar, textiles, and spices. The problem was that British officials were stationed in only a few ports, and at even fewer ports were they capable of monitoring the loading and unloading of cargo. So these bonds could be obtained for trade to only a very small number of ports.[72] Concerns about trafficking forced authorities to limit trade to a few ports that were closely regulated by colonial officials. These restrictions only expanded the economies of scale and regulatory advantages of steamships over dhows.

However, dhow traffics were not organized in such a bureaucratic fashion. *Nākhudās* used flexible itineraries, negotiable prices, and payment schedules to maximize their profits. By demanding heavy initial investments and long-term commitments, the bond system increased the costs of trade and forced dhow traffics to act like colonial businesses. But rather than resigning themselves to obsolescence, dhow networks adapted to their new role as illicit conduits of trade. *Nākhudās* developed a rather ingenious method of evading these bonds. They would import goods into Bombay for transshipment to ports in the Gulf or on the South Arabian coast. Goods for transshipment would not be charged import duties or subjected to bonds because they were ostensibly just passing through. Once dhows had left Bombay, en route to another Arabian Sea port, they would circle back and drop the cargo off at smaller ports on the Gujarati coast.[73] So even as the British Empire consolidated its control over legitimate trade, it was being subverted by the creativity of dhows.

Moreover, local rulers around the Arabian Sea were interested in fostering dhow traffics from which they could collect revenues. In the interwar period, British diplomats in Arab capitals were pressured to reopen trade, and these officials reluctantly relied on the word of local Arab officials to confirm receipt of restricted commodities. The sheikhs of Qatar and Bahrain had customs bureaucracies, and the British Political Agency pretended that the mere existence of a bureaucracy was a sufficient guarantee of cooperation.[74] As with much else, the production and circulation of official documents stood in for physical surveillance of commodities. It was almost immediately evident that far more restricted commodities than could be consumed locally were being transshipped through Bombay to Arab ports like Salalah, Shihr, and Jizan.[75] The most problematic port was Dubai, which was arguably the most important trading hub in the Gulf by the 1930s. British officials could do little to prevent Dubai's prominence and merely took consolation in the fact that most of these smuggled goods were headed for Iran.[76] These customs regulations produced a great deal of documentation about the movement of commodities across the Arabian Sea.[77] Yet the connection between all this paperwork and the actual movement of goods was tenuous at best.

World War II brought more of the same difficulties for imperial customs authorities in the Arabian Sea. Vichy-controlled Djibouti was a particular cause of concern because of its long history as the thorn in the side of British antitrafficking efforts. Djibouti was kept under constant blockade conditions for over two years.[78] The blockade had caused a sharp rise in the price of goods in East Africa and therefore was a significant inducement to smuggling.[79] Many restricted items were transshipped to other vessels while at sea, and shipping bonds were traded or reused to conceal illicit activities. A thriving commerce in these documents sprang up during the blockade, with many merchants and *nākhudā*s constituting a secondary market in bonds and export licenses.[80] *Nākhudā*s adapted to the bond system by producing the appropriate documents while making sure that the actual circulation of goods was not bound too closely to documentary circulation. While conditions in Djibouti were difficult under the blockade, it could not have lasted more than a few weeks without smuggling. Not only was Djibouti feeding itself through smuggling, but it even functioned as an entrepôt for Yemeni coffee headed for Europe to caffeinate Axis soldiers.[81] Vichy-ruled Djibouti thus lasted two whole years under the British blockade. Historians have credited the ruthless Vichy governor for sustaining the colony, but this evidence suggests that dhow traffics were key to the survival of Djibouti under otherwise impossible conditions.[82]

Ports like Djibouti and Dubai but also Sur and Gwadar were the nodes of an alternative network of trafficking in the Arabian Sea. These ports relied on their entrepôt trade to survive and thus emphasized their low taxes, minimal regulation, and "business-friendly" attitude toward all manner of exchanges. Negligent bureaucrats would only increase the attractiveness of such ports.[83] Gwadar, Goa, and Kuwait were all foreign enclaves that gave unregulated access to vast hinterland markets.[84] Sur was not so felicitously located, but its active seafaring community made it a hub for informal and illicit traffics in the Arabian Sea. The Suri diaspora in the Arabian Sea were well recognized as the most effective traffickers operating in these waters.[85] In official records these were insignificant ports, but it was common knowledge to sailors that these were hubs for the informal economies of these regions.[86]

With all the bureaucratic checks on commerce around the Arabian Sea, there was one fail-safe method of evading commercial regulations: bribery. The operation of regulations ultimately depended on government employees who were inspecting vessels, issuing licenses, and verifying documentation. Both European colonial officials and their Arab, Indian, and African subordinates were routinely swayed by social bonds and the temptations of money. Port officers might be bribed to make up a false license or to alter the details on a shipping document. Money often changed hands to purchase the negligence of customs officials.[87] Officials who might have been initially reluctant succumbed to a combination of threats from smugglers and the promise of generous payoffs.[88] Conniving officials organized elaborate scams in which small illicit shipments would be sacrificed to police in order to keep up the facade of vigilance, although even in such cases officials would take their cut of the sacrificed shipment before reporting the capture to their superiors.[89] These unsavory relationships between merchants and conniving officials were central to the operation of most large-scale or long-term smuggling operations. Effective regulation was utterly dependent on the propriety of the officials implementing regulations. As a result, commercial regulation in the Arabian Sea was built on sinking sand.

Regulations, antitrafficking protocols, and blockades were pivotal to funneling trade into major entrepôts and the holds of steamships. Wartime restraints were particularly powerful in bounding colonial markets and reducing trade to a limited number of highly regulated ports and colonial businesses. These policies concentrated trade and produced the economies of scale that justified new port infrastructures, larger steamships, and an ever expanding customs bureaucracy. However, while these processes displaced many dhows from their standard routes, they did not disappear. Rather, dhow traffics evolved with new regulations and found their flexible methods well suited to the newly illicit segments of trade. *Nākhudā*s and merchants learned how to evade documentation by operating through smaller entrepôts, or how to send the appropriate paperwork through the right regulatory nodes, while sending their cargoes elsewhere. These two separate but linked networks of ports consequently evolved in tandem, with goods and people easily moving between them.

ROUTES AND REBATES

The pricing of steamship journeys and the cost of their operations seemed to be public and determined by competition. In reality, these publicized prices elided the operation of cartels, subsidies, and racial preferences. Where regulation ostensibly protected consumers, in effect it protected steamship companies from the competition posed by dhows. In classical political economy, firms compete to provide the lowest price while still maintaining a profit, and the firm providing the lowest price sets the price for the market. The consolidation of a market price for transportation across the Arabian Sea was achieved through a very different mechanism. Market price in nineteenth- and early twentieth-century shipping was established not through competition but through intense collaboration. The close relationship between the management of different shipping companies and the close relationship between these companies and governments were essential to the consolidation of a particular form of price.[90] The market price mechanism for transportation in the Arabian Sea was exceedingly opaque because both steamship lines and passengers were manipulating pricing mechanisms to their own advantage.

European empires had a direct interest in the fostering of regular steamship lines and were actively involved in promoting particular firms. This promotion occurred not through explicit legislation but through social connections and racial biases. Shipping firms were one of the prime examples of what scholars have called "Gentlemanly Capitalism." This refers to the close social relationships between imperial policy makers and British businessmen, particularly in finance and the service industries.[91] The merchant marine by its very nature was tied to the empire. Ships were requisitioned during periods of war, and states were consequently interested in the success of their national shipping industry. British officials were anxious to promote the success of British firms and proud in noting their dominance over European rivals.[92] With colonial possessions on the coasts of the Arabian Sea, the

German and French governments were similarly interested in promoting their national shipping firms.[93] But even states with no presence along the Arabian Sea littoral were involved in this transoceanic carriage. Thus Russian, Dutch, and Japanese vessels were regularly found in Arabian Sea ports.[94] Shipping was not just any industry but one of imperial importance. So the firms that obtained imperial sponsorship also gained market dominance.

The privileges enjoyed by national shipping lines were numerous. In a highly regulated field, those firms with close ties to officials were able to avoid suspicions of trafficking and intensify enforcement against their competitors. They were also adept at obtaining exemptions from rules.[95] But the most powerful advantage that shipping firms could obtain was a government postal contract. The Peninsular and Oriental Company (P&O) maintained its contract to deliver mails between India and the United Kingdom for over a century until Indian independence in 1947. Mail contracts required a firm to regularly pick up and deliver government mails between various ports. In exchange, governments provided a generous subsidy that offset a proportion of the cost of maintaining a regular steamship service. Unsurprisingly, British businessmen who traveled in the same social circles as colonial officials obtained these contracts.[96] Despite their subsidies, these British firms often complained that their grants were smaller than those provided by the German or French governments. They employed national honor as a prod with which to procure higher subsidies from the British Empire.[97] The success of these firms therefore depended on their ability to negotiate the best possible terms with government officials.

Yet companies like the P&O did not use this subsidy to undercut the prices of their competitors. Indeed, their prices reflected a premium because they eliminated competition through the conference system. Shipping "conferences" were cartel agreements between European shipping firms operating along the same routes. The different firms cooperated to set prices, tonnage, and sailing times.[98] They agreed to cooperate, and any shipping firm that attempted to undercut the conference rates was subject to a rate war. This meant that conference firms, usually far better capitalized than their upstart competitors, offered freight prices at a severe loss in order to deprive new shipping companies of any cargo. Soon enough, the new company gave up or was bankrupted trying to compete. Immediately afterwards freight rates would return to their previous elevated rate.[99] The price of transportation between two ports was thus determined not by free competition but by the operation of cartels.

Despite their rhetoric of free trade, British governments supported this system. A number of companies opposed the conference system, but their attempts to circumvent it were quashed by the shipping conferences. The issue became a nationalist cause in India, and colonial officials were repeatedly accused of betraying the principles of free trade. The clamor was so great that a Royal Commission on Shipping Rings was convened. But after two years of collecting evidence and interviewing businessmen, the commissioners ruled in favor of their friends who ran the conference shipping lines. They were satisfied that the conference system provided a "handsome but not excessive" profit and therefore did not merit intervention.[100] Not only did the colonial government decline to intervene, but it routinely chided firms who declined to join the conferences.[101] For all its rhetoric of free trade and competitive markets, the British government openly supported price-setting cartels in shipping.

The shipping conferences favored large firms and thus encouraged mergers and acquisitions within the industry. The British India Steam Navigation Company (BISN) bought out the Persian Gulf Steam Navigation Company, the Ceylon Steam Navigation Company, James Nourse Ltd., Frank C. Strick and Co., and many others. Eventually the BISN itself merged with the P&O to create a global behemoth.[102] These myriad associated shipping lines shared ticket agents and even honored tickets from these related companies.[103] Thus, when the conference system itself was not enough, mergers and acquisitions provided another method of fending off competition.

Shipping companies even practiced their own policy of divide-and-rule. The different firms in a shipping conference agreed to let certain firms maintain monopolies over shipping between certain ports. Even between Japanese, German, and British firms, this cordiality was present to ensure that each firm could control its own niche.[104] This policy was extended to Indian firms on small unremunerative routes. Earlier we encountered Cowasjee Dinshaw & Brothers, which obtained the contract to deliver government mails in the Red Sea. There was some opposition, but ultimately it was the only firm interested in running a small fleet of steamers to serve the needs of the Aden government.[105] Similarly, the Bombay Steam Navigation Company and the Scindia Line were permitted to operate within the Indian coastal trade with relatively little interference from the BISN.[106] As long as these firms did not threaten the profits of the conference lines, they were permitted to dominate smaller niche markets.

But perhaps the most interesting and illustrative case was the tortuous relationship between the BISN and A. M. Jeevanjee. Alibhai Mulla Jeevanjee was a pioneer of the Indian community in British East Africa. He worked closely with the Imperial British East African Company to literally build the colonial city of Nairobi.[107] Jeevanjee is important to our story because his relationship with the BISN illustrates the tangled and personal nature of the shipping business in the Arabian Sea. Jeevanjee's close relationship with the BISN had led to a suggestion that he should purchase the Shah Line of steamers. The Shah Line operated, not along the conference lines, but on smaller routes between India and Mauritius and in the pilgrim traffic between India and Jedda. The BISN wanted Jeevanjee to purchase the company and then immediately shut it down and break up its ships for parts. The BISN agreed to pay him Rs. 100,000 for this service.[108] The BISN was interested in eliminating its competition and was willing to pay in the short term in order to monopolize trade in the longer term.

Jeevanjee purchased the Shah Line as instructed by the BISN but was rather slow in shutting down the firm and decommissioning its vessels. By continually professing his loyalty, playing on the egos of BISN executives, and playing the role of the bungling servant, Jeevanjee was able to extract extraordinary concessions from his patrons. He kept postponing and requesting extensions on the time within which he was to wind up the company's operations. Claiming penury, he obtained several loans, altogether worth Rs. 400,000, from the BISN and *still* continued to run his ships to Mauritius. Beguiled by Jeevanjee's charm and professions of loyalty, BISN officials continued to give him the benefit of the doubt even as he evaded the terms of their agreement. They took Jeevanjee at his word when he said that he did not want to compete with the BISN and assumed that he was a trustworthy, if incompetent, shipping manager.[109] As a result they were milked by Jeevanjee, who managed to string along the BISN for several years. The dominance of steamship liners in the Arabian Sea was the result of such convenient relationships rather than any competitive advantage.

On the other hand, the pricing of cargo and passages by dhow was fluctuating and negotiable. Arab dhows tended not to carry cargo at an agreed rate of freight; rather, the *nākhudā* and members of the crew purchased goods at one port and sold them at the best profit they could find. Passengers could negotiate their fare depending on services provided to the *nākhudā* or the exigencies of the voyage. Most dhows from Aden charged passengers the same fare whether they disembarked at Mogadishu, Lamu, or Mombasa.[110] The price of transportation on dhows was based not on a calculation of distance but on the variable costs of a trading voyage with the monsoon winds.

DISTANCES, IN NAUTICAL MILES, DIRECT FROM PORT TO PORT.

Place	Tilbury and Gravesend	Manchester	Cardiff	Marseilles	Port Said	Suez	Aden	Musca	Bunder Abbas	Lingah	Bahrein	Bushire	Mohammerah	Busreh
Tilbury and Gravesend														
Manchester	666													
Cardiff	500	280												
Marseilles	2001	2017	1846											
Port Said	3230	3241	3070	1510										
Suez	3318	3329	3158	1598	88									
Aden	4628	4639	4468	2908	1398	1310								
Musca	5843	5859	5688	4128	2618	2530	1220							
Bunder Abbas	6092	6103	5932	4372	2862	2774	1464	250						
Lingah	6148	6159	5988	4428	2918	2830	1520	300	106					
Bahrein	6372	6383	6212	4652	3142	3054	1744	525	345	245				
Bushire	6432	6443	6272	4712	3202	3114	1804	583	398	298	165			
Mohammerah	6576	6587	6416	4856	3346	3258	1948	727	542	442	309	174		
Busreh	6596	6607	6436	4876	3366	3278	1968	747	562	462	329	194	20	
Bagdad	7096	7107	6936	5376	3866	3778	2468	1247	1062	962	829	694	520	500

Suez—Jibuti 1284
Jibuti—Aden 133

DECK PASSAGES. NATIVE PASSENGERS OR SERVANTS, WITHOUT FOOD.

Fares, in Rupees.

Place	Port Said	Suez	Aden	Muscat	Bunder Abbas	Lingah	Bahrein	Bushire	Mohammerah
Suez	10								
Aden	40	30							
Muscat	70	60	35						
Bunder Abbas	75	65	35	4					
Lingah	76	66	36	5	3				
Bahrein	77	67	37	6	4	4			
Bushire	78	68	38	7	5	4	4		
Mohammerah	80	70	40	9	7	7	6	3	
Busreh	80	70	40	9	7	7	6	3	2

NATIVE PASSENGERS. SALOON FARES, WITHOUT FOOD.

Fares, in Rupees.

Place	Port Said	Suez	Aden	Muscat	Bunder Abbas	Lingah	Bahrein	Bushire	Mohammerah
Suez	15								
Aden	110	100							
Muscat	250	250	150						
Bunder Abbas	300	290	195	49					
Lingah	310	300	200	53	34				
Bahrein	320	310	210	62	40	35			
Bushire	330	320	290	86	56	45	25		
Mohammerah	350	350	250	108	70	63	45	23	
Busreh	360	350	250	113	75	68	45	30	7

FIGURE 2. Fare and distance chart for the Strick Line, 1902. Strick Line Handbook for 1902, SRI/19/6, Caird Library, National Maritime Museum, Greenwich, UK. Reproduced by kind permission of P&O Heritage Collection, www.poheritage.com.

The price of transportation on steamships concealed these material realities of maritime travel. Fares were publicly calculated by the rate charts published by shipping companies (see figure 2). The steplike organization of these charts expressed a standardized vision of travel that was not affected by currents or weather conditions. In fact, travel took longer and its costs were higher when it occurred against the monsoon and was cheaper with the monsoon, but this was not reflected in freights and ticket fares. Seasonality disappeared in this vision of transport, and prices instead fluctuated from year to year depending on the price of coal. Thus the rise of steamshipping appeared to regularize the cost of transportation and tie it to a new source of propulsion. Most important, it appeared to make transportation a commodity.

These appearances were of course deceiving. The invisible but essential component of freight charges for steamships was the rebate. Rebates ensured that businesses stayed loyal to one shipping company: the company charged a higher stated rate and then provided a rebate if at the end of a set period the business had not used any other shipping firm.[111] Rebate agreements provided lower costs, but only for customers of almost coerced loyalty. Shipping companies thus did not allow customers to compare prices, so again they mitigated the vicissitudes of the free market.

So as steamship companies introduced the public advertisement of freight charges, the actual costs and profits of transportation were obscured. Some firms, however, persisted in undercutting the operation of conference lines and rebate agreements. These shipping companies were derided as freight speculators and were inevitably organizations outside the tight fraternity of British shipping lines. Indians, Arabs, Iranians, and Germans were considered unscrupulous in quoting rates lower than those set by the shipping conferences.[112] British firms considered cartel arrangements more ethical than competition on price, which might deprive other companies of their business. This form of business ethics derived from the idea that market competition was feasible only when a market was sufficiently developed. In this view, the Arabian Sea was too undeveloped an area to justify capitalist competition.[113] To build up business and develop local economies, profits had to be secured by the coercion and collaboration of firms. This ensured that British companies would receive "handsome" profit margins on a smaller but more secure amount of business. Steamship lines provided the appearance of commoditizing distance even as they isolated themselves from the pressures of market competition.

On April 8, 1903, Abdulla bin Khamis, his son Salim, their servant Said bin Mubarak, and their traveling companions Musallim bin Sultan and Khalfan wad Bilal slowly disembarked from the British India Company's steamer, the SS *Chindwara*. An outbreak of plague had been reported in Bombay, so all passengers were requested to remain in Muscat under quarantine. But the final destination of these five men was not Muscat but the port of Sur, about a hundred miles further south. They were not particularly interested in what seemed to them a pointless obstruction to their travel, so they planned their escape from quarantine.

Abdulla bin Khamis, Salim, and Khalfan wad Bilal had purchased second-class tickets precisely because they knew it would help them avoid quarantine regulations. Second-class ticket holders were allowed into the city of Muscat and were requested to check in with the quarantine officials each day for a week to make sure they did not come down with symptoms. To these passengers, a second-class ticket was the price of avoiding imprisonment in a quarantine camp. Said bin Mubarak and Musallim bin Sultan had purchased third-class tickets, so they had to find a way to escape their quarantine enclosure. This did not seem to be a terribly difficult task, as they had arranged with Abdulla bin Khamis to meet at the edge of the enclosure, where he would be waiting with a dhow that would take them to Sur. They rendezvoused on the appointed night and sailed south with little difficulty. Everything was going according to plan until, about thirty miles away from Muscat, they saw a British steamship appear on the horizon in hot pursuit. All five men were captured and brought back to the quarantine camp.

The story might have ended there and been lost to history, except that Abdulla bin Khamis had one more trick up his sleeve. He claimed that he was a subject of neither the sultan of Muscat nor the king of England, but rather of the Republic of France. He produced documentation that he was a French protected subject and insisted that neither the sultan nor the British Navy had any right to stop his dhow or imprison his person. Abdulla bin Khamis was able to affix his interests to the long-simmering feud over jurisdiction in the Arabian Sea. His gambit was not ultimately successful, but this minor violation became a topic of international dispute, pitting two major world powers against each other and setting a precedent in the newly created Permanent Court of Arbitration at the Hague.[114]

This seemingly small incident could turn into a diplomatic dispute of global proportions expressly because it hit on so many of the contentious questions of maritime regulation. Abdulla bin Khamis had never visited a French colony, but the dhows that he captained carried French flags and registration papers obtained by his father. His ambiguous national status as well as the contentious status of quarantine regulations made this a particularly tough case to resolve. Abdulla bin Khamis and his traveling companions exhibited just how blurred the lines of jurisdiction and how weak the regulatory provisions were in the Arabian Sea. Furthermore, they demonstrated how easy and useful it was to move between formal and informal modes of transport. Abdulla bin Khamis took a steamship from Bombay to Muscat but a dhow from Muscat to Sur. The steamship allowed the party to travel against the monsoon winds in April, which would have been impossible by dhow. But only by dhow could they evade quarantine regulations, and only by dhow could they reach a smaller port like Sur. Regulations had firmly divided formal trade and travel by steamship from informal traffics on dhows, but the two networks of transportation developed in tandem and interdependent with each other. Steamship networks maximized economies of scale and standardized distances through cartels and subsidies. Dhows carried flexible and inscrutable traffics that subverted and circumvented regulations and surveillance. Dhow traffics became the informal capillaries that fed into the arterial routes of steamship lines.

The colonial imagination of dhows as a quaint anachronism served to efface this essential role in the infrastructure of colonial capitalism. The categorical ambiguity and physical malleability of dhows made them slippery objects to monitor or regulate. Eliding these dhow traffics allowed maritime transport to appear as a standardized commodity whose price was calculated by the objective distance between major colonial ports. Customs houses recorded only the goods and people that appeared to cross the sea on carefully monitored steamship lines, producing an image of the sea as an empty homogeneous space between clearly bounded colonial territories. Colonial officials could portray the diffuse geographic margins of colonial markets as sealed borders and well-regulated ports. Dhow traffics continued to frequent obscure ports, evade documentation, and carry illicit cargoes. Most notoriously, dhows were the preferred conveyance for enslaved persons, and it is to their plight that we now turn our attention.

TWO

Trafficking Labor

AS POLITICAL AGENT IN MUSCAT, S. B. Miles had heard some strange excuses from slave traders, but Abdulla al-Kasadi's excuse was stranger than fiction. Abdulla al-Kasadi, a merchant from the Hadhramout valley in present-day Yemen, was returning from a long sojourn in the Indian princely state of Hyderabad. Accompanying him were his family as well as two young Indian boys, Mohsin and Mubarak, whom he insisted that he had legally purchased in India. Al-Kasadi even produced a deed of sale on government-issued, stamped paper, registered and witnessed by the government of Hyderabad. Perplexed and outraged by this document, Miles sent a letter to the British resident in Hyderabad, demanding to know how it was possible that slavery was being legally recognized in British India. The resident eventually explained that the Hyderabad government had issued this document during the recent famine to facilitate parents or relatives wishing to hand over their child for "maintenance" to a charitable individual. This deed was issued to ensure that the biological parents could make no further claims over the child and to serve as official recognition of this charitable act of adoption. Though he was not pleased, Miles had to accept the exigency of the crisis in Hyderabad and the government's interest in protecting the rights of adoptive parents. Al-Kasadi, however, had attempted to resell the boys in the port of Sur, so he was arrested and the boys were sent to Bombay.[1]

The tortuous transactions of Abdullah al-Kasadi and the convoluted journeys of young Mohsin and Mubarak illustrate the vastly different ways that slavery was framed out of the Arabian Sea. The same transaction could be documented as selfless charity and as self-interested enslavement. As colonial officials and trading networks engaged each other across the sea, each sought to make visible different characteristics of their transactions. Colonial officials examined this traffic through the paradigm of markets, particularly the slave markets and the slave trades that they had encountered in the Atlantic World. Slave traders, like al-Kasadi, responded by framing their transactions as familial affairs. Colonial officials could not discern exploitation or slavery when it was obscured by relationships like marriage and adoption. European businessmen elided these same relationships of social dependence in order to portray their transactions as the operation of a market in free labor. Free labor was defined only in the negative: anyone that was not enslaved could be categorized as a free and independent market agent. Human beings were still entrenched in networks that constrained participation in social and economic life, but human bodies were decommodified.

The visibility of the slave trade was determined by the materiality of human bodies: their size, shape, and color, and how these bodies were affixed to ships and other people. A market in free labor necessitated the movement of free bodies, so abolishing the slave trade required the elusive distinction between enslaved bodies and bodies engaged in free labor. Consequently, abolition in the Arabian Sea was intimately tied to new racial distinctions, and the affiliation of certain kinds of bodies with slavery. Mobile African bodies were marked as slaves, while mobile Indian bodies were marked as free labor. Furthermore, determinations of age and gender would become flashpoints of conflict between traders and officials, and ultimately these bodies would be marked as labor or family through official certificates of marriage, adoption, and manumission. Bureaucracies attempted to disembody labor, but abolition was constantly subverted by traffickers who contrived to frame family bonds as exclusive of bonded labor.

Colonial officials imagined that if they destroyed slave markets and liberated slaves, a free market in labor would spontaneously form to distribute the labor of these former slaves. But while labor could be conceptually abstracted out of laboring bodies, it was much more challenging to disembody labor in practice. Human beings were neither commodities nor independent market agents; rather, they were enrolled in multiple socioeconomic networks. Absolute freedom was rarely very attractive; rather, people wanted control over which networks they were attached to and under what conditions. Thus we are confronted with slaves who, when offered freedom, emphatically wished to remain with their former masters. These slaves believed that they could sustain themselves more successfully by mobilizing the networks that they were situated in than by liberating themselves from all social bonds.[2] "Independent" freedmen tended to live a very precarious existence, or their independence was little more than a contrivance of colonial documentation. Transactions within colonial networks were documented as the movement of free labor, while similar transactions through Arab diasporas were maligned as slave traffics. Colonial regulations did not establish a labor market so much as they framed the flow of bodies through particular networks as the operation of a market in free labor.

Transactions in labor, rather than laboring conditions, were consequently the central concern of British officials. A number of historians have highlighted the persistence of relations of social domination after abolition. While the word *slavery* was slowly excised from colonial discourse, its characteristics persisted in everything but name.[3] Indeed, colonial officials across the Arabian Sea were hesitant to abolish slavery itself for fear of alienating cooperative elites and fomenting social revolution. So, for all their sanctimonious rhetoric, British officials were very much complicit in the perpetuation of slavery. Even their ostensible success in abolishing the slave trade did not prevent transactions in bonded labor. The illicit slave trade easily overcame the feeble imperial efforts to stop it.[4] Abolition also turned a profit for the British Empire, as the empire became the manager and beneficiary of a massive trade in Indian "coolie" labor.[5] This chapter consequently traces out these multifarious impacts of the abolition of the slave trade in the Arabian Sea. If abolition was a process of framing out slaves from the market, then the movement of bonded human bodies continued to undergird the market in free labor.

The process of abolishing the slave trade in the Arabian Sea began in 1822, when the British Empire negotiated a treaty with Sayyid Saʿīd al Bu-Saʿīdī, the sultan of Muscat and Zanzibar. Under this treaty, Sayyid Saʿīd prohibited the export of slaves from his dominions, declaring this "external" trade to be piracy. This label granted the ships of the Royal Navy the right to seize slave-trading ships beyond an imaginary line extending from Cape Delgado to Diu (see map 1).[6] In 1845, Sayyid Saʿīd signed another treaty prohibiting the export of slaves from his African dominions and the import of slaves into his Asian dominions.[7] Sayyid Saʿīd died in 1856, and with his sons warring over their late father's empire, British officials decided to play Solomon. In 1861, they divided the empire between Asia and Africa, severing the very maritime connection that had made it so wealthy and powerful. Finally, in 1873, the sultan of Zanzibar agreed to completely abolish the slave trade.[8] This treaty was supposed to be the culmination of Britain's abolitionist mission, but it proved to be mere window dressing: the commerce in human beings could not be so easily suppressed.

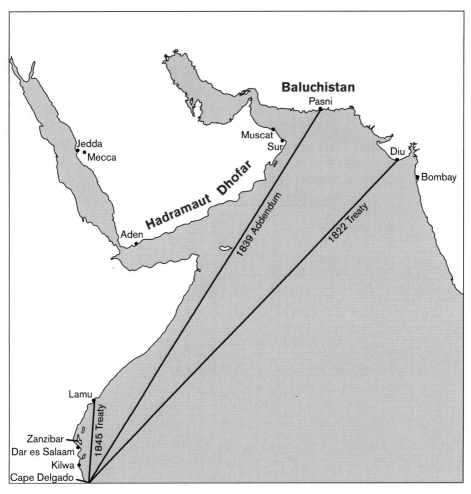

MAP I. Maritime borders of legal slave trading. Map by author.

The export of slaves from East Africa continued on a significant scale for a quarter of a century after the abolition treaty of 1873. This large-scale trade was mostly stanched by the de facto colonization of Zanzibar in 1897, yet despite the consolidation of colonial rule along the east coast of Africa a small traffic continued, particularly across the Red Sea. In the 1930s, a new slave trade from Iranian and British Baluchistan developed across the Gulf to the Arabian Peninsula. By the 1950s, when oil wealth of the Gulf states started to increase their demand for labor, these same networks were activated to supply labor from South Asia and Africa.[9] Thus the abolition of the slave trade altered and rerouted the flow of bonded labor without stopping it.

This chapter argues that abolitionist efforts neglected the smuggling traffic, condoned those slave transactions that resembled kinship transactions, and privileged British businesses in transactions of "free" labor. From their experiences in the Atlantic, British officials assumed that the Arabian Sea slave trade was structured by slave markets. However, the trafficking of slaves across the Arabian Sea did not depend on markets but was largely facilitated by dispersed social networks. Abolitionism in the Arabian Sea had three consequences. First, it produced a distinct smuggling traffic in slaves. Second, adoption and marriage became nonmarket exchanges by which the substantial traffic in women and children was legalized. Third, British bureaucrats and businessmen simply replaced slave traders in profiting from the disposal of laboring bodies. Subtle semantic shifts allowed British official to document a victory against the slave trade by overlooking, condoning, and co-opting labor traffics for their own benefit. The abolition of the slave trade was supposed to establish a free market in wage labor. Instead, both imperial officials and diasporic merchants contrived to frame out enslaved bodies from the market, while facilitating a traffic in bonded labor.

THE OTHER MIDDLE PASSAGE

Mohsin and Mubarak's journey from their families in Hyderabad to Muscat bore little resemblance to the slave raids, barracoons, and plantations that characterized the Atlantic "middle passage." Their parents had sold them into slavery during one of the most destructive famines of nineteenth-century India; Mohsin's widowed mother sold him to a woman for just four rupees. This woman took him to Hyderabad city, where she hawked him about until she found a buyer in Abdulla al-Kasadi. Mohsin lived with al-Kasadi for two months before going to Bombay, where they caught a trading dhow to Sur. Mohsin and Mubarak would have traveled as regular passengers, no different from Al-Kasadi's own children. There was little chance that a naval officer would ever have suspected that they were enslaved.

From the moment of enslavement to final sale, this slave trade was a highly contingent and improvised affair. The sale of children by their parents or guardians was not an uncommon practice in India, Africa, and even the Middle East. It was tied to wider practices of debt bondage and occurred most often during periods of famine.[10] In many of these cases, slave traders and avaricious relatives preyed on orphaned children, profiting from the absence or destitution of their parents. It is heartrending even to imagine Mohsin's mother weighing imminent death by starvation against a life of slavery for her children and a morsel of food for herself. This is not to say that these cases did not profit the purchaser of the slave or that they were not frequently abusive. Nonetheless, in conditions of extreme distress slavery provided the only hope of escape and saved the lives of many children who would otherwise have starved to death.

However, for many slaves in East Africa during the nineteenth century, enslavement occurred when prisoners were taken in internecine warfare. Since almost all the evidence we have comes from the conjectures of European observers, we cannot be certain of the percentages of slaves taken in warfare, debt bondage, or other methods. Nevertheless, violence was a fact of life. For each slave working in a household in the Arabian Peninsula, many casualties were incurred in Africa. The arduous journey from the great lakes region to the coast took thousands of lives a year, and virtually all accounts from David Livingstone onwards agree that the greatest brutality of the slave trade occurred in Africa itself. Slave caravans from the hinterlands of East Africa to the coast were equally ivory caravans: slaves were usually the porters carrying huge tusks hundreds of miles to the coast.[11] Heavy labor, limited provisions, and disease caused death on a massive scale: by one count, eight to ten slaves died for each slave that reached the coast.[12] Though in other ways the cruelty of the Indian Ocean slave trade was more restrained than that of the Atlantic middle passage, this original violence cannot be ignored.

Once slaves boarded a trading dhow, forms of exploitation became far more varied. On board, slaves were no more confined than any other passenger: they ate the same food and lived in the same spaces.[13] Slaves were rarely treated as commodities to be traded; rather, passengers and crew took full advantage of them as laborers. This component of the slave trade was less dehumanizing but perhaps more exploitative than in the Atlantic. Slaves often worked as sailors and domestic servants on board the ship, serving both their masters and others passengers. Slaves also traveled differently depending, for example, on whether they were an Ethiopian eunuch, a Circassian concubine, an Indian orphan, or a Swahili sailor. *Nākhudā*s charged different fares and provided different accommodations depending on their status.[14] As a result it is almost impossible to speak of slaves as a uniform category, or this "middle passage" as a unified enterprise.

At the other end of the journey, the circulation of slaves was also an essential part of the local economy. Slave brokers in Sur and Muscat sent newly arrived slaves to harvest dates on the Batinah coast of Oman. While working the date harvest, the slaves would be taught Arabic, and their temperament and capacity for labor would be ascertained. So, by the end of the harvest, the brokers would have gained sufficient knowledge to appropriately price their sales to other Arabs and Iranians.[15] Slave labor was needed to harvest dates, but the harvest was simultaneously an integral component of the slave trade. Imagine a slave carrying tusks of ivory from the great lakes to the coast of East Africa, then serving as a sailor aboard a dhow crossing the Arabian Sea, then picking dates on the Batinah coast, and finally serving as a shepherd in the mountains of Oman. The movement of slaves from capture to final disposition was a multiplicity of different activities, none of which could be exclusively defined as a slave trade.

The trading of slaves in the Arabian Sea was likewise not the province of specialized merchants concerned solely with slaves. Rather, the slave traffic was part of the general trade of these regions: *nākhudā*s shipped slaves along with any manner of cargo that was available. Slaves could be bought and sold in markets or in isolated transactions. Yet they were also received in lieu of money as part of a transaction, as pawns and pledges for future service, or as security on loans. Just as often, they were exchanged in nonmarket transactions, perhaps received by a patron as tribute or given as part of a bride's dowry.[16] Quite often someone possessing a slave would not have full ownership over that slave and might never have desired a slave. However, slaves were such an integral part of commerce in the Arabian Sea that traders had to deal in them. In this sense, there was no slave trade in the Arabian Sea because its participants and infrastructure were inextricable from the wider commercial environment.

The coherence of the slave trade was further dissipated by the fact that it had no set routes or timings. As we saw in the previous chapter, a *nākhudā* made his profits from intimate knowledge of local conditions and the acumen to seize the right opportunity for an advantageous transaction. So if most *nākhudā*s were carrying a few slaves among their cargo, they could easily sell them at a loss, or loan them out, or take on new slaves if this contributed to the overall profits of the trading voyage. Even basic provisions for the slaves were negotiable if the right opportunity presented itself. A dhow might be carrying inadequate supplies on the assumption that they could get more at an intermediate port or might be carrying an excess of provisions in the hope of selling them at a remunerative rate.[17] This is not to suggest that the trade was arbitrary or unorganized but rather that it was structured to react quickly and flexibly to changing conditions.

The flexible nature of this trade was a result of the fact that trade hinged on networks of brokers, not on markets. Markets certainly existed and played an important role in facilitating commerce, but transactions occurred in a wide variety of locations. Where slave markets did exist they could quickly be closed and reconstituted elsewhere, or the transactions dispersed to various locations.[18] Merchants did not seek to buy and sell all their goods within the sphere of a single market. Rather, they sought out individual buyers, isolated ports, and remunerative markets, coasting through any number of ports to make the best profit possible.[19] It is clear that many if not most transactions in slaves occurred privately between trusted partners. Of the precious few letters of correspondence between slave traders that remain in the archives, all indicate the consignment of a slave to either a particular buyer or a trusted broker who would dispose of slaves at the best price that could be obtained. Furthermore, most slaves were either accompanied by their owners or sent in the care of a trusted agent.[20] The slave trade in the Arabian Sea was a highly personalized commerce, dependent far more on social networks than on institutional infrastructures. While this system had its limitations, it still sustained a transoceanic trade involving tens of thousands of slaves annually, and it had the resilience to survive the onslaught of British abolitionism.

ABOLITION

It is not surprising that British naval patrols did not notice Mohsin and Mubarak: they were busy looking for ships coming from Africa packed with shackled black bodies. This oversight perfectly illustrates the futility of British efforts to suppress the slave trade: an improvised slave traffic built on personal networks easily eluded efforts to suppress a systematic market-centered slave trade. Anti–slave trade patrols were ineffective because they tried to apply the lessons of the Atlantic to the Indian Ocean. In the Atlantic, almost all slaves were exported from Africa and imported into the Americas, while in the Indian Ocean there was a demand for slaves everywhere, and slaves could be supplied from a variety of places. Slaves were captured along the Swahili Coast, in Ethiopia, India, Baluchistan, and the Caucasus, and on the Arabian Peninsula itself. Slaves of many races, cultures, and languages rode the waves of the Arabian Sea, yet naval officers assumed any African on a boat was a slave about to be sold. Any number of dhows were boarded, interrogated, and burned because Africans were on board, while Indians or Caucasians passed freely under the assumption that they couldn't be slaves.[21]

There was also tension between naval officers charged with abolishing the slave trade and civilian officials who dealt with its impacts onshore. British policies had to be formulated in cooperation with local rulers, so on terra firma abolitionist zeal was tempered by the interests of local potentates. Treaties condoned domestic slaveholding because the institution was enshrined in the Quran, was regulated by Islamic law, and hence did not appear to partake of the dehumanizing extremes of Atlantic slavery.[22] Thus slavery itself was not a target of abolition in the Arabian Sea until the twentieth century. Moreover, slave transactions that never left the shore were at best neglected by British officials, condoned by Italian officials, and possibly commissioned by German officials.[23] Since the Royal Navy was the main instrument of abolitionist policies, British efforts were limited to seaborne trade. Only after the consolidation of colonial rule in East Africa was the overland slave trade included in anti–slave trade efforts.[24] British abolitionism focused on the maritime slave trade because of the limitations on British power and the expediency of compromising with local rulers.

One of the primary infrastructures of the slave trade in West Africa was barracoons, and these became one of the primary targets of the Royal Navy in East Africa. Barracoons were buildings purpose-built to hold slaves and facilitate their transportation by slave ships. Naval patrols were instructed to destroy barracoons along the East African coast.[25] Destroying this infrastructure was so important that it merited a special addendum to the slave trade treaty of 1845. Sayyid Saʿīd allowed the Royal Navy to sail up creeks and rivers in his dominions for the sole purpose of destroying barracoons.[26] Yet in thousands of pages of official correspondence from over half a century, there was only one documented case of the destruction of a barracoon. This was a consequence of the fact that the slave trade in East Africa did not use barracoons. West African barracoons were dehumanizing holding pens that kept slaves concentrated and available for shipping at a moment's notice. In East Africa, the situation was perhaps less dehumanizing though probably no less arduous. Slaves were not merely commodities to be sold; rather, they were of immediate use as agricultural and domestic labor.[27] So keeping slaves unutilized in barracoons made little sense. Barracoons reduced the transaction costs of a trade in commoditized bodies, whereas in the Arabian Sea slave traffics profited from constantly employing slaves as bonded laborers.

The singular case where a barracoon was destroyed is the exception that proves the rule. The account comes from the rather self-congratulatory narrative of Commander Bunce of the HMS *Dee*.[28] In 1850, an Indian merchant was convicted of slave trading and in exchange for a reduced sentence agreed to lead officials to a nearby barracoon. He brought Commander Bunce to two settlements at the mouth of the river "Mozamba."[29] To catch the culprits red-handed, Bunce ordered a surprise attack on a stone structure on the bank. His marines stormed the building, but no slaves were found. They did find considerable quantities of ivory, piece goods, promissory notes, muskets, and other merchandise belonging to merchants in the region. Nonetheless, Bunce persisted in asserting that this structure was a barracoon and summarily burned it as an example to those who might dare engage in slave traffic. Bunce further boasted that this was the only barracoon on the entire coast and that its destruction would be a "death blow" to the East African slave trade.[30]

Commander Bunce's triumphalism rings hollow if we consider it with any degree of skepticism. The assertion that the only barracoons on the coast would be located near the relatively insignificant towns of Keonga and Mapani, rather than the major hubs of Kilwa, Dar-es-Salaam, or Bagamoyo, is highly questionable. At best, Bunce had destroyed a former barracoon built by Portuguese slave traders but now used as a warehouse. The self-promotional tone of the account, the unreliability of a coerced informant, and most of all the simple lack of slaves in an alleged barracoon stretch the limits of plausibility. A far more likely scenario was that the Indian informant pointed out an ordinary warehouse, which may well have been a competitor's property. Imperial officials placed a premium on the destruction of barracoons on the East African coast, but, unfortunately for naval officers less imaginative than Commander Bunce, they didn't seem to play much of a role in the slave traffic.

If barracoons were important to abolitionist ideas, the slave market was a symbol of all the evils of the slave trade for British administrators. Henry Bartle Frere, the official responsible for negotiating the 1873 abolition treaty, was disgusted by the sight of people buying and selling slaves and generally lounging about in the Zanzibar slave market. He argued that "nothing can tend more to keep up a depraved feeling on the subject of the Slave Trade generally than the existence of an open slave-market."[31] Bartle Frere consequently believed that if slave markets could be eliminated the trade itself would disappear.[32] But, as we have seen, the slave trade did not depend on markets. In fact, the Zanzibar slave market was nothing more than an open square in town where buyers and sellers of slaves congregated.[33] There was little physical infrastructure to destroy and little difficulty in establishing a market elsewhere. When the markets were closed, the traffic was quickly reconstituted outside of Zanzibar town, in private houses and by simply depending on brokers to connect buyers and sellers.

The efforts of the Royal Navy in the waters of the Arabian Sea were focused on intercepting "slavers." Slavers were fast ships designed specifically to transport slaves, akin to the notorious Baltimore clippers that so dominated the trans-Atlantic carriage of slaves. In particular, the treaties were written to identify slaving vessels by slaving equipment: shackles and decks designed to carry the maximum amount of slaves in the space available, and minimum provisions and crew members. But these ships, with their investments in special outfitting of holds, were basically nonexistent in the Indian Ocean slave trade. While dhows were often fast and maneuverable ships like Baltimore clippers, they were not engaged solely in the carriage of slaves.[34] Dhows were not designed to maximize efficiency in carrying slaves, so it was a futile endeavor to identify "slavers" in the Arabian Sea.

Since slaving dhows did not exist, British officials had to create them. New regulations required that any dhow carrying slaves was to be conspicuously marked as a slaver. During the 1860s dhows engaged in the legal slave trade were ordered to carry special passes and to exhibit distinctive marks on their hulls to indicate that they were carrying slaves.[35] Yet this system was soon found faulty because the passes issued to one ship were purchased by other ships engaged in the illegal trade to the Arabian Peninsula.[36] Furthermore, those distinctive marks were easily painted over. Free Africans had to carry certificates of liberation from the political agent in Zanzibar, and whether free or slave they needed to be entered in a manifest of "Negro passengers." They were also permitted to travel only on ships with passes that explicitly stated their itinerary.[37] Another policy required that all African passengers should wear a linen cloth around their wrists with a consular seal to indicate that they were not being transported for sale.[38] This regulation disturbingly echoes the practices of certain slave traders who tied a black cloth with the name of the consignee around the necks of their slaves.[39] Thus, in order to render passenger traffic legible to British cruisers, imperial administrators marked African bodies in the same way that slave traders did. Africans travelers now needed a variety of official papers to permit them the mobility they had enjoyed prior to abolition.

This slew of regulations halted only a small percentage of the slave trade, even as it interfered with the bulk of regular trade between East Africa and the Gulf.[40] One administrator estimated that anti–slave trade patrols captured less than 1 percent of the slaves brought to Arabia.[41] Observers attributed this to a variety of different causes: naval officers argued that not enough cruisers were on the water, others suggested that the pass system was unenforceable, and still more believed that the whole project was impossible if slavery itself was not abolished.[42] Regulations against the slave trade were ineffectual, so officials were constantly expanding the jurisdiction of British courts and the cruising grounds of naval squadrons. The colonial bureaucracy could not control the traffics that connected the shores of the Arabian Sea, but the impact of the anti–slave trade campaign was not insignificant. The abolition of the slave trade in the Arabian Sea was the justification for Britannia ruling these waves, and this would have lasting effects on exchanges across the Arabian Sea.

"A DISTINCT TRAFFIC"

The British political agent in Muscat could rescue Mohsin and Mubarak in the territories of the sultan of Muscat because British administrators claimed extraterritorial jurisdiction over diasporic Indians across the Arabian Sea. Indian merchants had been a fixture in the trade of Arabia and East Africa for centuries and as a result were intimately involved with all aspects of the traffic in slaves along the coasts of the Arabian Sea. Given that slavery was an accepted institution in India and an integral component of the general trade between these regions, Indians were often slaves, slave owners, slave traders, and potentially all three simultaneously. Yet as the slave trade and slavery were being abolished in British India in the early nineteenth century, Indians involved in the slave trade in Africa and Arabia were largely unaffected. British efforts to eliminate Indians from the slave trade became the wedge that forced open a larger campaign to separate and ultimately eliminate the slave trade.

In the 1860s, as the suppression of the slave trade was being enforced by British officials outside India, these British Indian slaveholders provided a perfect point of entry for abolitionist policies. In both Oman and East Africa, British officials informed Indians that they could no longer possess or trade in slaves.[43] This caused a furor, particularly on parts of the Swahili Coast where Indians held significant numbers of slaves.[44] Some three thousand slaves were emancipated simultaneously, and the economic consequences were almost apocalyptic: "When these slaves were emancipated, the value of the estates fell proportionately; heavy loss was sustained by our subjects; credit was shaken . . . and hence no man would advance on security of any landed estate. The circulation of money was checked in the source; commerce in general became affected; the value of all property, house or landed fell."[45] The events were certainly dramatic in the moment and would have significant longer-term effects on the financial structures of East African commerce. Perhaps most importantly, regulation of Indian slaveholding succeeded in removing the main mercantile community from direct participation in slavery. Consequently, the slave trade became one step removed from the general trade of the Arabian Sea.

Colonel Rigby was the political agent in Zanzibar who instituted these regulations on Indian subjects in East Africa. Yet he conceded that anti–slave trade patrols had actually doubled the quantities of slaves traded in the 1860s. Patrols had increased prices of slaves and profits of slave traders without effectively intercepting the transportation of slaves. Moreover, he himself argued that only *after* the British intervention did the slave trade became a "distinct traffic."[46] The removal of Indians from the traffic, naval patrols, and regulations instituted by customs officials forced those *nākhudā*s committed to trading in slaves to develop a dedicated traffic that could evade these regulations. Only when the commerce in slaves became illicit did it emerge as a distinct slave trade.

Perversely, one accomplishment of abolition was the creation of some of the very horrors it set out to abolish. Beginning with the process of enslavement, the suppression of the slave trade had detrimental effects on the experience of slaves moving through the Arabian Sea. If enslavement had occurred in a variety of ways, the suppression of the slave trade caused a particular spike in the use of kidnapping, or "man-stealing" as the British often called it.[47] Thus the fear and even terror of enslavement became palpable. One official described Zanzibar as "a city with a hostile army camped in its neighborhood. Every person who is able to do so sends his children and young slaves into the interior of the island for security. People are afraid to stir out of their houses after dark, and reports are daily made of children and slaves kidnapped. And in the suburbs of the town they even enter the houses, and take the children away by force."[48] While slaves may well have been kidnapped before British anti–slave trade efforts, they were not kidnapped in the numbers that they were after anti–slave trade operations commenced, and certainly not from Zanzibar. The ban on slave markets did not stop Arab merchants from catering to the demand for slaves; it merely made this demand more explicit by forcing traders to "steal" what they would otherwise have purchased.

The abolition of slave exports from Zanzibar had merely made visible the opaque violence that slave purchasers had already been perpetrating. The notion of a "slaver" had not existed in the Indian Ocean up to the early nineteenth century.[49] However, in response to increasing patrols, slave traders began to run large cargoes of slaves on old and barely seaworthy dhows. These ships always sailed within sight of the coast so that if they were chased by a British cruiser the dhow could be quickly crash-landed into the rocky shoreline. The slaves were then evacuated and marched into the hinterland. A British cruiser might pursue, but the time it took to anchor and send a small boat to navigate through the rocks without being damaged invariably meant that the slaves would have long disappeared into the surrounding regions.[50] These slaving dhows were old and cheap so that in precisely these instances the sale of the landed slaves would compensate for the loss of the dhow. Atlantic slavers were vessels engineered to maximize the horrific efficiencies of a capitalist trade in human beings; Arabian Sea slavers were defined only by the fact that they were disposable.

The limited military and financial resources that the British Empire committed to combating the Indian Ocean slave trade meant that there were gaping holes in its enforcement. The Royal Navy rarely deployed more than half a dozen ships to combat the slave trade in the western Indian Ocean; more often the number was much lower, and those ships had to serve a number of additional functions.[51] This handful of ships was meant to monitor thousands of miles of coastline in East Africa and the Arabian Peninsula, not to mention the thousands of square miles of open seas in between them. As one official bemoaned: "Under existing adverse conditions, the operations of the fleet have been by common consent, absolutely futile and these conditions unaltered and the powers of cruisers further restricted, its labour will continue to be thankless and barren of good result, nay, harmful."[52] Both the merchants and the sailors knew that the odds were good for smuggling and that no amount of crafty positioning of cruisers could capture even half of the traffic.[53] Consequently, the shifting instructions and redeployment of cruisers in the Arabian Sea over the course of thirty years became almost comical. Ships were sent at one moment to Muscat and Zanzibar, then to choke points like the Straits of Hormuz, next spread along the southern coast of Arabia, only to be transferred to the choke point between the island of Socotra and the Somali coast.[54] This game of cat and mouse continued, much to the chagrin of naval officers, who rescued ever fewer slaves. The limited number of cruisers, the vast expanse of the ocean, and the flexibility of *nākhudās* almost guaranteed that slave traffics would remain just out of reach.

Slave traders also developed an extremely comprehensive intelligence network, especially when compared to the Royal Navy's. British attempts to gather information on slave trafficking was woefully inadequate, on several occasions falling prey to false rumors and misleading intelligence.[55] Slave traders, on the other hand, could find innumerable places to hide from British cruisers, having had long experience in these waters. Slave traders also developed a system of flag signals by which informants onshore could convey the location of British cruisers and how to evade them.[56] Moreover, local townspeople, fishing boats, and bedouins actively supported slave traders, whether by acting as informants or by concealing landed slaves. This also extended to the connivance of local customs officials who out of sympathy or bribery overlooked the import and export of slaves from their territories.[57] Indeed, in Oman and the Gulf the slave trade benefited exponentially from the support of the local population.

Slave traders found a particularly effective method of evading detection by exploiting land routes that, while often more expensive and more destructive, were unmonitored. Slave caravans that had formerly ended at Kilwa and Bagamoyo for the dhow journey to Zanzibar and onwards now marched north to Lamu and even Somalia.[58] From there it was a short journey to the southern coasts of Arabia. Some slave traders circumvented British surveillance altogether by crossing the Red Sea where British cruisers could not patrol Ottoman and later Saudi waters.[59] Similarly, in the Gulf there was a long history of the enslavement of Baluchis. With the decline of slave imports from East Africa, worldwide economic depression, and political unrest in Baluchistan in the 1930s and '40s, growing numbers of Baluchi slaves found their way into Oman and the Gulf.[60] Many Baluchis were kidnapped, were sold into slavery, and even became slave traders themselves as a result of the harsh conditions in Iranian and British Baluchistan. Others were recruited to the Arab side of the Gulf on the promise of work, only to be enslaved when they arrived.[61] Both in the Red Sea and in the Gulf, slave traders could easily spirit their human cargo across the waters on a dark night with almost no chance of capture by British cruisers. Anti–slave trade patrols thus pushed the slave trade from a primarily seaborne journey to primarily an overland march.

Yet slave traders could also follow their normal maritime routes by removing their dhows from British jurisdiction. Earlier in the nineteenth century,

British officials complained of Spanish, American, and even Mexican ships loading slaves at Zanzibar in blatant disregard for the anti–slave trade treaties signed by Sayyid Saʿīd.[62] By the late 1860s, these European nations had largely disappeared, but the Ottoman and Qajar Empires continued to provide immunity from search by British cruisers.[63] But as we saw in the previous chapter, toward the end of the nineteenth century the French flag would become the most effective cloak for the slave trade. By the mid-1870s, the protection of the French flag was so notorious that a British naval interpreter was publicly taunted on the point when at Sur.[64] Indeed, Sur had always been an important port, but in this period, it became infamous as a center for slave trading because of all the dhows sailing under the French flag. Suri *nākhudās* flaunted their immunity in the face of British officials, who despaired: "One thing is certain, as long as the native craft can buy the French colors for a mere song, so long the slave trade will exist."[65] The case of Abdulla bin Khamis, recounted in the previous chapter, led to an Anglo-French compromise and a limit on Suri dhows carrying French flags. Yet well into the twentieth century slave traders continued to evade detection on French-flagged dhows.[66]

The increasing presence of British patrols in the waters of the Arabian Sea had fundamentally altered the dynamic of trade. To suppress the slave trade, imperial regulators forced all traders to abide by a number of new regulations. Before these regulatory interventions, traders had used improvised sailing plans, intelligence networks, and amenable political patrons to further their commerce. With slight modifications, these would prove to be effective strategies for developing an illicit slave traffic in the era of abolition. The slave trade was thus extricated from general commerce and evolved as a smuggling traffic. Naval patrols had made this traffic more cruel than previous modes of transporting slaves, but they could not suppress the traffic completely. The sea was too large to effectively control, and land routes and foreign flags provided protection from seizure by British cruisers. Slave traders had found myriad ways to evade patrols, but they equally endeavored to frame this traffic as outside the market.

TRANSACTIONS IN KIN

Mohsin and Mubarak were not the only slaves traveling on the dhow to Sur that day. Another Arab from Hadhramout was transporting a small girl from Hyderabad named Haleema. Mohsin was about ten years old, but Mubarak

FIGURE 3. Cargo of child slaves rescued from an Arab dhow. "East African Slaves Taken Aboard the HMS *Daphne* from an Arab Dhow," January 11, 1868, FO84/1310, National Archives of the United Kingdom, Kew, UK. Reproduced with the kind permission of the National Archives of the United Kingdom.

and Haleema were so young that they could not give an account of how they were enslaved. It was not an anomaly that all three slaves traveling on board this dhow were children: women and children constituted the majority of slaves being trafficked across the Arabian Sea (see figure 3). Since children were more impressionable, learned Arabic faster, and quickly forgot their past, they were preferred as slaves. This was largely because the slaves tended not to be employed as agricultural labor except along the coasts of East Africa and the Indian Ocean islands. The agricultural production of the Gulf did not demand large laboring populations, and the infrastructures simply did not exist to efficiently coerce a hostile labor force.[67] Rather, slaves were employed mostly as domestic and sexual labor, and as such, the ability of women and children to assimilate into Arab society was more prized.

Since colonial officials mostly condoned domestic slavery, slave trading evolved to appear closer to domestic slavery. Slave traders discovered that the best way to avoid detection was not to be invisible but rather to make slaves perfectly visible to British authorities as servants. Despite the creation of a distinct illicit trade in slaves, most traders shipped their human cargo singly or in small groups on dhows that were carrying a varied cargo. As many officers put it, slaves were transported "in driblets."[68] From letters recovered from slave-trading vessels it is also clear that many merchants preferred to transport their slaves on regular vessels and not on slaving dhows.[69] Crews were more likely to convince naval officers that this slave was just the servant of a passenger if there were only one or two aboard. By the twentieth century, the most effective method was probably to transport slaves on British steamships. Naval officers never imagined that these paragons of British enterprise and modern technology could carry slaves. However, in 1935, a League of Nations Committee reported that Africans were being transported as passengers on steamships, only to be sold into slavery when they arrived in Muscat.[70] Thus, as long as they called their slaves servants or passengers, merchants could operate just as they had when the slave trade was legal.

The pilgrimage to Mecca also proved to be a successful cover for transporting slaves, as British officials could not inquire too forcefully into a religious obligation that engaged such huge numbers each year. Nonetheless, they feared that "the annual gathering at Mecca gives the principal impetus to the present Slave Trade of the world."[71] Jedda and Mecca hosted large slave markets, and many brokers used the hajj as an opportunity to realize a profit on their slaves.[72] But for many Muslims this transaction appeared in a completely different light. Manumitting a slave while performing the hajj was considered a particularly pious deed for a pilgrim. One hajji interrogated for trading slaves explained it as follows: "On my voyage to Mecca as it is customary among Mahomedans to give liberty to bondsmen and bondswomen and this is considered [a] good action, I purchased one in Mecca and one in Jedda and gave both their liberty as a charitable action and gave them their choice of either serving me or going where they choose [sic]. They preferred to serve me and I therefore brought them with me. . . . As they are children and require a guardian to bring them up I have kept them out of charity."[73] Officials both accepted this particular explanation and approved of it as charity. Indeed, there is little reason to believe that this was not meant as a genuinely charitable act. At the same time, this case perfectly exhibits the blurred distinctions between slave trading and charity. Unscrupulous individuals could legally manumit their slaves while maintaining control through powerful social bonds.[74] The difference between a charitable act of manumission and an unscrupulous cover for slavery was the extent to which the owner/guardian exploited the dependence of his ward. Adoption was a noneconomic transaction that could not be distinguished from child slavery. Unfortunately, the hajj provided a perfect venue for countless transactions of this sort each year.

One of the most important methods of disguising slave transactions in the Arabian Sea was as the sale/marriage of girls to their owners/husbands. Though their numbers fluctuated according to place and time, an important characteristic of the slave trade in the Arabian Sea was the predominance of females. British officials were particularly horrified and titillated by the cases of women from the Caucasus who interchangeably served as slave, concubine, and wife to aristocratic Arab men.[75] The stories of white-skinned Circassian (from the Caucasus region) beauties inhabiting the harems of the Ottoman sultans had captured the imaginations of British officials. Therefore, the records of a handful of women from the Caucasus in the Arabian Sea are particularly rich and detailed.

Naz al-Bustan was one such Circassian beauty. She claimed that she had been purchased in Istanbul and brought to Muscat by Sayyid Thuwainī ibn Saʿīd, then the sultan of Muscat. Thuwainī's death resulted in several years of turmoil until his brother Turkī ibn Saʿīd established himself on the throne. In her account, Turkī married Naz al-Bustan, but after seven years of marriage he divorced her and she went to live with Thuwainī's daughter. Then she was aggressively courted by the *wali* (governor) of Dhofar, Suleiman ibn Suweilim. She felt at first that as merely a servant of the sultan he was beneath her. But with much pressure from the royal family she eventually married Suleiman, settled in Dhofar, and bore him a son.

Not surprisingly, after a few years Naz became unhappy with her life in the wilderness of Dhofar. She particularly complained that her husband had taken away the jewelry given to her by Sayyid Thuwainī and Sayyid Turkī. She decided to leave her husband and returned to Muscat, seeking refuge with Thuwainī's daughter. But Naz had miscalculated: the princess rebuffed her, saying that Naz was not Suleiman's wife but his slave and so had no choice but to return to Dhofar. A less self-confident woman would have accepted her fate, but Naz al-Bustan was clearly a force to be reckoned with. She surreptitiously escaped Muscat and found place on a dhow going to Bombay for herself, her child, and even her nanny! After arriving in a city where she lacked both social networks and social status, Naz had to somehow find a means of support. She eventually found a patron in Sheikh ʿĪsa ibn Khalīfa, a wealthy pearl merchant from Bahrain. Despite protests from her erstwhile husband and their own uneasiness, colonial officials allowed her to remain with her son in Bombay.[76]

In the course of her life, Naz al-Bustan went from slave to wife to slave to wife to slave, finally ending in some sort of indeterminate state of dependence on Sheikh ʿĪsa. She was a slave whose closest companions were royalty and who condescended to governors. Her experience was far from the norm among slaves crossing the Arabian Sea, but the indeterminacy of her status was very common. The blurred line between the Muslim practice of a husband's payment of *mahr* (a gift of money or property providing some financial independence to the wife within the marriage) and the purchase of a slave could well have misled Naz al-Bustan, just as it was a source of continuing frustration for imperial administrators.[77] Under Islamic law, even if Naz were a slave, her son would be free and his father's legitimate heir, and she had the right to be free on Suleiman's death.[78] For Naz al-Bustan and many enslaved women, the threshold between dependency and exploitation or between guardian and slave owner was never clearly delineated, so the condition of slavery remained ambiguous.

If women like Naz al-Bustan straddled the border between slave and wife, many slave traders passed off their slaves as wives in order to circumvent British officials. Customs officers were often told that newly purchased slaves were married to the passengers that brought them, but these officers eventually became wise to this ruse and demanded to see marriage contracts.[79] Official documentation of marriage subsequently became a requirement for the legal importation of women into the Arabian Peninsula. As a result, marriage contracts were drawn up and signed by *qāḍi*s (Islamic judges) in order to facilitate the trafficking of domestic slaves. This was such an effective system that on the eve of World War II it was apparently still being used in Saudi Arabia:

> It would of course be possible for Shaikh Yusuf to import women for the Saudi royal family without transgressing any law, human or divine, that he recognizes. He has only to marry a girl in Syria and to divorce her on arrival in Riyadh; there she could easily be constrained to marry one of the princes, who in a few weeks or even days would divorce her and pass her on, always in accordance with Moslem law, to a younger brother or to some friend . . . Dr. Midhat, who arrived in Saudi Arabia some years ago as a penniless refugee, is now a rich man, and it is unlikely that his wealth is due solely to his medical skill. . . . It is not unreasonable to suspect him of acting as pimp to the royal family.[80]

This account is probably exaggerated, and it is quite possible that these marriages were not even the orthodox Muslim marriage known as *nikaḥ* but the rather more dubious practices of temporary marriage (*muta'a*) or secondary/slave marriage (*sūria*). Nevertheless, British officials could not tell the difference and declined to interfere or categorize these marriages as slavery.[81]

There was one significant exception to British acceptance of marriage contracts of this sort: marriages between Arab men and African women. Such contracts were always under suspicion as a ruse to conceal domestic slavery, and officials would not accept the marriage contract on its own. Saleha, for example, was an Ethiopian girl brought through Muscat to Bushehr by an Iranian merchant named Sayyid Ibrahim. Saleha claimed to be a free Arab born in Mocha and said her mother had given her in marriage to Sayyid Ibrahim at Mecca. Sayyid Ibrahim said she was a free-born Ethiopian and he had paid a *mahr* of fifty dollars to her father in Mecca; he presented an official marriage certificate signed by a *qāḍi* and the Iranian consul in Jedda.[82] The discrepancies in their stories made the investigating officials presume that this was a case of slave trafficking. Saleha firmly denied understanding the "Abyssinian" language but knew only a few words of Arabic. The political agent in Muscat concluded that she was a slave and needed to be rescued. Over her protests, the political agent removed Saleha from Sayyid Ibrahim's custody.[83] In the mass of conflicting evidence, it is difficult to disentangle the thoughts and motives of Saleha or Sayyid Ibrahim, but clearly Saleha's race trumped both her own statements and Sayyid Ibrahim's documentation. British officials found African women to be inherently suspect as slaves and assumed a patronizing role that they did not for women like Naz al-Bustan.

For better or for worse, the mobility of Africans in the Arabian Sea was more rigorously interrogated by British officials. Anti–slave trade operations, while cognizant of the diversity of enslaved persons, were focused on the enslavement of Africans by other races. Yet marriages to Baluchi, Arab, and Circassian slaves were less suspicious. Hence the ease with which Sheikh Yusuf, referred to above, could traffic Syrian women into Saudi Arabia. In the twentieth century, as anti–slave trade operations made the mobility of African women immediately suspect, the supply of female slaves from other regions began to compensate. Since only marriage to Africans bore the stigma of slavery, the trafficking of slaves from other parts of the world continued. The trafficking of sexual labor had certainly changed in the course of the suppression of the slave trade. In particular, the trafficking of African slaves was limited and the total numbers dwindled. Yet the practice continued by maneuvering around British regulations: it was twisted into the guise of marriage and shifted away from European racial stereotypes.

FREE SLAVES, FREE LABOR, AND FREE MARKETS

Mohsin and Mubarak were both left with the Bombay police commissioner in 1878 for disposal among the inhabitants of the city. We know that in the following year the children were placed in the households of Mahomed Reza Benaresi and Abbas Ali Sheriff. We do not know anything specific about these two men, except that the police commissioner considered them "respectable native gentlemen," and from their names we can assume they were Muslim.[84] As children alienated from their own community networks, Mohsin and Mubarak were completely dependent on these Muslim Bombayites for opportunities to live and labor. Other than a change of scenery, their condition probably would not have been different from slavery in Sur. We can only speculate about their lives subsequently, but clearly they had no control over their lives or the disposal of their own labor. One can hardly blame the police commissioner, as their age and status left him few options. However, the notion that emancipation would spontaneously produce a free market in labor is belied by the thousands of freed slaves shuttled about the Arabian Sea by imperial fiat.

Britons had worked determinedly to obtain freedom for African slaves throughout the nineteenth century: little did they realize that freedom would bring almost as many problems as slavery. Anti–slave trade measures, while not overwhelmingly successful, had created a growing population of liberated slaves at various ports around the Arabian Sea. British officials imagined that this free labor would be an irrepressible, self-perpetuating force for good, increasing profits and wages. The political agent in Zanzibar argued: "Let the nucleus of this free force be established & fostered, inherent powers of increase will come into play, and a numerous population of free descendants will dwell in Zanzibar, a stout phalanx in the path of slavery."[85] Colonial officials assumed that their only responsibility was to emancipate these laborers. So initially slaves were handed their certificates of manumission and released wherever their slave ships were condemned. The political agents in these locations often assisted a free slave in finding domestic labor with respectable merchants, but it soon became apparent that these positions were virtually indistinguishable from the lot of domestic slaves and sometimes worse. "I maintain that the slave handed over and assigned for service to private individuals is in a worse position, than one that is purchased; a man will take care possibly of property for which he pays."[86] Thus officials quickly discovered that if they had any pretension of improving the lives of slaves, their responsibility did not end with emancipation.

Perhaps the central problem was that freedom was a highly unstable condition for slaves. Manumission was a common occurrence in the Arabian Peninsula, but so was re-enslavement. No matter what one's legal status, being of slave heritage placed one in a position of subservience that was difficult to break out of.[87] In much of East Africa and in the Arabian Peninsula re-enslavement was common for manumitted slaves, as names and physical characteristics indicated slave heritage and free populations were complacent about such breaches of Islamic and colonial law. Dozens of slave accounts evidence this trend, with the narrators recounting how even after manumission they were kidnapped or their former masters reasserted ownership.[88] British officials had placed so much importance on the emancipation of slaves that they did not confront the reality that manumission made little difference to the economic opportunities and social status that determined living standards for freed slaves.

British officials had put great store in the certificates of manumission that they issued. These documents were supposed to be bulwarks against re-enslavement, but canny slave traders discovered that they provided the perfect method of transporting slaves. Slave owners held on to manumission papers and pulled them out only to pass off their slaves as free persons when questioned by officials. When they reached their destination or a good enough price was offered, they gave up the pretense and sold the slave. The process had apparently been streamlined in Mecca, so that slave purchasers from India could obtain certificates of manumission directly from a *qāḍi*, with slaves themselves never seeing the document.[89] It also appears that in Zanzibar some employers drew up formal labor contracts for former slaves either to evade scrutiny or to preempt any question of their free status.[90] The legal structures of emancipation were no match for the continuing social power of slave owners.

Imperial administrators consequently decided that they should send freed slaves to locations where Britain had greater powers of surveillance and control. By location, the best destination for slaves was Aden, which had been a British colony since 1839. But very quickly the numbers of liberated slaves overwhelmed this port city, which had no agricultural production, little industrial work, and few households wealthy enough to take on additional servants.[91] Fear of a smallpox epidemic meant that slaves were quarantined on a small, barren island in Aden Harbor. As their numbers grew, conditions on the quarantine island were so abysmal that one official admitted: "Their condition as freemen is not superior to that from which they have been removed."[92]

Unlike Aden, the Seychelles were an archipelago of islands with plenty of fertile land that could support sugar plantations and potentially a community of freed slaves. The Church Missionary Society had also established a mission in the Seychelles, hoping to make it the Indian Ocean equivalent of Sierra Leone.[93] The problem in the Seychelles was not lack of opportunity or land but the freed slaves themselves. The small population of slaves brought to the islands was proving to be a thoroughly reluctant workforce, as the civil commissioner of the islands noted: "Even under the most favourable circumstances, [freed slaves] can do but a minimum of good to any country could they be disposed of as labourers, but . . . under the present aspects of the labour-market, will put the Government to very heavy expense. The islands are now overstocked, not only with the African in his normal state, but with his offspring, the fecundity of the women being quite remarkable. Twins are very common; and upon two occasions I have seen three at a birth."[94] Officials continued to speak of freed slaves as if they were chattel ("overstocked"), and were concerned not with their well-being but with their excess supply in this market. Their arrival on the sugar plantations of Mauritius occasioned similar indifference, and in the following years imperial administrators in the West Indies, Fiji, Somalia, and Borneo all declined to accept freed slaves after finding out that they were uninterested in plantation work.[95] It was clear that, despite lifetimes of enslavement, plantation discipline did not agree with liberated slaves from the Arabian Sea.

It was not surprising then, that colonial officials concluded that they needed to impart some discipline in order to prepare these freed men and women to "use well the freedom that awaits them."[96] Though it was never implemented in Zanzibar, a form of apprenticeship was proposed by which freed slaves would become free labor.

> There is no reason why free labour may not be as nearly cheap & as certainly manageable as slave labour in Zanzibar. I do not use the word "free" in the sense that the freedom we have given is to bear no fruit of obligation. Unless, by a benevolent compulsion these freed folk are taught to labor they probably will not, & it will be essential to the proper working of the measure that a large control, under Consular supervision, be given to the Planter, & that an

obligation be laid upon the quondam slave to discharge certain duties for a certain term as the price of his liberty & civil rights.[97]

Contrary to Adam Smith's contention, free labor was not cheaper than slave labor because of market competition. Free laborers had to be disciplined under benevolent compulsion, but it was compulsion nonetheless. Their indiscipline was likely due to the fact that many slaves worked as domestic laborers, concubines, and sailors. So they were unaccustomed and unwilling to accept the strenuous labor of a plantation. Moreover, they were probably frustrated by the notion that even after being "liberated" they were sent about the Indian Ocean by bureaucratic fiat and given occupations in which they had no interest. Freed slaves complained that colonial officials continued to treat them as if they were enslaved, and in private, missionaries admitted it. One official argued that "so long as, they are in a child stage of development, they must accept what those over them think best for them."[98] The routes of labor mobility had changed after abolition, but laborers themselves still had little say in what routes they would take.

Very early in the suppression of the slave trade, French plantation colonies in the Indian Ocean attempted to obtain labor through the engagé system.[99] Under this system, French plantation owners and ship captains ostensibly contracted with free Africans for five years' indentured labor in sugar colonies like Réunion. What incensed British administrators was the fact that the recruitment "bonus" was paid to slave owners and was equal to the price of a slave on the Zanzibar market. Slave owners and brokers consequently freed their slaves, ordered them to work for the French recruiters, and pocketed the recruitment bonus.[100] The French recruiters and their consul did not believe they were doing anything wrong; indeed, they saw themselves as rescuing men from slavery.[101] But British officials were outraged, arguing this was merely a continuation of slavery under another name, especially since this demand for free labor would still cause the enslavement of Africans in the hinterland.[102] Thus freed slaves had to be protected from French schemes even as they had difficulty being placed in British colonies.

French businessmen and Zanzibari slave owners believed British outrage over the engagé system had much more to do with undermining the British indentured labor trade from India. For all their outrage, British officials were deeply invested in forms of bonded labor that could be publicized as free. Indentured laborers or "coolies" drew on precisely the same populations that had fed the smaller slave traffic coming out of India: famine-stricken, impoverished, and otherwise desperate individuals.[103] British officials advocated for indentured labor because officials, brokers, and shipping companies all benefited from promoting the "coolie" trade. Freed slaves, on the other hand, were only a burden on the government exchequer. Both liberated slaves and coolies were forced by desperation or coercion into laboring in far-off lands. While coolies were transported by labor recruiters motivated by profit, freed slaves were transported by bureaucrats motivated by expedience. In both cases, the experience was similar from the perspective of the laborer, and it looked nothing like a free market for labor.

Since children were a large component of the slave trade, colonial officials were stuck with large numbers of dependent children. These children could not be "set at large" unless one of the adult slaves asserted that he or she was the child's parent.[104] The remaining children were placed with "respectable families." Though it is never explicitly stated, the names of the adoptive families and British fears that these freed children would convert to Islam indicate that these families were overwhelmingly Muslim. These families would almost certainly have been Arabs or Indians from the Ismaili, Khoja, and Bohra sects of Islam who predominated in the trade of the Arabian Sea. These would also be the only communities able to speak Arabic or Swahili, the languages that freed slaves might understand. So these families who might have purchased domestic slaves previously now received them in Bombay free of charge.

In 1885, when fears of conversion were heightened, active efforts were made to find schools where these children could obtain a Christian education, preferably one not run by French Catholics. Bombay was a train ride away from three mission schools: the Ahmednagar Mission School, the Deccan Industrial School at Shirur, and the African Asylum at Nashik. Since the 1850s, these institutions had served as orphanages for freed African boys and girls. After 1885, they would serve as the destination for all rescued slave children under the age of seventeen.[105] Boys would usually be taught a trade and girls trained for domestic service. Both would receive instruction in a language, perhaps Marathi or Hindi, and only the smarter ones would be given lessons in English.[106] Nashik in particular would become famous in Africa for producing missionaries who would return to proselytize their fellow Africans. The government paid the missions for this service, and the system seemed to work well for several years. But then the schools began to have more problems with the children's discipline, and the treasury started to complain about the costs of maintaining the children.[107] In 1889, the commissioner of police complained that Bombay was overrun with ex-slaves who had become an "excitable and turbulent element in the population" and requested that in the future liberated slaves should be sent elsewhere.[108] Only after the turn of the century, when the Royal Navy reduced its efforts to patrol the sea, would the Bombay police commissioner be relieved of this particular burden. But in the meantime Bombay would witness the development of a substantial community of freed slaves.

Girls and women among this freed population presented a particularly thorny problem for officials in Bombay. Initially they had been left to their own devices, but while men could occasionally find work it became evident that women were turning to prostitution. This was a shocking realization, and some officials suggested it would be better to leave such women in slavery in Arabia. "Respectable gentlemen" were again sought out who could employ these women as domestic servants or would take them as brides.[109] These women had little choice in who they married or what kinds of domestic and sexual labor might be required of them. So little had changed between slavery and marriage. This trajectory is illustrated by the case of Amina, who had been kidnapped in the Caucasus and ultimately purchased by a relative of the sultan of Muscat. She lived in Muscat but after a few years was sold to an Iranian man, who was taking her to Bandar Abbas, when she was rescued by the captain of their steamship. British officials eventually sent her to Bombay, where she was completely out of place, speaking only Arabic and refusing to leave the house unless she was fully veiled. Moreover, as she was completely incapable of performing domestic service, local administrators could think of only one resolution: she had to be married off. But no "respectable" men were willing to marry this former slave, so for several years she was dependent on the government. Finally, a suitable man was found when the deal was sweetened with a gift of clothing, jewelry, and other wedding accoutrement costing the colonial exchequer over Rs. 100 .[110] In Mecca men were paying *mahr* to obtain a slave as a wife, but in Bombay British administrators were paying dowries to dispose of a former slave as a wife. British officials were not merely duped by slave purchases disguised as marriages. When the circumstances required, they were perfectly willing to pay to rid themselves of a slave in the guise of marriage.

But this history is not completely bleak, for the archive turns up some rather extraordinary people who overturn our conceptions of freed slaves in the labor traffic of the Arabian Sea. Freed male slaves were usually "set at large" in Bombay; after about 1890 they were "put in the way of obtaining employment," and after about 1900 they were "handed over to the head of the *Sidi* community" in Bombay.[111] These three phrases were virtually identical in meaning because even in the earliest instances these freed slaves were often handed over to their "country people." The Sidis were originally Ethiopians who had been settled in India for centuries, but by the late nineteenth century in Bombay the term referred mostly to freed slaves from East Africa and the Middle East.[112] In 1902, Abdullah bin Nasib was the head of the Sidi community, and we know that he was a freed slave who had been born in Bahrain. He had lived in Bombay for twenty-five years after his liberation, and somehow he had become a *serang,* or labor recruiter for the Bombay shipping office. He received freed slaves from the police commissioner and for a cut of their wages placed them into jobs on steamships. By the turn of the century, most of these liberated male slaves were gainfully employed, almost exclusively by steamship companies.[113] Abdullah bin Nasib's place in the structure of the Arabian Sea labor traffic was almost identical to that of slave traders; he was a broker for other people's labor. But he was a man respected and valued by the laborers he controlled.

The large numbers of freed slaves formed a social network and support structure in Bombay, at the center of which was a labor broker. The community of freed slaves in Bombay put this man at the head of their community because they could not fend for themselves in an economy where labor was employed at the discretion of slave smugglers, imperial administrators, and *serangs.* Under Abdullah bin Nasib, the community could tap into the networks that distributed labor, and the benefits were redistributed to support women, children, and the unemployed. Thus the commissioner of police was willing to place women and children with Abdullah bin Nasib, and liberated slaves as far away as Basra asked to be sent to the Bombay Sidi community.[114] They were no less dependent than previously, but in Bombay they were also invested in a community of freed slaves. Well into the twentieth century, Africans would be a major component of the maritime labor force of the Arabian Sea. We do not know whether like-minded *serangs* succeeded Abdullah bin Nasib or whether this became just another avenue of exploiting transactions in labor. But the *serang* system continued, and brokers continued to determine employment for freed slaves. The British Empire had suppressed the slave trade in the Arabian Sea, but they replaced it with a trade in labor that seemed to differ only in that it was condoned by British officials.

Perhaps the canniest slave we meet in the archives is a Swahili woman named Khatamishi. According to her, she was purchased in Zanzibar as a concubine for sixty Maria Theresa thalers by an Indian merchant named Abdulla Remtulla. Remtulla demurred, saying that he had merely hired her from her owner and paid her wages as his servant. In either case, it appears that Remtulla became very sick and feared he was nearing death. It is not clear what his condition was, but he wrote out a will that freed Khatamishi and left his estate—including another slave girl named Chousi—to her. Remtulla had no other heirs and was utterly dependent on Khatamishi to nurse him through his illness, so he may have been blinded by sickness or possibly held hostage by his own slave on what he believed to be his deathbed. Whatever the circumstances, Khatamishi obtained a *waraqa*, a written deed, in which Abdulla Remtulla testified to her freedom and her inheritance. So when Remtulla recovered and attempted to get rid of Khatamishi and renege on their agreement, she was armed with the right documentation.[115]

Barring this *waraqa*, Remtulla would almost certainly have evaded any repercussions. It may have even been the case that he did not own Khatamishi but rather legally rented her services as a domestic and occasional concubine. It would have been easy to sustain the legal fiction of employment even as he enjoyed the benefits of ownership. But if Abdulla Remtulla understood the value of legal documentation, so did Khatamishi. She recognized that Remtulla's illness was a moment in which the master's dependence on the slave was most pronounced. Not only did she extract the promise of her freedom and his estate, she had Remtulla write down this will, and then she maintained possession of the *waraqa*. Khatamishi understood just how tightly her life was bound up with the right piece of paper. This document made her body visible as a liberated person and property owner. She exploited the same documentary ambiguities that had kept her legally a laborer and practically a slave to turn the tables on her owner/employer.

Labor and human bodies were brought under a new regime of documentation and visibility in the Arabian Sea. Abolishing slave markets and the legal underpinnings of the slave trade was supposed to unleash a free market in labor. In practice, abolition did not create free choice for laborers; it merely changed the channels through which labor was distributed. Abolitionist policies attacked markets and neglected brokers, allowing a smuggling traffic to flourish. The sphere of family, and the kinship transactions that constituted such families, were off limits to state intervention, so adoption and marriage were contrived as means of appropriating labor. Lastly, the labor of freed slaves became the de facto property of the British Empire, to be disposed of at the convenience of imperial officials. The profits derived from the

Indian coolie trade made liberated slaves a burden by comparison. Yet this neglect opened a small avenue for freedmen in Bombay to enter the labor traffic on their own terms. The discourse of abolition across the Arabian Sea was revolutionary only in that it allowed British participation in labor traffics.

The human body consequently served as a key intermediary object between the market and society across the Arabian Sea. It was framed within the market as a buyer, a seller, a broker, or embodied labor, and it was framed out of the market as a spouse, child, or slave. Free labor remained an equivocal concept, defined only as the absence of the slave trade, whereas the precise nature of human bonds and economic relationships was continually renegotiated between colonial bureaucrats, traders and laborers themselves. Laborers had to document themselves in order to frame their role in the market, while traffickers contrived to frame their transactions outside the ambit of market exchange. Violence, of course, had a central role in framing human bodies as private property or free labor; consequently the following chapter will explore this contentious aspect of market exchange.

THREE

Disarming Commerce

RATANSI PURSHOTTAM WAS RUINED by the SS *Baluchistan*. With its stumpy topmasts and bland, functional exterior, the SS *Baluchistan* did not look particularly nefarious. Yet this ship carried in its hold a cargo that threatened to explode the foundations of the free market. In the winter of 1897–98, the SS *Baluchistan* set off on a six-week journey from London through the Suez Canal, across the Arabian Sea, and finally up the Gulf to Bahrain. This seemingly innocuous itinerary would have all of the intrigue and plot twists of a spy thriller: secret caches of Russian weapons, traffickers scrambling to forge documents, diplomats forcing through secret treaties, and even a boat chase on the high seas. The turmoil surrounding the SS *Baluchistan* did not concern the ship itself so much as the eight thousand rifles and seven hundred thousand ammunition cartridges in its cargo hold.[1] Many of those rifles and cartridges belonged to Ratansi Purshottam. When these weapons were confiscated by the Royal Navy, the losses were not immediately disastrous for Purshottam, but they were a harbinger of larger changes in the framework of trade around the Arabian Sea. The detention of the SS *Baluchistan* and the seizure of its combustible cargo marked the turning point of a long history of arbitraging across markets, legal categories, and the colonial distinction between state and market. This was the dramatic climax of colonial efforts to reformat the relationship between violence and private property.

Ratansi Purshottam was not exclusively an arms trader; indeed, his firm had been established as a general trading concern in the middle of the nineteenth century. Purshottam had arrived in Muscat from Mandvi in the Indian princely state of Kutch to work for his uncle. He branched off from his uncle's shop, and over the decades his profits grew. Eventually his sons took over the firm, though it continued to do business as Ratansi Purshottam.[2] The firm became so deeply involved in the arms trade because it had become the most profitable line of business in Muscat by the last decade of the nineteenth century. Indeed, the arms traffic was the primary reason for the resurgence of Muscat as a major entrepôt in the Arabian Sea.[3] Around the Arabian Sea littoral there was a large demand for precision firearms, and Muscat emerged as the main node for the import and distribution of these weapons. European producers, diasporic traders, and the sultan of Muscat's customs all raked in large revenues in servicing this demand. In some ways, these precision-manufactured firearms exemplified the benefits of industrial production and capitalist free markets. The problem was that firearms were many things to many people: to Ratansi Purshottam they were a profitable commodity, to Pathans and Somalis they were a defensive tool against colonial oppression, and to imperial bureaucrats they were a threat to the security of private property.

We tend to think about private property rights as something endangered by intrusive states trying to confiscate or nationalize private property. Yet it was precisely the expansion of state power that made it possible to enforce private property rights in the first place. Traders around the Arabian Sea had dealt with rebellions, banditry, and piracy for millennia, but beginning in the nineteenth century British traders started to demand that the Royal Navy secure their property rights. Rather than bearing the risks of a violent maritime world and assuming the costs of their own security, British and British Indian traders could outsource the efforts and the costs of securing their property to the empire. British gunships became the foundation of free trade and private property rights around the Arabian Sea. Historians of the British Empire have long argued that free trade ideology was a key driver of imperial expansion.[4] Similarly, recent work on piracy in the Indian Ocean has uncovered the methods by which certain forms of maritime violence were legitimized and others were rendered as piracy.[5] Scholars have even begun to examine the arms trade and its links with late imperial expansion and competition.[6] However, this literature is fundamentally concerned with violence as a political act, because colonial bureaucrats thought of the arms trade as a political problem of consolidating political authority. As important and compelling as this scholarship is, it leaves unexplored the possibility that violence is a continuing and constitutive element of free markets.

In capitalist political economy, violence has no place within the market; the only coercion permitted is that of the competitive market. The history of the

Arabian Sea arms trade reveals that this idea was far from natural; rather, it was deeply contested, contingent, and ultimately incomplete. In the previous chapter, we examined the production of the capitalist concept of labor as a result of framing out slavery. This chapter takes up the next pillar of capitalist ideology, private property and its negative corollary, coercion. While private property might be associated with peace, it is a peace stalked by the threat of state violence. In neoclassical economic theory, property is conceptualized as a "bundle" of rights: the right to use, rent, profit from, and sell property. Perhaps the most important right in the bundle is the right to have the government enforce one's property rights.[7] In other words, for private property rights to be secure, a state must use violence to ensure that those property rights are respected. Violence pervades free market exchange but only when exercised by a sovereign. The Weberian concept of sovereignty as a monopoly on the legitimate use of violence was therefore foundational to a capitalist understanding of private property. The safety of private property and the freedom of the market resulted not so much from the elimination of violence as from its monopolization by the state. The boundary between "the state" and "the market" was delineated by a distinction between legitimate state power exercised outside the market and criminal coercion that trespassed into the market. The violence of the sovereign state and the freedom of the market were inextricable, yet they had to be framed as discrete and detached realms.

The foregoing discussion is abstract and perhaps hard to engage when we consider commodities like cotton or land, yet it is a very concrete problem when we consider firearms and ammunition. Firearms were both a form of private property and a threat to private property rights. Depending on your point of view, they could be commodities or contraband, instruments for self-defense or for violent coercion. Rifles and ammunition were thus intermediary objects that bridged the conceptual division between state and market. The artificial division of firearms into commodities in one moment and instruments of violence in another makes them a rich object for examining the framing out of violence from colonial markets. Firearms became a particularly fettered form of property, with a much smaller bundle of associated rights. Regulations limited the ways a firearm could be used, where it could be taken, and to whom it could be sold or even given away. Nevertheless, these limitations had to be enforced mostly at the moment of importation. The history of the arms trade consequently traces a procrustean effort to frame violence outside the market without impinging on property rights in firearms.

So private property rights were enforced by controlling the arms traffic in the Arabian Sea. The aim of these regulations was never to completely halt the flow of firearms across borders but rather to filter these flows so that trade could flourish without threatening private property. This process required naval officers and customs administrators to make three distinctions: between a trade and a trickle, between contraband and commodity, and between state and society. British officials had to distinguish what amount of firearms and what routes of importation might constitute a threatening trade or merely a negligible trickle to authorized individuals. They also had to determine which weapons were contraband and which were harmless commodities. Lastly, they needed to distinguish between consumers associated with the state, who were sanctioned to possess firearms, and those subjects who might undermine the state's monopoly on legitimate violence. But each of these distinctions was not only difficult to make but fundamentally ambiguous. Colonial officials exercised a wide discretion in determining who could purchase weapons, what weapons could be purchased, and how they could be purchased. The coercive power of the colonial state was therefore central to the definition of property rights.

The effort to remove violent coercion from commerce required that bureaucracies deploy violent coercion to monitor and police the arms trade. Violent coercion was never monopolized by colonial bureaucracies, but it was certainly concentrated in its bureaucratic and military apparatus. The "colonial state" was never a unified agent but rather the effect of bureaucratic rules and distinctions to regulate the market.[8] Since there was no consistent boundary between the state and the society it governed, merchants capitalized on these ambiguities to exploit the state's supposed monopoly on the use of violence.[9] This concentration of coercive violence produced substantial benefits to those with access to the colonial bureaucracy. Regulators trusted firms connected to the bureaucracy, so the legitimate arms trade was dominated by European firms and those connected to local rulers. However, the cooperation of bureaucrats was equally critical to the success of the illicit arms traffic. Corrupt or simply careless bureaucrats were essential to the success of these illicit traffics. Colonial officials also secretly supplied firearms to rebels who undermined the interests of their enemies. Consequently, the licit and illicit trades were not distinct but interdependent. Large consignments of rifles and ammunition for military forces were legally imported into the Arabian Sea littoral, only to be illegally resold to private purchasers. A legitimate trade expanded, but it fed an illicit demand. Colonial policies did not create a monopoly on the legitimate use of violence, but colonial bureaucracies monopolized the import of firearms for both licit and illicit traffics.

This chapter demonstrates how colonial policies attempted to remove violence from commerce in the Arabian Sea by regulating the traffic in firearms. Campaigns against piracy had proved insufficient to secure free trade, so British diplomats forced rulers around the Arabian Sea to prohibit the private importation of firearms. Yet border guards, customs officials, and naval patrols could not eliminate the traffic in firearms. The arms trade was rife with ambiguities and problematic slippages: trade that was organized for legitimate purposes and yet supplied an illicit demand, weapons that could be used for both sport and banditry, and individuals who were both sovereigns and subjects. The arms trade was structured by ambiguous distinctions between trade/trickle, commodity/contraband, and state/society, as well as by the ability of merchant networks to arbitrage across them. Regulation established a set of diversions and bottlenecks that channeled the arms traffic without controlling it. Imperial regulation did not establish the rules by which trade was organized; rather, state bureaucracies became the central conduit of arms traffics. Firearms and private property rights were not universal but the preserve of those with access to sovereign privileges. Thus private property was the result of a contentious process of framing out violence from free trade.

MONOPOLIZING VIOLENCE

In 1866, the *banias* (Hindu merchants) of Muscat took all of their movable property out of their homes and shops and carried it to ships waiting in Muscat harbor. Ratansi Purshottam—still a young man at the time—was almost certainly among them, carrying goods from his uncle's shop to the waiting ships. This community of traders from Gujarat and Sindh in western India were concerned that the recent death of the sultan of Muscat under suspicious circumstances would lead to general violence in the town. Their property was an attractive target for looting, and their usurious practices and strange religion chafed against the social and religious values of their Muslim neighbors. Taking their valuables offshore was a strategy deployed by the community multiple times and was encouraged by British diplomats. Naval cruisers protected the movable property of these merchants. British cruisers could not, though, protect the landed property of Ratansi Purshottam or guarantee the collection of his outstanding debts.[10] Foreign traders visiting different ports had to be wary of the constant possibility of violence and could never take for granted the security of their property. But as the nineteenth century wore on, the Royal Navy increased its presence in the Arabian Sea, and colonial power became more pervasive along the littoral. By the twentieth century, rulers more forcefully asserted a monopoly on the legitimate use of violence, and property rights became sacrosanct, at least for British subjects.

Violence had been a facet of trading activities in the Indian Ocean for centuries. Maritime raids were a common occurrence because the seas were open and ungoverned territory. Such raids were undertaken both with and without the sanction of political entities and were acknowledged as a legitimate form of economic activity, especially when it was the only method of survival for populations occupying barren terrain.[11] Traders, in turn, were often armed and traveled in large convoys with military escorts in order to defend themselves against attacks. The protection of property rights was guaranteed only at a cost to the owner. Success in trade was as contingent on managing protection as on minimizing costs.[12] Classical political economy holds that one of the main functions of the state is to protect private property rights. British officials, schooled in classical political economy, could not stand by as the lives, property, and trade of British subjects were threatened. So over the course of the nineteenth century, British officials ensured that British trade would be protected by state violence.

Within their own colonies, European powers consolidated their authority, crushed rebellions, policed populations, and tried to enforce a monopoly on violence. Only in wartime was the confiscation of property a legitimate act, and even then only with the official sanction of the metropole. Those areas not directly ruled by a European colonial power were pressured to protect private property, particularly that of European subjects. But these rulers were often lax in their enforcement and even more so when the violence took place beyond their shores at sea. It was in the ungoverned space of the sea that property was at the greatest risk of violence. So if Britannia did not literally rule the waves, the Royal Navy certainly positioned itself as the guardian of property rights in the Gulf and the Arabian Sea. Yet all these claims were continually frustrated by the resilience of piracy and private violence across the sea.

From Pirates to Gunrunners

The British East India Company became concerned with maritime violence in the Gulf early in the nineteenth century. Attacks on British and Indian trade in the Gulf led the East India Company to mount a punitive expedition against the Arab sheikhs of the so-called "Pirate Coast." A sustained campaign of bombing forced the rulers of the Arab coast of the Gulf to sign the General Treaty of Peace in 1820.[13] The terms of this treaty introduced a sharp distinction between the legitimate violence of states and the illegitimate violence of individuals. The relevant article is worth quoting in full: "If any individual of the people of the Arabs contracting shall attack any that pass by land or seas of any nation whatsoever, in the way of plunder and piracy and not of acknowledged war, he shall be accounted an enemy of all mankind and shall be held to have forfeited both life and goods. And acknowledged war is that which is proclaimed, avowed, and ordered by government against government; and the killing of men and taking of goods without proclamation, avowal, and the order of a government, is plunder and piracy."[14] Thus the proclamation of a government became essential to the legitimation of violence, and without such a proclamation physical coercion became piracy. This was not the imposition of imperial conquest, but it was an ideological imposition. Arab rulers could acknowledge the right of a hostile state to deploy violence, whereas private individuals were denied this right. The aim was not to shore up the power of local rulers or even to assert British influence but to protect "any that pass by land or seas of any nation whatsoever." The British Empire conferred on the Gulf sheikhs a monopoly on the legitimate use of violence in order to protect British trade and private property.

In the following decades, the Royal Navy increased its reach in the waters of the Gulf and the Arabian Sea in order to secure British trade. The Gulf sheikhs were not particularly interested in investing their resources to enforce the General Treaty of Peace, so the Royal Navy took on the responsibility of enforcing its terms. Eventually the sheikhs ceded their abilities even to engage in "acknowledged war" over the waters of the Gulf, and the cruisers of the Royal Navy assumed a monopoly over the legitimate use of seaborne force.[15] In Aden, similar concerns over piracy resulted in the conquest of this port city in 1839.[16] As discussed in the previous chapter, the suppression of the slave trade gave the Royal Navy even broader authority to seize ships, confiscate cargo, and patrol the waters of the Arabian Sea. Gradually the British Empire came to monopolize the use of force on the high seas.

Yet increased patrols with modern steamships could not eliminate the profits of maritime raids. In the late nineteenth century, reports of piracy cropped up all around the Arabian Sea. Even near the center of British naval power in western India there were piratical attacks for which the perpetrators were never found.[17] In the early twentieth century, a notorious pirate named Ahmed bin Salman gained fame and fortune raiding pearling boats in the Gulf. The sheikh of Qatar turned a blind eye to his depredations and happily accepted his money in local markets.[18] Similarly chronic problems were reported at the maritime bottlenecks of the Shatt al-Arab and the Gulf of Aden. Neither British, Iranian, nor Iraqi officials had much success in policing these heavily trafficked waters. In one instance, the sheikh of Mohammerah became so desperate that he was forced to employ local prostitutes to try to ferret out these brazen raiders.[19] Raiding, banditry, and theft were pervasive, so imperial administrators turned to the arms traffic to contain the violence of local communities.

"At a thousand yards the traveler falls wounded by the well-aimed bullet of a breech-loading rifle. His assailant, approaching, hacks him to death with the ferocity of a South-Sea Islander. The weapons of the nineteenth century are in the hands of the savages of the Stone Age."[20] The young Winston Churchill, quoted here, was perhaps the loudest voice decrying the role of modern rifles in undermining the Pax Britannica. Churchill's account of fighting the Pathan tribesmen of India's Northwest Frontier was published in several installments in London's *Daily Telegraph* over the summer of 1897. While his reportage covered many aspects of the fighting, his main analytical digressions focused on the dangers of putting modern firepower in the hands of "savages." He lamented the smuggling of weapons from the settled regions of British India to the frontier, and the narrowing gap in weapons technology that barely allowed British Indian forces to overcome their adversaries.[21] Churchill's strident reportage, as well as the prominence of the Malakand campaign in which he participated, undoubtedly encouraged the upper echelons of the imperial administration to redouble their efforts against the arms trade.

Throughout British rule in India, the Northwest Frontier was an open and festering sore on the body of the colonial state. Pathan tribes repeatedly sloughed off the yoke of colonial rule, and the British Indian Army was repeatedly sent to subdue them until the next bout of unrest. Moreover, looming beyond the frontier were the questionable loyalties of Afghanistan and the ever-present tensions of the Great Game with Imperial Russia. At the other end of the Arabian Sea, the Indian Army was confronting a similarly prolonged war with the forces of the so-called "Mad Mullah" in the interior of British Somaliland.[22] The language of savagery and irrationality deployed against Somalis and Pathans was just the extreme of a racialized discourse that marked certain communities as uncivilized and consequently unable to participate in the free market. These two regions most persistently resisted colonial rule and became a magnet for precision rifles filtering into the Arabian Sea.[23] The Indian Army attempted to pacify these populations through punitive military expeditions and co-optation of local power brokers, but by the early twentieth century stanching the flow of weapons came to take on ever more importance in imperial policies.

In Iran and the Arabian Peninsula British colonial rule was not directly threatened, but the security of British and British Indian trade was a serious concern. Piracy had elicited concerted government intervention in the early nineteenth century, but by the end of the century the freedom of trade was the main justification for engagement by the imperial government. As the British resident in the Gulf argued:

> While the continuation of the arms traffic affects the Persian and other States bordering the Persian Gulf in a directly vital way, there can be no doubt that its suppression is equally important to legitimate British trade, for the extension of which a firm Government and security to life and property are essential. Our trade with these parts has increased enormously of late years, and will go on increasing if the merchant can be certain that his goods will reach their destination in safety, but trade routes are delicate plants to foster, and easily destroyed, and once those into Persia are forsaken in consequence of want of suitable protection, it may be years before they can be reopened.[24]

So it was essential for the expansion of British business that trade routes in Iran be secure and conducive to completing transactions. In the short run, the arms trade was enhancing the prosperity of local economies. But in the long run it armed rebel groups and bandits, served to destabilize the Qajar Empire, and ultimately endangered the "delicate plants" of British trade. The conflicts in Somaliland and on the Northwest Frontier of British India, along with a desire to increase British trade in Iran and Arabia, provided a powerful incentive to seal territorial borders against the destabilizing importation of illicit firearms.

Closing Borders

Following the 1857 Rebellion, the British Raj instituted rules to harden the borders of British India against the importation of arms and ammunition. Those communities and districts that rebelled against the East India Company were "pacified" by the army and "disarmed" by legislative enactment. But with mixed success in implementing these regulations, additional arms legislation was passed in 1860, in 1866, and again in 1878, unifying British India under a single regulatory regime.[25] Customs officers would now be on the front lines of the effort to disarm the Indian population. On British India's western border, the Qajar government of Iran was slowly losing control of its outlying districts. In the hope of choking the supply of weapons to rebellious groups within the country, the shah closed Iran's borders to the private importation of arms in 1881. The shah's minister for foreign affairs argued: "Since the right of purchasing arms and introducing the same into Persia belongs to the Persian Government ... and if this absolute right were not exclusively confined to the Government, and everybody who thought fit to do so were allowed to purchase such articles and introduce them into the country, this great governmental privilege would become obsolete, and considerable evils would result to the state."[26] Thus the Qajar rulers asserted a government monopoly on the importation of precision firearms into Iran in order to shore up state power and secure Iran's territorial integrity. British administrators in India were fully in support of this action, hoping that a stable neighbor could reinforce the stability of India's western border and better protect British trading interests. India and Iran constituted the northern and eastern coastline of the Arabian Sea, which were now off limits to the arms trade.

Confronting significant rebellions, European colonies in Africa could barely maintain the fiction that they had a monopoly on the use of force in their territories. A key clause of the General Act of the Brussels Conference in 1890 prohibited the sale of arms to consumers in the African continent between the latitudes of twenty-two degrees south and twenty degrees north and one hundred nautical miles off the African coast.[27] So the Brussels Conference erected another border against the arms trade, closing off the entire western shore of the Arabian Sea.

Sandwiched in between Asia and Africa was the Arabian Peninsula. In the first years of the twentieth century, British diplomats and administrators made a strong push to convince Arab rulers to enforce a prohibition on the import of arms for commercial purposes. Yet these rulers did not face internal rebellions and were not particularly interested in expending their resources to halt a profitable trade. By the first decade of the twentieth century, British officials could only pressure the Arab rulers of the Gulf to prohibit the *export* of guns to Iran or India.[28] Weapons were still imported into these territories, but at least they could not be legally exported to regions where they might endanger British rule. Subsequently, British diplomatic efforts slowly pushed to monitor and

MAP 2. Major distribution paths for illicit firearms. Map by author.

then close the coasts of the Arabian Sea to the importation of precision rifles. The preservation of property rights around the Arabian Sea would depend on effective control over these borders. However, pivotal gaps at Muscat and Djibouti frustrated this cordon sanitaire along the littoral (map 2).

TRADE/TRICKLE

In 1906, Ratansi Purshottam was filled with anxiety over what might be occurring at yet another conference of colonial powers meeting in Brussels.

Failing to regulate the arms trade in 1890, and again missing the mark with the capture of the SS *Baluchistan* in 1898, colonial bureaucrats gathered once more in 1906 to find a way to enforce their sovereign rights. The conference discussed ways to limit the arms trade in Asia and Africa, and there were indications that the delegates would institute a ban on the export of arms to Muscat. Schwarte & Hammer, one of Ratansi Purshottam's trading partners in London, was not particularly concerned. They insisted that even if a ban was instituted they would merely deliver a large number of small shipments to comply with the restrictions.[29] In small enough consignments, Schwarte & Hammer did not have to report their transactions, and customs officials could not possibly monitor every little shipment that passed through the docks. A number of small consignments of firearms consequently did not constitute an arms trade.

Customs officials were very concerned about the threat that firearms posed to the security of property rights. However, regulation required economies of scale: small customs establishments could only monitor commodities that were concentrated in sufficient numbers. An arms trade could be supervised, but a trickle of weapons seeping through the customs house was almost impossible to trace and thus was written off as insignificant. Systems of surveillance and rubrics of classification were developed to distinguish a threatening trade from a negligible trickle. What amount of goods constituted a significant trade? What routes of transport were used by legitimate traders? And what methods of exchange opened the possibility of an illicit trade? Colonial officials developed strategies to make the arms trade visible, and mercantile networks developed tactics to subvert these regimes of classification.

Not Quite Trading

Arms regulations were intended to constrain a substantial trade that might threaten private property and the state's monopoly on violence. So from the earliest arms regulations in the 1870s, traffickers imported firearms into British India in small lots, and colonial officials were mostly oblivious.[30] By the 1890s British administrators were struggling to understand how significant numbers of arms ended up in prohibited areas in the absence of an observable arms trade. One official came to a seemingly contradictory conclusion: "I am not of [the] opinion that there is a regular direct trade . . . but at the same time there is most probably a steady flow of arms into Afghanistan from the country below."[31] What persisted into the middle of the twentieth century, despite all efforts to stop it, was a "trickle" or the importation of arms in "driblets."[32] One merchant in Bombay shipped a large amount of sulfur for making gunpowder in 270 lots of exactly ten seers (one seer ~ 10 kg).[33] Ten seers was the limit beyond which sulfur had to be declared in customs forms, so in this way the merchant avoided customs and licensing regulations and could deny engaging in the ammunition "trade." Increased transportation costs were balanced by the invisibility of not quite engaging in trade.

Colonial regulations defined trade not just by quantity but also by trajectory. If merchants did not engage in wholesale trade and merely facilitated arms imports for a licensed consumer, they were not regulated as traders. Merchants facilitating such imports did not need a trading license, and European consumers could even claim a rebate on import duties.[34] Such firearms were required for the self-defense and personal use of Europeans and other loyal subjects of the British Empire. These weapons were ostensibly imported for the protection of property, so the British administration had hoped that granting rebates would steer weapons into the hands of loyal subjects and property owners. But rather than protecting property and securing colonial rule, this policy merely illustrated the ignorance of the administration. Alarming numbers of weapons were being imported for which no rebate was claimed, and officials could only conclude that these were ending up in the hands of unlicensed consumers.[35] What appeared to be individual direct consignments was ultimately revealed as a cunningly designed wholesale trade in arms.

Regulators also confronted the problem that in frontier areas arms regulations appeared to promote theft and raiding. Bandits and thieves easily obtained weapons through illicit methods, while law-abiding subjects could not obtain firearms for self-protection and found themselves defenseless against criminals. Thus local officials, overwhelmed by the depredations of "the criminal classes," pleaded for a more liberal interpretation of arms-trafficking regulations: "It is impossible to deprive the criminal classes of arms, they can procure them for purposes of aggression without the least difficulty, to refuse arms to the more respectable Patels [headmen or chiefs] is therefore to place them at the mercy of the dangerous classes. In districts where dacoity [banditry] is common the people should be encouraged to defend themselves. I have known more than one instance in which an attack on a village has been defeated by a show of resistance and a few matchlocks being fired off from the interior of the houses."[36] Colonial bureaucrats' efforts to disarm the population actually made subjects more vulnerable to violence than they had been previously. Disarmament was so all-encompassing that peasants were increasingly subject to attacks by wild animals that damaged their crops.[37] The inability of the colonial bureaucracy to protect property from the violence of criminals or animals meant that officials had to backtrack and more liberally interpret the provisions of arms regulations.

Similar concessions were made on the waters encircling the Arabian Peninsula, where maritime raids continued to afflict trade. When two dhows were plundered off the coast of Aden in quick succession, the senior naval officer questioned the ability of the Royal Navy to protect British-registered vessels. He even suggested that imperial administration should provide Martini-Henry rifles and ammunition to dhow captains at cost price so that they would be able to protect themselves.[38] But inevitably this concession opened up another avenue for the illicit trade in firearms. Dhow captains realized that rifles permitted for self-defense could provide a profitable addition to their regular trade.[39] Colonial authorities were unable to secure the property rights of their subjects and consequently permitted them to arm themselves. Much to their chagrin, officials found that self-defense just as quickly became an opening for an illicit arms trade and only perpetuated the insecurity of property rights. Small consignments of firearms and ammunition continued to be a remarkably effective method of circumventing restrictions on an arms "trade."

Flexible Trading

Customs authorities had to accept that a trickle of firearms would still flow into their territory, but they hoped to ensure the validity of these transactions by constraining the routes through which this traffic flowed. Regulators tried to identify consumers and register all the intermediary transactions in order to map out exactly how the arms traffic was operating. Securing the free market did not mean disarming the population so much as monopolizing the arms trade and restricting access only to responsible subjects. The need for economies of scale required that legitimate trade be routed through major hubs. Customs authorities ordered that all arms intended for the western Indian coast be funneled through Bombay, where transactions could be more easily monitored.[40] Yet as entrepôts like Bombay and Zanzibar were brought under increasing scrutiny from colonial regulations, trafficking networks shifted their operations to Muscat. Muscat had the perfect infrastructure to mediate the licit and illicit components of the arms trade in the Arabian Sea. The sultan of Muscat lightly taxed imports and did not monitor exports, and his long and loosely governed coastline made it easy for firearms to be surreptitiously sent to consumers as close as Bandar Abbas and as far away as Somalia.[41] As a result, Muscat became the premier arms-trafficking hub in the Arabian Sea. This of course antagonized imperial officials, who redoubled their efforts to impose the same standards of transparency in Muscat.

The sultan of Muscat resisted British pressure until 1912, when his growing debts left him no choice but to comply. A licensing and warehousing system was put in place that minutely scrutinized the quantities of weapons and ammunition purchased by each individual consumer.[42] The bottleneck created by this new regulatory system created ferocious resentment among the Omani tribes of Muscat's hinterland. These angry consumers subsequently rallied behind a rival to the Bu-Saʿīdī dynasty and almost deposed the sultan. While there were other grievances behind the revolt, arguably the major driver was the imposition of the arms warehouse at Muscat.[43] Thus arms regulations intended to secure the state's monopoly on violence almost caused the destruction of the state. British warships propped up the sultan's rule, but Muscat's role as a trading hub was devastated, as were the profits of firms like Ratansi Purshottam. Yet even as Muscat's arms traffic declined, many merchants shifted their operations to Kuwait, Djibouti, and the Omani port of Sur.[44] Kuwait's rise as an arms-trading hub was subsequently constrained by British pressure to stamp all imported arms with the *wasm* or family emblem of the sheikh.[45] This limited the re-export market and the resale value of these weapons. Yet once again the arms traffic adapted, and until World War II Qatar would take up the mantle of arms-trading hub.[46] The ease with which arms-trading networks shifted from one port to another reflects how arms regulations diverted trade flows without actually disciplining them.

Even those traffickers who could not hop from one accommodating port to another found other ways of evading the gaze of customs authorities. The wholesale trade particularly concerned British officials because it was so opaque. Wholesale traders "speculatively" imported rifles in the hope that they could be resold at a profit, so they had the largest incentive to dispose of their inventory through illicit sales. Customs officials subjected these dealers to rigorous surveillance in order to render the trade more transparent. But rather than comply with demands for transparency, arms traffickers used vague terms in their documentation. Ratansi Purshottam's cargo on the SS *Baluchistan* was "consigned to order" rather than to a specific purchaser. Imperial authorities assumed that this vague designation was proof of the shippers' intent to engage in illicit sales. British, Indian, and Arab shippers all responded that local consumers would not pay for a weapon they could not visually inspect. And if they took possession of the weapon before paying, consumers would never actually pay. Moreover, merchants needed to keep goods in their own name for the duration of a journey in order to secure financing and insurance.[47] Ratansi Purshottam, then, was prosecuted fundamentally for trading methods that accommodated the exigencies of local trade. Other traffickers took the more blatant step of consigning their goods to fictitious firms, or falsely consigning goods to reputable firms whose name would forestall suspicion.[48] Merchants also frequently exercised the option to alter the port of consignment mid-journey in order to take advantage of price fluctuations at different ports.[49] Imperial bureaucrats imagined that trade was a preplanned process; shippers countered that trade was unpredictable and that they had to constantly adapt to shifting markets.

Surveillance was not a neutral activity: it involved the diversion, concentration, and reordering of trade flows. Not only were Indian imports channeled through Bombay, but Bombay arms dealers were required to keep government-issued account books, detailed records of their transactions in English, and to make these records available for periodic inspection.[50] These regulations reformatted the smallest details of transactions in order to make them visible. So these efforts pushed traders into more overtly illicit activities and had the perverse effect of skewing what meager information was already available. The political agent in Kutch complained: "To require retail dealers to keep books, might so impede sales of licensed imports, that smuggling would take place, and that the present information as to the quantity of caps [a type of ammunition] entering Cutch would become less reliable."[51] Much as Heisenberg's uncertainty principle suggested for electrons, the act of identifying the routes through which firearms flowed made it impossible to ascertain the quantities flowing through these routes and vice versa. Regulation did not facilitate legitimate trade, it stanched the flow of legitimate trade by increasing the transaction costs and reducing the flexibility of traders. Merchants moved instead into illicit trading or to transactions far removed from what imperial bureaucrats conceived of as trade. Attempts to make arms traffics more transparent actually resulted in their becoming more opaque.

Ratansi Purshottam repeatedly requested that their Belgian-manufactured rifles be inscribed with the phrase "Made in England" rather than "Made in Belgium." When the dealers answered that customs authorities in Europe would not permit such a request, he asked that they engrave the name of the London arms dealer through whom the purchase was arranged. But the manufacturer could not comply with this request either, so Purshottam asked that they simply leave out any indication of the place of manufacture. The compromise was finally reached that the Belgian proof marks would be on the underside of the barrel so that they did not show, and that the shipment would go directly from Antwerp to Muscat and hence avoid British customs and the application of the Merchandize Marks Act, which prohibited such a practice.[52] Ratansi Purshottam never put much effort into obtaining British rifles; indeed, they were focused on Belgian and German manufacturers. So why were they were anxious to give the impression that these rifles were in fact British?

The advantage of a British proof mark was not its indication of higher quality, because Belgian, German, and French rifles were all highly regarded around the Arabian Sea. Rather, British rifles passed through searches by British customs officers with greater ease than rifles from other European countries. Distinguishing which rifle was a legal import and which was not depended on a variety of complex and ambiguous calculations about the style of the weapon, the ammunition it took, the final purchaser, and how it would be used. The great difficulty of regulating firearms was that they were perfectly normal commodities in production and circulation and became problematic only in certain forms of consumption. Firearms "consumed" in hunting animals or games of sport were perfectly respectable consumer goods. But when firearms and ammunition were consumed in acts of murder, theft, or extortion they presented a much more problematic commodity. Officials had to predict how the firearms would be used on the basis of the appearance of the weapon and sometimes little more than a description. Customs officers depended on importers to be truthful and forthright in their declarations, and on vague categorizations to distinguish between commodities and coercive instruments. So rough heuristics—rules of thumb—had to compensate for the lack of prophetic ability. The most important heuristic device was simply that customs officials tended to trust manufacturers from their own nations, but various other easy—if imprecise—rules played a key role in the work of arms regulation. Arms traffickers were keenly aware of the difficulties of differentiating licit from illicit firearms, so they quickly found ways to manipulate these rules of thumb.

Porous Categories

One of the primary methods by which traffickers evaded regulations was the classic trope of concealing a weapon in some other cargo. Firearms and ammunition were intensively regulated commodities, so merchants disguised their weapons as unregulated commodities. Ammunition could be concealed in virtually anything, and customs authorities had little chance of discovering it. Bullets were slipped into packages of dates, perfumes, spices, and "sundries" and were rarely discovered, while other shippers sent ammunition simply unconcealed in passengers' baggage or in boxes labeled "packets and books."[53] Rifles, on the other hand, were large and heavy objects that could not be easily concealed. Fortunately for smugglers, cotton was a major item of trade and easily concealed large firearms. When hidden within large bales of cotton, rifles were invisible to customs: "The bales were so packed that they appeared to be exactly like those of piece-goods which merchants generally despatch by rail . . . [but were] found to contain very cleverly arranged, in separate pieces of straw, two military Martini-Henry rifles, one ordinary Martini-Henry rifle, one B.L. carbine and 3,290 military ball cartridges."[54] While the imperial administration became aware of this method of trafficking, the sheer volume of the cotton trade meant that they could do little about it. Similar cases of trafficking arms in cotton bales were uncovered between Muscat, Somalia, Iran, Bahrain, and many other places.[55] Another set of smugglers concealed small pistols in specially designed compartments cut out of the pages of books. This method had the benefit not only of being shipped via the postal system but also of being shipped by the cheaper rate of book post rather than first-class mail![56] Given that this plot was uncovered in 1910, one wonders whether an Indian smuggler might be at the origin of this trope of spy novels.[57] Winston Churchill admiringly recounted an escapade where rifles were smuggled in a coffin with a piece of rotting beef to approximate the smell of a corpse, as well as to discourage officials from investigating too thoroughly.[58] Though some of these smugglers were particularly creative, ultimately their schemes all relied on making contraband visible to the regulators as unregulated commodities.

Such elaborate schemes of concealing weapons could also be obviated by the use of a very vague but accurate description of rifles and ammunition.

Perhaps the most common means of transporting arms without detection was to label them as "hardware" or "merchandize." According to shipping regulations, all the cargo that a ship carried had to be specified in the ship's manifest, but by labeling arms as hardware shippers could be truthful in their declaration, and customs officials never imagined that "hardware" might signify firearms.[59] When customs officials proscribed this practice, shipping companies responded that it was mercantile custom and that when arms were shipped along with other metal goods it was the *only* accurate description.[60] Given the millions of items that passed through customs posts each year, authorities relied on importers to be not only honest but also forthright in their declarations.

The category of firearms that officials most frequently permitted through customs was sporting rifles. The sporting rifle was a convenient classification that allowed regulators to assume that the firearm would be used for peaceful purposes. The British administration in India could hardly prevent Britons and Indian rajas from participating in the time-honored pastime of hunting.[61] The problem was that sporting-pattern rifles were easily substituted for military-pattern rifles. Figure 4 is taken from the correspondence between Ratansi Purshottam and Joseph Winterhoff, a London merchant. It depicts a military-pattern rifle and a sporting-pattern rifle manufactured by the same firm. The differences are evidently slight, amounting to little more than a safety bolt as opposed to a wooden stock fitted for a bayonet. Winterhoff even felt it necessary to handwrite which image accorded with which pattern of rifle.

There was no substantial difference in the design of sporting rifles as opposed to that of military rifles: the difference was ultimately how the weapon was used rather than any greater capacity for violence. The finish of sporting rifles, as indicated in this catalog, was available in all the same caliber ranges as those for military-pattern rifles and could be customized to consumer specifications. Indeed, many consumers around the Arabian Sea saw firearms as personalized luxury goods, so the customizations and engravings on sporting rifles were more appealing than military rifles.[62] The distinction between sporting and military pattern rifles was essential to regulation, yet effectively meaningless because they were equally dangerous to colonial rule and property rights.

A potentially clear line of distinction appeared when a firm requested permission to import Winchester repeating rifles "for *bona fide* sporting purposes." These "repeating" or "magazine" rifles could shoot five to ten rounds without reloading, and this technology was of little benefit in gentle-

FIGURE 4. Military and sporting rifles. Joseph Winterhoff to Ratansi Purshottam, May 7, 1907, Arms Trade, Ratansi Purshottam Archive, in possession of Vimal Purecha, Muscat, Oman. Reproduced with the kind permission of Vimal Purecha.

manly sports, so one would imagine that British administrators would have pounced on this as clear evidence of the manipulation of the category of sporting weapons. The bureaucratic correspondence indeed did question whether such repeating rifles were necessary for sporting purposes.[63] One official with uncharacteristic humor commented: "It is no doubt true that such arms *might* be used for sporting purposes, as also might an Armstrong 12 pounder [a field artillery piece operated by nine men] for shooting elephants, but they are not sporting rifles properly so called & should not be passed as such."[64] Yet despite this withering sarcasm, the Government of India did not prohibit the import of these rifles and instead dealt with them on a case-by-case basis. This essentially allowed European firms to import magazine rifles, but not other firms. Magazine rifles were some of the most common rifles imported into Muscat, so much so that they were given Arabic names. Rifles with ten cartridge magazines were known as *Abu-'Ashra* (father of ten), and those with five cartridge magazines were known as *Abu-Khams* (father of five).[65] Not only was the category of sporting rifles manipulated by smugglers, but officials stretched the limits of these categories when it was convenient. Both physically concealing weapons in other commodities and conceptually concealing them in ambiguous classifications allowed contraband to pass as commodities.

National Industry and Colonial Regulation

Given the difficulties of parsing licit from illicit rifles, customs officials often turned to an easier heuristic for illicit trade: national origin. As we saw with

Ratansi Purshottam, British officials were suspicious of firearms from France, Belgium, Germany, and Russia. King Menelik of Ethiopia humiliated Italy on the battlefield of Adowa in large part because he was supplied with weapons by Russia. British bureaucrats were anxious to avoid the same fate in the Northwest Frontier Province and Somaliland. In fact, it was Russian ammunition cartridges that prompted surveillance of the SS *Baluchistan*.[66] Belgian and French arms and ammunition faced similar difficulties in British colonies around the Arabian Sea. British officials presumed the loyalty and respectability of British merchants and the duplicity of their competitors. This heuristic device was simultaneously easier to deploy and more beneficial to British interests than an unbiased administration of regulations.

British weapons were in turn discriminated against on other shores of the Arabian Sea. At the end of the nineteenth century, the Iranian customs administration was run by Belgians, who appeared to be less rigorous in their regulation of Belgian weapons than of British weapons.[67] Traders around the Arabian Sea recognized this tendency and were anxious to purchase Belgian rifles.[68] This certainly contributed to the dominance of Belgian weapons in the Gulf at the turn of the twentieth century. Moreover, arms traders utilized government markings to facilitate their transit through customs. Ratansi Purshottam and other merchants requested rifles engraved with the Qajar Imperial seal to indicate a government purchase, whether or not the rifles were actually intended for the Qajar military.[69] Yemen and Somalia, given their proximity to the French colony of Djibouti, were well supplied with French Gras rifles and their ammunition. Djibouti was the hub of the arms trade for the East African coast and the Red Sea, and French administrators were only too willing to turn a blind eye to the thriving commerce that filled the government's coffers and those of French manufacturers.[70]

That French rifles could predominate in a British colony like Aden was deemed a failure, and British administrators were determined to correct this state of affairs. The political resident in Aden resolved that British arms should be liberally sold to tribal leaders at cost price so that they would have no reason to purchase French weapons. The language they used betrays economic competition as the central impetus driving British arms policies: "[The resident] recommended a full and sufficient supply of arms for the actual needs of the tribes which will compete in price and popularity with the French weapon."[71] So, rather absurdly, the British method of constraining the illicit arms traffic in Aden was to liberally provide Arabs with British weapons.[72] Far from disarming the population, arms regulations frequently meant ensuring that colonial rulers dominated the supply of weapons to colonized consumers.[73] The key dynamic seemed to be the competition between colonial bureaucracies to monitor and monopolize the distribution of arms.

Regulation as a method of promoting British industry was particularly egregious in the case of ammunition. The black market for ammunition around the Arabian Sea was glutted with British military-issue cartridges.[74] The frequency of pilfering, embezzling, and outright theft of government ammunition suggests that the Indian army was quite liberal in distributing ammunition and unconcerned that its supplies were hemorrhaging into the illicit trade. It was widely known in Bombay that anyone who knew a soldier could not only purchase ammunition but do so at the military discount.[75] Moreover, Belgian manufacturers designed rifles specifically to take British government cartridges, in order to compete for markets around the Arabian Sea.[76] The only explanation for this negligence seems to be that officers were so concerned that soldiers be liberally provisioned with ammunition that they were reluctant to impose too strict control over supplies. Nevertheless, the negligent attitude toward government-issued ammunition subtly allowed the colonial government to stimulate British industry even as it threatened colonial property.[77]

Yet this promotion of British ammunition was also undercut by the maneuvers of local merchants and consumers. Arab and Indian consumers sought out *badl* ammunition. *Badl* can be roughly translated in both Arabic and Urdu as "substitute," which indicated the spent cartridges of European ammunition that were reloaded with locally produced bullets. These were cheap and plentiful because Arabs and Afghans were very careful to recover spent cartridges. As one official noted: "It is interesting to observe how zealously an Arab afer [sic] firing will collect his cartridge cases, and nothing will usually induce him to part with them."[78] Indeed, empty cartridges became a commodity in and of themselves, with enterprising traders selling them at a profit in Afghanistan and Somalia. New British cartridges were known as *wilayati* in Muscat, a term that makes little sense in Arabic but in Urdu this term indicates something English or European.[79] These cartridges were comparatively expensive and were purchased only by wealthier gun owners. Imperial officials were incensed at the production of *badl* ammunition and revised Indian statutes to prevent its production, which no doubt helped the sales of *wilayati* cartridges.[80]

The inconsistent policy of the British Empire with regard to the import of arms and ammunition was subtly tied to the effort to maintain the competitiveness of British industries. Administrators did not wish to regulate British exports when such actions would "only mean its [the arms trade] passing into the hands of other nations."[81] Instead, they maintained a profitable tension between punishing arms traders in the Arabian Sea and promoting the arms industry back in Britain. One official stated this quite frankly: "The English Government does not desire to cause loss to its own manufacturers in England but prefers to shift the burden of any loss to the native purchasers in Maskat."[82] Imperial policies were formulated from the dueling imperatives of metropolitan and colonial interests. These interests were reconciled by the loose regulation of British businesses and the harsh regulation of their competitors and colonial subjects. The difference between licit and illicit arms trade was ultimately determined by the discretion of regulatory officials. None of the European states administering customs regimes around the Arabian Sea littoral had an explicit agenda of promoting their national manufactures; rather, customs officials simply trusted the manufactures of their own nation and questioned the manufactures of other nations. Merchant networks were of course quick to exploit this gap between regulatory categories and the nationalist biases in their interpretation.

STATE/SOCIETY

Until 1912, the Muscat customs farm was auctioned every year to the highest bidder, and Ratansi Purshottam frequently entered the winning bid. Almost without exception, the customs administration was farmed out to one of a handful of well-capitalized *bania* firms operating in Muscat. As Muscat's customs revenues were propelled upwards by revenues from the arms trade, this position became ever more profitable. Indeed, the increase of the import duty on arms in 1897 was justified to British officials as a means of limiting the arms trade. Its actual effect was to increase the customs revenues collected by Ratansi Purshottam.[83] Ratansi Purshottam's role as customs farmer not only was an additional source of revenue but provided a number of vital benefits that came from exercising state authority. The firm administering the customs farm could import firearms without being taxed, so they had an upper hand against other importers. If the customs farmer was responsible for regulating the trade in firearms, there was little incentive to effectively administer regulations unless they increased revenues. As colonial officials attempted to secure a state monopoly on violence, they were undermined by the overlap between the state and the merchant networks they were regulating.

The regulation of the arms trade was organized around a nebulous distinction between the state and the society that it ruled. Colonial governments sought a monopoly on the use of violence, and they pursued this by limiting the ability of their subjects to purchase firearms. While the legislation was clear in its conceptual division of state from society, in practice this boundary was continually trespassed. The state was made up of individuals who were also part of society, and parts of society were routinely co-opted into the state apparatus. The racial dynamics of British colonialism separated out the European population of British colonies and effectively made them sovereign agents.[84] Simultaneously, states often contracted out certain responsibilities to private commercial firms, like the sultan of Muscat farming his customs to Ratansi Purshottam. This outsourced logistical hassles, but government policy also became subject to the conflicting incentives of profit. Lastly, colonial bureaucrats recruited soldiers from the societies they governed. This fluctuating military population had to be armed and disarmed as their numbers changed in accordance with political exigencies. There was no state that was totally separate from society. Colonial efforts to define and control populations through taxation, military service, and racial preference produced the distinction between the state and the society that it ostensibly governed.[85] This ambiguous state/society distinction was especially performed through efforts to monitor, manage, and monopolize the arms traffic.

Europeans in the State

Europeans were given a relatively free hand in importing precision firearms because they were part of the ruling class. In a surprisingly candid moment, the judicial secretary for the Government of Bombay admitted that "all precautionary measures of this nature [arms regulations] are adopted mainly with a view to the security of the British Government and the protection of the lives of Europeans."[86] Thus arms regulations were instituted as much to protect the ruling minority from the potential violence of the colonized as to promote peace within colonial society. Europeans and sometimes Eurasians were considered almost sovereigns and were encouraged to carry firearms.[87] The restrictions on arms dealers assumed the trustworthiness of European dealers and quite overtly targeted Indian dealers. The intention was "to keep the trade of arms and ammunition as much as possible in the hands of the

European merchant."[88] This legislation worked to displace the Bohra community that was already well established around the Arabian Sea as arms dealers. Bohras were Gujarati Muslims who dominated the import and trade of weapons in Bombay, Zanzibar, Muscat, and Bushehr.[89] In the interests of securing the lives and property of Europeans, the arms licenses of Bohras were revoked, while licenses for Europeans were approved in their stead.[90]

Even as British officials were equating the interests of the European race with those of the imperial state, they started to recognize that racial solidarity could not be counted upon from "Europeans of a certain class."[91] British arms dealers had an obvious conflict of interest between racial solidarity and personal profit, and for many such dealers the latter won out. Messrs. Walter Locke and Company sold a large consignment of ammunition to a fraudster claiming to be an honorary magistrate because he appeared to be a respectable "well dressed native."[92] The firm of Latham & Co. in Bombay shipped guns to a planter in the princely state of Travancore without verifying his identity. It was later discovered that the firm sold dozens of weapons to a single arms dealer who repeatedly returned to the shop in a novel disguise and bearing a new identity to purchase yet another rifle.[93] It is conceivable that this man was a brilliant actor but more likely that Latham & Co. were trying not to notice the same man behind the fake moustache. Furthermore, not only established arms dealers but also profit-minded Europeans were involved in selling arms to unlicensed Indians. Itinerant traders, a former inspector in the Bombay city police, and even a "traveling dentist" were discovered selling firearms.[94]

Indian and Arab merchants quickly noticed this predilection in the enforcement of arms regulations and consequently employed British agents to handle their business.[95] British firms handled imports and customs formalities, but then they would sell to Arab and Bohra dealers who could manage the final retailing to consumers around the Arabian Sea.[96] Thus British arms regulations in India and the Gulf counted on Europeans as an extension of the sovereign state, but many European civilians were not particularly fastidious in protecting their sovereign privileges.

Merchants in the State

If British colonial authorities privileged European civilians in the administration of arms regulations, Arab and Iranian authorities similarly privileged certain firms with close ties to the ruler. The practice of tax farming was common across much of the Arabian Sea world. Therefore, the government's interest in securing a monopoly on the import of arms was filtered through the profit motive of the commercial firms collecting customs duties. In Bahrain, the sheikh had officially prohibited the import of firearms for commercial purposes. However, the sheikh had also proclaimed a state monopoly on the import of arms for resale on the Arab coast of the Gulf. The sheikh had given this monopoly to his *wazir* (minister), who then contracted it to a certain Agha Muhammad Rahim, who finally sold this concession to the firm of Fracis Times, which was the largest British arms trader in the region. The *bania* customs farmer and Fracis Times became embroiled in a dispute over the taxable value of this monopoly, after which the sheikh of Bahrain was forced to intervene and revoke the concession.[97] The intricate relationships that secured this monopoly over the arms trade and those that destroyed it illuminate the extent to which the state's power was exercised by private firms. State privileges had become negotiable commodities. But as long as merchants continued to fill the functions of the state, there would be openings for the arms traffic to proliferate.

In Kuwait a similar monopoly was given to the Marafi family, which was closely connected with the sheikh. When the sheikh of Kuwait finally succumbed to British pressure and limited the importation of rifles, it was the Marafi family who dictated the time line so that they could stockpile enough weapons to take full advantage of the increased prices. The Marafi family's influence was so pervasive that British diplomats refrained from criticism, despite their evident irritation.[98] Like the fox guarding the henhouse, the firms who were the object of arms regulations were responsible for implementing those same regulations. Moreover, as British pressure slowly chipped away at the influence of these favored firms, another category of favored firm came into prominence. French businesses could own and charter ships that were immune from search by British cruisers. As British regulations were tightened, firms like Goguyer et Cie. were pushed into the forefront of the arms trade. Monsieur Goguyer both capitalized on the protection of the French Empire and further entrenched his connections with local rulers by providing favorable loans.[99] Thus the political connections of arms dealers were far more significant to their success than their efficiency or innovation.

The Arabian Sea was also bordered by large states that were not so easily pressured by European empires. British officials complained vociferously about the corruption of the customs authorities in Iran, who had little incentive to stop the arms trade and large incentives to facilitate it.[100] For most of the nineteenth century, customs revenues were farmed out by province, as in the Arabian Peninsula, while trade was administered and facilitated by merchant guilds. Thus the *moin-ut-tujjar* (deputy of the merchants), who British observers thought was a customs official, was in fact an officer of the merchants' guild. Therefore we see the *moin-ut-tujjar* resolving disputes not merely by proclaiming judgments and punishments but by facilitating trading activities, purchasing abandoned goods, and selling extraneous ones.[101] Merchant guilds handled many of the functions that at the end of the century would be handled by the Belgian customs regime. Yet the same accusations of favoritism and bias also plagued the more bureaucratic Belgian administration; the difference was merely which segments of mercantile society gained the benefits. Very similar criticisms were leveled at the *näggadras*, or "heads of the merchants" in Ethiopia. The *näggadras* were prominent merchants who in the late nineteenth and early twentieth centuries became increasingly central figures in the fiscal administration of the Ethiopian Empire. Individuals like *näggadras* Haile Giorgis came to dominate the local economy by means of their special access to state power.[102] These shifts make clear that the implementation of arms regulations was determined by the incorporation of mercantile interests into the bureaucracy.

Soldiers in Society

Governments incorporated merchants and other subjects into the state apparatus, but the most pervasive way that the colonial bureaucracy transformed subjects into state functionaries was through the military. Soldiers and sailors were recruited in large numbers to serve all the states around the Arabian Sea littoral. Access to firearms was essential to their roles, but many soldiers found that this access could be a source of additional income. British enlisted soldiers, usually from the lower classes of society in Britain and Ireland, had a great deal more to profit from subverting their status as trusted government functionaries than from enforcing the hierarchies of imperial rule. Soldiers arriving from Britain provided a steady flow of weapons into India. Their customs declarations were not inspected and no systematic monitoring was made of their imports because they were responsible for maintaining their own weapons. Indeed, it was notorious in Bombay that Europeans who had joined the volunteer corps were a ready supply of ammunition for the general population. British sergeant-armorers in particular had extensive access to military stores of weapons, and a number were discovered to have run arms-trafficking syndicates in India. They could easily pilfer arms and ammunition from military stores, could purchase them from officers finishing their tours, and knew arms regulations well enough to make everything appear above board.[103] The allure of profit overcame the loyalty of many British soldiers who were only too happy to profit from their meager privileges.

Far more Indian soldiers populated the ranks of the British Indian army than Britons. Because of their larger numbers and dispersal through different parts of the subcontinent, Indian soldiers collectively had access to a vast market of consumers. Each soldier had family and local village networks that facilitated questionable transactions and allowed firearms to penetrate far beyond the circuits of European officials. Some soldiers themselves became small-scale traffickers, while others became suppliers to Bohra arms dealers.[104] In Kuwait, soldiers were similarly implicated in the rising tide of the arms trade. British officials could not question Sheikh Mubarak's requests for arms because he claimed that these weapons were for his military. He justified the vast size of his purchases by arguing that each year Kuwaiti youth were coming of age and that they all would need new firearms to take their place among the sheikh's retainers. The sheikh of Kuwait took British notions of the state's monopoly on arms imports to their logical conclusion: the entire adult male population of Kuwait was a reserve for the army, so they were all part of the state.[105] Soldiers thus incorporated almost all of society, and this state consequently had no society to regulate and protect from dangerous weapons. In fact, in this same period, the entire population of Kuwait cooperated in the ingenious efforts of *nākhudā* Abbās bin Nakhī to outwit the British Navy and conceal guns smuggled from Muscat. Today a short film commemorates Bin Nakhī as a national hero, and this effort as evidence of the resolute national unity of the country.[106] When the regulators and the regulated population became indistinguishable, arms regulation became an absurd task.

Sailors also played an important role in the arms traffic because they were similarly exempt from many arms regulations. Bengali sailors were noted as particularly gross violators of arms regulations, while Somalis were identified as inveterate arms smugglers and were described as a "most shameless and treacherous people" who "did not care at all . . . [to do] everything for their pecuniary gain."[107] But even Goan Christians, who were given trusted responsibilities as stewards, were discovered stealing and smuggling weapons.[108] German sailors working on the Hamburg Amerika Line and the Austrian Lloyd Triestino Line apparently made a tidy profit: as there were no regulations on sailors taking arms out of Europe and on arrival in India, they apparently could be "easily concealed in the palm of a large seafaring hand."[109] Whether German seafaring hands were quite so large is debatable, but nonetheless they were making handsome profits. Sailors were merely another category that blurred the imaginary boundary between state and society.

Perhaps the largest influx of arms into the Arabian Sea littoral occurred in the aftermath of wars. Wars necessitated an expansion of the military and armament of soldiers, but in their aftermath militaries decommissioned and disarmed their soldiers. After World War I, colonial powers had an oversupply of weapons and a dearth of cash. For many governments, the simple solution was to demobilize soldiers and sell off their weapons to the highest bidder. The conquering army of the Arab Revolt returned to various corners of the Arabian Peninsula with as many rifles and as much ammunition as they could carry. Newly unemployed and holding rifles costing more than twice as much in Iran as in Syria, these soldiers made the rational decision to sell their weapons. The problem became significant enough that one British administrator even suggested sending "bogus traders to buy on our behalf" and consequently repurchasing what the British Empire had so liberally distributed just a few years previously.[110] Weapons used in the Italian conquest of Ethiopia in 1935 similarly leaked across the Red Sea to threaten British influence in Aden.[111] Similarly, the sultan of Muscat's military was mostly manned by Baluchi mercenaries who frequently crossed the Gulf of Oman with their weapons. But when the Baluchis were replaced with British Indian troops, these demobilized soldiers quickly evolved into effective arms traffickers.[112] The demobilization of soldiers explicitly involves the reincorporation of state functionaries into civilian society and presents a natural conduit for the transfer of arms from the state to society. The minimal value of these weapons to the colonial bureaucracy and its desire for funds after wartime presented a uniquely powerful combination of incentives and opportunities to undermine arms regulations.

Most perversely, the colonial authorities were also involved in the illicit arms traffic when it was in their interest. Even as the Royal Navy was scouring the waves of the Gulf to catch illicit arms traffickers, British diplomats were illicitly supplying arms to Abdul Aziz ibn Saud. Officially, the British were working with the Ottoman Empire to halt the illicit imports of arms into Ottoman territory, but they surreptitiously supplied Ibn Saud with the latest firearms to use against his Ottoman-supported rival Ibn Rashid.[113] These weapons were sent through Kuwait, contributing to its own rise as an arms-trafficking hub. When World War I arrived, the British Empire no longer had to disguise its support of anti-Ottoman forces and actively supplied weapons to both Ibn Saud and Sharif Hussein during the Arab Revolt. Indeed, this virtually unlimited supply of firepower probably contributed in far greater proportion to the success of the revolt than the more photogenic activities of T. E. Lawrence.[114] French and Russian officials similarly supplied their favored protégés with the latest weaponry.[115] So even as European powers signed agreements to restrict the arms trade, they actively subverted these policies when other interests intervened. Thus arms regulation was handicapped by the fact that state policy was conflicted and the state itself was not a cohesive or coherent entity. Not only was the distinction between state and society ambiguous, but the officials responsible for parsing this distinction were not always motivated to keep these categories distinct.

The detainment of the SS *Baluchistan* was a pivotal moment in the economic fortunes of Ratansi Purshottam because it marked the dominance of a conceptual model of the market that was free of violent coercion. From this point onwards, private violence was an anathema to the proper functioning of the market. At the same time, the specter of imperial violence was essential to the ordering of this market. Ratansi Purshottam's carefully cultivated relationships with the sultan of Muscat and myriad consumers around the Arabian Sea were devalued as colonial power reformatted commercial exchange. The firm's success in the arms trade irritated the British agent in Muscat, so he rigorously enforced regulations against the firm and they tried to sue him in return.[116] In the first decade of the twentieth century the firm's correspondence begins to betray desperation as they chased deals with manufacturers and merchants. By the end of World War I, Ratansi Purshottam was no longer the preeminent merchant in Muscat. The firm of Ratansi Purshottam neither delved into the illicit traffic in firearms nor could develop the colonial connections that would allow them to profit from the licit trade.

The declining effectiveness of Ratansi Purshottam is emblematic of the changing structures of trade around the Arabian Sea. Before the nineteenth century violence was an integral part of trade, where the protection of property had to be calculated into the costs of doing business. Beginning in the early nineteenth century, capitalist ideas of political economy began to penetrate trading networks across the sea, particularly through the Royal Navy's campaigns against piracy. Piracy and private violence became delegitimized as colonial empires asserted a state monopoly on the legitimate use of violence. By the end of the nineteenth century, this conceptual separation of violent coercion from market exchange was almost complete except for the nagging vexation of firearms. The private trade in firearms threatened colonial rule as well as colonial states' ability to secure private property rights. Yet firearms were simultaneously owned as private property and traded as legitimate commodities. Firearms were violence commodified. Customs officials and colonial regulators were charged with the impossible task of decommodifying the violent potential of firearms.

Firearms became a peculiar form of property, in that the rights to use, transfer, and profit from it were severely curtailed. But since colonial empires did not have the resources to regulate the everyday use of these weapons, the primary method of enforcement was to regulate their import and export. Customs officials attempted to separate property from predation by distinguishing a trickle from a trade, commodity from contraband, and state from society. Yet these distinctions were elusive, so they were interpreted by rules of thumb like quantity or nationality. Trafficking networks exploited the slippages in these heuristics, and arms regulations succeeded only in entangling the state in both the licit and the illicit arms trades. Traffickers arbitraged across the conceptual boundaries of colonial capitalism and thus participated in framing the security of property rights.

In colonial political economy, violence was essential to the functioning of the free market, but only when this violence was framed out of the market itself. State violence directed toward the protection of private property was a crucial institutional pillar of the market economy, yet it had to be framed as acting outside the market. If sovereign bureaucracies claimed a monopoly on the legitimate use of violence, they also claimed a sovereign monopoly on the issuance of currency. Like firearms, monetary instruments proved to be contested intermediaries that were *in* the market, yet somehow not *of* the market. The next chapter takes up this paradox of money that frames capitalist exchange.

FOUR

Neutralizing Money

GANGA RAM HAD A BRILLIANT PLAN. It was the end of May 1940, and wartime conditions had caused a surge in the price of gold in Iraq and around the Gulf. The British government had prohibited the export of gold from India; nevertheless, merchants, sailors, and ordinary travelers from India packed gold sovereigns in their luggage and made staggering profits selling them on arrival in Arab ports. But the SS *Varela*, due to arrive in Bahrain on May 22, had been detained in India. The war had already limited maritime transport between India and the Gulf to a minimum, so this additional delay powerfully affected the local market for gold. The price of gold in the Gulf surged even higher with the obstructed supply from India. This is when Ganga Ram went into action. Indian and Arab travelers were not very familiar with the recently established routes of British Imperial Airways. Air travel was quite expensive and hence was largely the preserve of Europeans. If Ganga Ram could get to Bahrain before the SS *Varela* arrived in the Gulf, the astronomical prices for gold would easily defray the high cost of air travel. So Ganga Ram booked a flight from Karachi to Bahrain and packed £1,000 worth of gold sovereigns in his bags. But when he arrived at Karachi airport his scheme was foiled by a very simple fact. On a ship surrounded by thousands of other Indians and Arabs, one man with some heavy luggage would have been inconspicuous. On a plane with a few dozen European officials, Ganga Ram stood out like a sore thumb.[1]

Ganga Ram's ingenious—though poorly executed—plan is emblematic of the subtle dynamics of visibility and invisibility that channeled monetary flows across the Arabian Sea. Before the outbreak of war, customs authorities had tried to make visible the flows of money across international borders. But since gold was not subject to tariffs, it was a low priority in British India, and officials were satisfied with the self-reporting of imports and exports of gold across the border. During the war, not only were imperial authorities more anxious to make currency flows visible, but they were also attempting to halt these flows. Customs authorities instituted more invasive search procedures, particularly against populations they deemed to be inveterate smugglers. Ganga Ram rendered his gold invisible by concealing it in his bags, but his body, clothing, and behavior made him conspicuous to the roving eyes of the customs authorities. Colonial bureaucrats rendered visible global monetary flows even as they attempted to render invisible the invasive ways that state bureaucracies collected this information. Traffickers concealed their money from colonial bureaucracies by making it visible as some other commodity or by making themselves visible as loyal and trustworthy subjects. The history of money in the Arabian Sea was a struggle over when and how money would be visible.

The monies circulating around the Arabian Sea littoral until the twentieth century were almost breathtaking in their diversity. Ottoman, Qajar, and Mughal coins continued to circulate in the regions that these empires had ruled. Smaller rulers in western India, the Arabian Peninsula, and East Africa produced their own currencies and utilized commodity currencies like salt bars, cowry shells, and bitter almonds. Coins were minted by private individuals, cowries were pulled out of the ocean, and bitter almonds literally grew on trees. European coins were also widely used, so that many currencies of the Arabian Peninsula are still called Riyal, an arabicization of the Spanish *Real*. Muslim rulers regulated the circulation of multiple coins through a market inspector known as the *muhtasib*. The *muhtasib* was responsible for administering *hisba,* or the obligation of Muslim rulers to enjoin the good and discourage evil. By his physical presence in the market and prominent display of the instruments of punishment, the *muhtasib* strove to prevent usury, counterfeiting, and other financial crimes.[2] He could permit a wide variety of coins to circulate because they were nothing more than specified weights of metal.

Islamic notions of money incorporated two of the three functions of money in classical political economy: it was a store of wealth and a medium of exchange. The novel component of European political economy was to suggest that money was also a standard of value. Money was supposed to be a neutral standard by which all other commodities could be valued. Whereas coins around the Arabian Sea were themselves measured and evaluated for their metallic content, colonial authorities attempted to make a standardized coinage that would permit a universal method of calculating value. Marx's famous formula M-C-M' (the transformation of money into commodity into money plus profit) could operate only where money was a singular and stable standard of exchange value. This new conception of money required eliminating the diversity of monies in circulation. Moreover, it required changing the relationship between people and money both as a concept and as a physical object. It demanded interventions in the rates at which people exchanged money, how they handled these physical objects, the emotional resonance these objects held, and indeed the power that money wielded over people. Colonial authorities would have to decommoditize money so that it could function as a neutral and transparent measure of real value.

However, coins were also problematic for the *muḥtasib* because they were intimately connected with usury. Moneylending that did not incur interest was permitted in Islamic law, as was investing in a business that yielded profits, but lending money at a specified rate of interest was considered usury. In most schools of Islamic law, usury was classified as an unequal exchange: a certain weight of gold could not be exchanged for a smaller/larger weight of gold. The money regulated then was metallic coinage: one could exchange coins, but one could not rent capital.[3] This prohibition was inconvenient for Muslim and non-Muslim commerce in the Arabian Sea, and it was regularly circumvented in practice.[4] On the other hand, capitalist political economy conceptualized money as a measure of value and an avatar of capital. Interest was the price of renting that capital for a specified period of time.[5] But we are not going to investigate the complicated and subtle history of credit and interest here because we must first confront the different conceptions of money itself that give rise to these attitudes toward usury/interest. Money could become capital only after coins were framed as objects that facilitated market exchange without actually shaping transactions. Capitalism first had to transfigure money from a lump of solid metal into a transparent veil.

The conception of money as something obscuring market exchange can be traced back at least to the eighteenth-century writings of David Hume. He conceived of money as something that was separate from—while flowing through—market exchange. Thus with classical political economy money became a rather elusive and illusive force. Classical political economists were attempting to persuade governments that the fetishizing of gold by mercantilist thinkers was a mistake because money was just a veil that shrouded the reality of barterlike exchange.[6] Yet monetary theory from Hume to Keynes and beyond was largely focused on debates over the quantity of money in an economy.[7] These authors were concerned with money supply and its effect on price levels, interest rates, and consequently national economies.

Few questions arose about money as coinage, how coins would be made uniform, or how to neutralize their use as a speculative commodity.[8] As debates in monetary theory marched on in Europe and India, colonial authorities around the Arabian Sea continued to struggle with the frustrating multiplicity and volatility of monies. Money was metal coins and paper notes: a physical intermediary between the conceptual free market and sweaty pockets or dirty hoards. Diasporic networks exploited this physicality to frame coins as cultural artifacts in order to arbitrage their value across the sea. Piercing the monetary veil in this littoral zone required erecting national borders, demonetizing competing currencies, and decommoditizing money.[9] What was discussed in Europe as merely revealing the true nature of money required a fundamental reordering of exchange relations in the Arabian Sea.

Colonial political economy consequently required a very different set of policies and a new kind of monetary authority. The administration of *ḥisba* was concerned with physical coins and how they circulated within a human community. It was not limited to the market and did not recognize the economy as a distinct sphere of human life but rather attempted to govern the morality of people generally. Money changers were monitored more intensively than other individuals, their schemes were investigated, and potential fraud was deterred by the visible presence in the marketplace of the *muḥtasib*.[10] Colonial monetary policy on the other hand, attempted to operate invisibly. Officials stayed away from markets, banks, and the booths of money changers but nevertheless sought to act upon the circulation of money. They collected information about the quantity and velocity of money in their attempt to make money universal, standardized, and stable. Colonial economic policy was interested, not in people or in coins, but in the financial statistics and national accounts that assumed neutralized money as a standard of value. Since money was framed out of the market, laissez-faire ideology sanctified intensive intervention and management of this lifeblood of market exchange.

Yet how did distant financial authorities affect the circulation of coinage without a visible presence in the marketplace? To a significant extent this was accomplished through a vast network of mediators. Both British banks and Indian merchants played a vital role in colonial efforts to demonetize old monies, introduce new financial instruments, and stabilize exchange. Monetary authorities could tweak the money supply, but the impact of these policies on the ordinary artisan or fisherman was mediated by merchant bankers. Diasporic merchants not only mediated between colonial policies and colonial populations but also exploited the arbitrage opportunities that these policies introduced.[11] Banks and merchant bankers were treated as normal market agents even as they took advantage of their key mediating role in monetary policy. Coins occupied a similar space at the margins of the conceptual market: they were the physical objects that instantiated monetary theory, yet they easily moved in and out of the market. This chapter consequently examines how colonial political economy framed money as a neutral standard through which it could visualize and intervene in the economy, but simultaneously how diasporic networks mobilized to exploit the blind spots in the colonial gaze.

FRAMING A COMMON CURRENCY

Ganga Ram was quite unusual in that most gold smugglers in South Asian history were attempting to bring gold into the subcontinent, not out of it. During the war, gold was the only truly liquid means of payment across battle lines. Iraq had apparently become a conduit for gold to the Axis powers, and Indian merchants had exported hundreds of thousands of pounds worth of gold in a matter of two months. Colonial authorities were suddenly faced with the rather awkward realization that India's gold hoards were feeding the Nazi war machine. They hurriedly imposed an export ban, which only egged on Ganga Ram and his compatriots.[12] Colonial monetary policies were implemented first to constrain gold hoarding and then to prevent the dispersal of those very hoards. These tumultuous swings of monetary policy were a result of the gap between the colonial conception of money and its everyday reality.

Communities around the Arabian Sea were in the habit of saving money in the form of gold and silver. Money was used as a store of wealth, but with changing conceptions of political economy in Europe what had once been an admirable trait became an irrational obsession. As early as the Mughal era, India was maligned as a nation of hoarders, an inexhaustible sink for the world's precious metals. Colonial monetary policies were consequently directed toward constraining the inflow of precious metals into British India. The introduction of gold coinage was always limited for fear that the global money supply would be endangered by India's insatiable appetite for gold.[13]

Hoards were filled not only with coins but also with bullion and jewelry. Jewelry was considered a more effective store of value than coins because it had the mobility and security of being fastened to one's person. As one colonial official commented: "Women and children['s] ... bodies are made the banks of their husbands and parents."[14] Many individuals even punched a hole in their coins to incorporate them directly into jewelry.[15] Money was a malleable object whose shape and content could easily be altered to serve the purposes of any consumer. It took different forms and entered or disappeared from circulation at the whim of Arab bedouins or Indian peasants. Over the course of the nineteenth century this consumer control over state-issued coinage would be eroded, and the British Empire would seek to monopolize the production and direct the circulation of money around the Arabian Sea.

The East India Company commenced its monetary policies by taking over the mints of rulers it had displaced and continuing to produce the same coins. In 1835, the company issued its own silver rupee for the first time and declared the Company rupee as legal tender across its territories. Yet at this stage, the company's coin was merely one of many current coins in their territories.[16] It was not until the East India Company gave way to direct crown rule that alternative forms of money were invalidated by British policy. Sections 230 to 254 of the Indian Penal Code of 1860 addressed the counterfeiting of coins and defined coins as "metal used as money stamped and issued by the authority of some government in order so to be used." As with violence in the previous chapter, colonial legislation made money a government monopoly in the nineteenth century. Government coinage had long circulated alongside commodity currencies and privately minted coins. The circulating medium for arguably the majority of the population was not government-issued currency but cowry shells and unstamped pieces of copper known as "dumps." "Dumps" probably had evolved from both the Mughal copper coinage called *dam* as well as the dumped or left-over bits of copper from minting coins with holes at the center. The Indian Penal Code explicitly excluded both cowries and dumps from protection, yet admitted that they might nonetheless function as money.[17] Even as colonial authorities acknowledged these diverse forms of money, they consciously chose to ignore this diversity. With one deft move, this law rendered these forms of money invisible for the purposes of monetary policy, even as they continued to operate as media of exchange.

Monetary authorities hoped to replace the circulation of cowries and dumps with their own copper coins. British mints stood to gain substantial seigniorage revenues, which were the profits gained from the difference between the face value of a coin and its cost of production. Yet while it was relatively easy to change a law, British authorities found it rather more difficult to persuade their subjects to accept coins at their face value. The circulation of money depended on its consonance with the systems of mental arithmetic used by the population. In the decimal system, numbers divisible by ten are easy to calculate with, but in parts of western India people calculated with a base of four, a unit known as a *gunda*. Special accounting symbols were employed to express fourths, sixteenths, sixty-fourths, and two hundred fifty-sixths.[18] Following the monetary system of the Mughals, the East India Company minted subsidiary coins of silver and copper. The rupee was divided into sixteen *anna*s and the *anna* was divided into four *pice*. When British mints started producing a half-*pice* coin it was speedily adopted into circulation because it was equivalent to an existing unit of account called an *adhela*.[19] But the practice of minting coins that matched local units of account was stymied by the fact that different methods of calculation predominated between mercantile and agricultural populations. In their account books, merchants calculated with a unit called a *pie* (worth one-twelfth of an *anna*). British mints thus coined copper *pie* pieces for circulation, but while this unit was used for commercial calculations it had no popular equivalent. So the value of the *pie* piece depreciated until it settled at a more congenial rate of one-sixteenth of an *anna:* the value at which cowry shells circulated.[20] Even as cowry shells were pushed to the margins of the economy, their role as a unit of value could not be displaced. Colonial mints could standardize the coins in circulation, but they could not standardize the way that different populations counted.

If cowries continued to shape monetary practices amongst fishermen and peasants, gold *mohur*s persisted in ceremonial gift giving among aristocrats. In 1874, the Bombay High Court heard a case regarding the counterfeiting of gold *mohur* coins, which had been minted under the Mughal emperors. The court had to decide whether these *mohur*s were to be considered money and hence protected by the counterfeiting provisions of the Penal Code. The Bombay High Court—channeling classical political economists—defined money as "a general standard of value and medium of exchange."[21] These *mohur*s were in general circulation, but their price fluctuated regularly and was known only by merchants who dealt specifically in these coins. Hence, the judge decided that they might have been a medium of exchange but they could not be a standard of value. The fact that the value of these *mohur*s was not transparent to the wider public persuaded the court that they could not be money. Since *mohur*s were not a universal standard of value, these transactions were categorized as gift exchange and consequently outside the ambit of monetary protections.[22] Merchants of course took advantage of this decision. According to one estimate, 85,000 counterfeit *mohur*s were produced annually just in Bombay.[23] By excluding the circulation of *mohur*s and cowries from the official economy, colonial policy makers could imagine that colonial coins constituted a transparent and universal standard of value. Nevertheless, *mohur*s, cowries, and counterfeits continued to circulate within these populations even if monetary authorities refused to see them as money.

The Mughal gold *mohur* was not the only monetary relic that continued to pass current along the coasts of the Arabian Sea. Indeed, perhaps the most important coin circulating around the Arabian Sea bore the busty image of a German empress who had been dead for over a century. The Maria Theresa thaler was a silver coin of the Hapsburg Empire, first minted during the eighteenth-century reign of the eponymous empress. Its high silver content and excellent minting made the thaler a sought-after coin in North and East Africa and around the Arabian Peninsula. When the Empress Maria Theresa died the coin was withdrawn from circulation within the Hapsburg Empire, but the Vienna mints continued to coin the thaler for consumption around the Arabian Sea. The wide acceptability of the coin gave it a value well above its silver content and made it profitable for Austrian mints to continue coining the thaler well into the twentieth century. Numerous governments attempted to displace or control the circulation of the Maria Theresa thaler but could not seem to overcome the potency of the coin and its appeal to populations around the Arabian Sea.[24] Much of the monetary history of the Arabian Sea was consequently a tale of two currencies: the rupee, backed by power of the British Empire, and the thaler, backed by the peoples of East Africa and Arabia.

Both the rupee and the thaler would be severely undermined by the emergence of the international gold standard.[25] The international gold standard necessitated the demonetization of silver coinage, and this had an almost immediate and negative impact on trade in the Arabian Sea. Silver was the predominant metal of coinage around the Arabian Sea, so as Europe and America demonetized silver it flowed east.[26] The value of silver coins in the region suffered a precipitous decline, and alternative uses for silver became increasingly attractive. A group of cunning silversmiths discovered that by adopting a new technology called electroplating they could put silver to two uses at once. Electroplating involved placing a piece of bullion and a second object in a chemical bath and then connecting them with electrical wires. When an electric charge was sent through the water an almost imperceptible layer of silver atoms was "sweated" from the metal and deposited on the exterior of the second object. The British administration had no objection to this new procedure, but a problem arose when coins provided the silver. Unlike melted, clipped, or filed coins, rupees used for electroplating were indistinguishable from full-weight coins even to trained experts. It was not a crime to use coins for the purposes of electroplating, nor was it counterfeiting. It was only the knowledgeable exchange of a coin that had been sweated, which could be prosecuted as the lesser crime of cheating.[27] Given that it was virtually impossible to identify such coins, much less prove someone's knowledge that they were passing sweated coins, this was a perfect crime. Silversmiths had both full-value coins and silver-plated objects; they could have their proverbial cake and eat it too.

Populations around the Arabian Sea recognized that coins were often not what they appeared to be, and thus they relied on alternative forms of authentication, in particular *shroff* marks. *Shroffs* can be loosely defined as the merchant bankers of the Arabian Sea littoral. While *shroffs* were mostly Indians by the late nineteenth century, their name derives from the Arabic *ṣarraf*, meaning "money changer."[28] The myriad variety of coins, the prevalence of debased and counterfeit coins, and the fluctuations in the value of gold, silver, copper, and commodity monies created a wide demand for *shroffs* to evaluate different forms of money. A *shroff* would impress a small hole upon the coin's face to test the metal, and this became known as a *shroff*'s mark. A *shroff*'s mark, even as it defaced the original minting, usually enhanced the reliability and hence the value of this piece of metal.[29] By the 1870s, with the rapidly declining value of silver, the value of the rupee was determined not by the colonial government but by *shroffs* in each marketplace.

It was an anathema to colonial administrators that *shroff* marks might deface a government-minted rupee and that their subjects questioned the reliability of government mints. So as part of a larger effort to make the colonial government the final arbiter of monetary circulation, *shroff* marking was prohibited.[30] Yet these policies could not fully eliminate *shroff*-marked rupees; they only made them circulate at a discount outside the vision of monetary authorities. District collectors then attempted to monitor fluctuations in the value of British coins and to bring discounted coins back to their face value.[31] The value of British coins fluctuated with supply and demand, but colonial political economy demanded that coins function as a measure of value rather than having their own fluctuating values. These efforts went some way toward making British Indian currency behave in the way that classical political economy predicted, but they were always subject to the manipulations of *shroffs*.

By the 1890s, the devaluation of silver inflated the value of colonial India's gold-denominated debts that were becoming impossible to repay. So in 1893 a committee was appointed to look into the possibility of closing the Indian mints to the free coinage of silver bullion. Drawing on expertise from the preeminent economists of the day, the committee recommended that India adopt a managed monetary standard in which the value of the rupee would be pegged to gold but the circulating currency would be silver.[32] A mere five years later this new currency regime had proven a failure and another committee was charged with addressing the problem. Drawing on more damning evidence and new economic theories, this committee recommended that India adopt a full gold standard. But the committee's recommendations were resisted by the India Office, which feared that gold coins would disappear into hoards and also that the costs of purchasing sufficient quantities of gold would be prohibitive.[33] They subsequently attempted to achieve the same goals with a more refined gold-exchange standard, but every few years a new currency commission would be resurrected to address the continuing instability of the rupee.

These currency commissions identified princely state coins as one of the main obstacles to a stable currency in India.[34] A number of princely states along the western coast of India continued to exercise the royal prerogative to mint their own coins. The colonial government tried to cajole and coerce them to close their mints, but with little success.[35] In fact, after 1893, when British mints were closed to the public, princely mints happily accepted the public's silver. The coins of native states did not usually circulate at par with British Indian rupees, but when the supply of rupees was constrained they were a perfectly acceptable circulating medium. As their currencies spilled into British-administered territories, Indian princes profited from the seigniorage.[36] Thus colonial monetary policies were frustrated because they would never have a monopoly on the production of money in their territories.

Colonial efforts to demonetize princely coinage were simultaneously facilitated and exploited by *shroffs*. British treasuries found it inconvenient to convert small amounts of coins, so they paid merchants a premium to collect coins from the peasantry and present them in bulk at British treasuries.[37] *Shroffs* happily complied because impending demonetization forced peasants to sell their hard-earned savings to merchants at a discount, and *shroffs* turned around and sold these coins to the colonial government at a guaranteed premium.[38] Indian peasants, Indian princes, and British treasuries were all milked by the manipulations of *shroffs*. Colonial policies attempted to produce a universal medium of exchange, but the unification of currency instead guaranteed a line of profit for the mercantile classes.

Indian merchants were of course not limited to the Indian subcontinent: they had for centuries been operating in all corners of the Arabian Sea littoral. Gujarati traders dominated the commercial life of southern and eastern Arabia and brought the rupee everywhere they traded. The rupee had been legal tender in the colony of Aden and the wider Aden Protectorate since the early nineteenth century. In the 1910s, building on the commercial penetration of Gujarati traders, British officials gained control of customs, postal correspondence, and shipping services in Muscat and Bahrain. British rupees were the only accepted currency for paying these fees, despite the preference of local Arabs for Maria Theresa thalers. By the turn of the twentieth century, the Indian rupee was current in every Arabian port from Jedda to Basra.[39] When British banks were given monopolies to operate in these countries in the mid-twentieth century, they too insisted on operating only in rupees.[40] Exactions by the ruler were handled in rupees, but local commerce continued to be transacted in thalers. Colonial statistics demonstrated ever increasing penetration of British Indian business interests, but they also elided the continued circulation of the thaler.

Monetary circulation in East Africa followed a similar trajectory. When the Imperial British East Africa Company (IBEAC) was established, it minted its own version of the rupee. Local populations in East Africa were discerning consumers and easily resisted the imposition of foreign coins that held little value within their markets. Indian merchants were therefore the only population the company could effectively tax, and they preferred the Indian rupee they were familiar with. The IBEAC rupee had a tepid reception, and in 1905 a currency commission legalized the de facto dominance of the Indian rupee. This commission hoped to eliminate the circulation of noncoined commodity currencies, but officials failed to collect taxes except in labor, cowry shells, hippo teeth, and even young elephants and zebras.[41] The Indian rupee spread into Africa with Indian merchants and laborers, but it could not displace the myriad forms of currency used by African peoples. The expanding circulation of the rupee did, however, provide a method of conversion between diverse transregional transactions and a single standard of value. The Indian rupee thus translated a seemingly inscrutable world of African exchange into a form comprehensible to colonial political economy. But it did so only by obscuring the rich diversity of economic life beyond the ambit of the rupee's circulation.

The First World War exacerbated the contradictions of colonial monetary policy. Wartime governments required far more money than there was gold available, so they pushed the limits of fiat currency within their borders but relied on gold in international transactions. Diasporic networks and seafaring peoples were only too happy to exploit this contradiction by smuggling gold and silver across the seas. After the war colonial officials in East Africa tried to establish a new gold standard currency, but the introduction of the East African florin was a tortuous process. The Indian trading community was attached to the rupee because it stabilized trade with India. But they also recognized that the demonetization of the rupee provided an opportunity to extract profits. Indian traders imported millions of rupees into East Africa to have them redeemed by the East African Currency Board at a vastly inflated price. The demonetization of the rupee was far more expensive than expected because it was achieved only after Indian traders had extracted their pound of flesh from the colonial government.[42] Only after hemorrhaging florins and being forced to devalue this new currency could colonial authorities claim some progress in eliminating the multiplicity of monies in East Africa.

The anxieties of World War II created a welter of regulations and smuggling, and the dawn of the postcolonial era only exacerbated the possibilities for smuggling. Many of the currency controls instituted during the war were continued to allow Britain to service its debts. The Indian rupee was still the official currency of colonial India, the Arab Gulf states, Aden, and Somaliland, and along with British East Africa these countries were incorporated within the Sterling Area monetary system. This coordinated but divergent set of monetary policies was a magnet for smugglers. The creation of the Pakistani rupee in 1947, the devaluation of sterling currencies in 1949, and the 1951 conversion from rupees to East African shillings in Aden and Somaliland all created opportunities for arbitrage (map 3). Gold smuggling became rampant in this period, ultimately forcing both the Indian and Pakistani state banks to introduce special Persian Gulf rupee notes to prevent the hemorrhaging of currency reserves.[43] Monetary policies consequently became ever more nuanced to accommodate the complexities of exchange across the Arabian Sea, but they always appeared to be one step behind the innovations of trafficking networks.

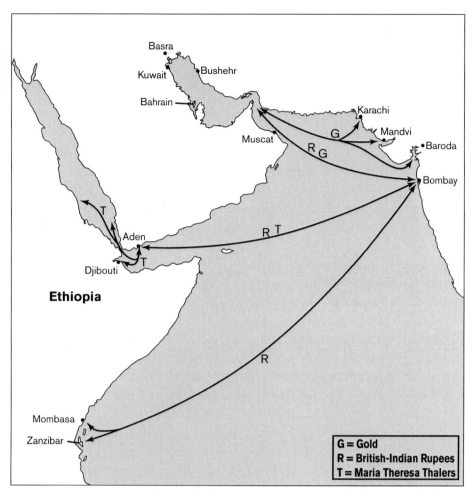

MAP 3. Major currency and specie flows. Map by author.

CONCEALING COUNTERFEITS, SMUGGLING SILVER

Apparently, Ganga Ram was not a seasoned criminal. We can imagine him being interrogated in the Karachi customs office and quickly caving under pressure. He divulged the names of four accomplices who together intended to transport about £21,000 worth of gold sovereigns. It turns out that Ganga Ram was just a small part of a substantial operation managed by a *bania* firm called Dhamanmal Isardas. The firm had arranged the operation so that they were buffered from the actual smugglers like Ganga Ram.[44] While remaining in the safety of their family home, the firm could arrange vast traffics of coins, currency notes, promissory notes, and bills of exchange. It was precisely their ability to obscure these forms of money that produced the largest profits. By operating beyond the perception of colonial authorities, firms were able to obtain contraband and circulate counterfeits. Customs officers were constantly working to ensure the visibility of monetary flows, while smugglers were equally working to obscure the vision of colonial officials.

At the most basic level, the illicit circulation of currency was exemplified by a group known as the Chapparband tribe. The colonial police produced a fascinating ethnography of these Muslim peasants from the district of Bijapur in central India. The men cultivated their fields and raised chickens while the women knitted quilts. When a favorable omen was obtained, the men of a village would assume the guise of wandering mendicants or fakirs and would journey on foot to the nearby princely state of Hyderabad. They coined rupees by a simple process of baking a mold out of lime and mud, melting down tin from the local bazaar, and pouring it inside the mold. This minting would occur in the evenings as the troupe camped by the side of the road. As they walked down dusty roads and through village markets, they would beg for alms and pass off counterfeit rupees to women and "simple people." After journeying about the country, they returned to their villages with perhaps twenty extra rupees in their pockets and once again resumed work in the fields.[45]

This account must be taken with a grain of salt, based as it was on rumors and Orientalist speculation. Nonetheless, these reports had apparently been collected for over fifty years, and sheer repetition would seem to lend some weight to their description.[46] Yet despite extensive surveillance of the Chapparbands, their activities were not important enough to elicit prosecution. Officials justified their inaction because these activities were on such a small scale and yielded almost no lasting trace. Whereas other counterfeiters could be identified by metal dies or specialized instruments, the Chapparbands destroyed their moulds in the process of extracting the counterfeit coins. The counterfeits that they produced were so crude that most market-goers would not trust the coins as legitimate. By targeting women and "simple people," the Chapparbands exploited those who had the fewest options in terms of trading partners. More experienced market participants would be able to spot such counterfeits and would avoid transactions with unknown purchasers. Moreover, the Chapparbands minted counterfeits not in their own villages but while traveling far from home. By the time their counterfeits were discovered they had already moved on to the next village.

The Chapparbands avoided prosecution because they left no visible trace of their activities, because they transacted with people at the margins of society, and because they were perpetually mobile.

Ultimately, the Chapparbands were a small-scale operation that never posed a danger to the money supply. It was the ability to bring substantial amounts of false money into circulation that really fueled the fears of monetary authorities. While more refined counterfeiting techniques contributed, it was ultimately the authority and reputation of *shroffs* that facilitated the circulation of counterfeits. Coins and notes did not bear their own authority but were valued on the reputation of the person paying out that money. The legal adviser to the Bombay presidency insisted: "It has often been remarked that the difficulty is not in forging currency notes but in putting the forged notes into circulation. A man, therefore, who by his wealth and position is able to pass forged notes … is doubtless deserving of the severest punishment."[47] Since gold and silversmiths were often lower-class artisans, it was *shroffs* who were the main orchestrators of counterfeiting schemes. Counterfeits had to pass the discerning eyes of *shroffs* to circulate widely. So it was passing off counterfeits, a crime called "uttering" in colonial jurisprudence, that merited the greatest concern and the harshest penalties. Ever more complicated designs and innovative devices were added to colonial coins and notes, but they did not seem to hinder the production of counterfeits. Thus, in order to standardize the money supply, monetary authorities needed to discipline the networks through which coins circulated.

The production of high-quality counterfeits involved machinery, which, if found, provided tangible evidence of counterfeiting and guaranteed a conviction. The production of counterfeits was consequently located beyond the jurisdiction of the relevant authorities. Counterfeits of British coins were produced in princely states, and counterfeits of princely state coins were produced in British-administered territory. Each government administered lighter punishments and was lax in enforcing provisions against counterfeits of foreign coins. With exceedingly porous borders, counterfeits could be produced in foreign territory and easily smuggled back in. Even if such smugglers were caught, they could easily plead that they had no idea that the coins they were carrying were counterfeit. So counterfeits were minted in territories where regulations were lax and distributed where their value was highest.

The lax British regulation of foreign counterfeits was not limited to the Indian princely states. Police discovered a veritable mint operating in Bombay that was producing counterfeits of monies used in Turkey, Central Asia, and

America. None of these coins were legal tender in India, so it was difficult to prosecute anyone. The business was booming, employed dozens of smiths, and apparently produced in about two and a half years over four hundred thousand coins. To the great frustration of the Bombay police, these counterfeiters could be prosecuted only in Ottoman Turkey or Central Asia.[48] Therefore, the production of foreign coins insulated counterfeiters from effective prosecution; the real dangers arose only where these coins circulated as legitimate currency. Not until 1929 would an international convention be signed to suppress these kinds of transnational counterfeiting circuits. Yet this treaty was not binding on the princely states of India or independent states like Muscat and Iran.[49] International borders thus proved quite efficient at veiling counterfeiting operations.

The closing of Indian mints to the coinage of silver in 1893 delinked the circulating value of the rupee from its metallic content, which had for centuries been the basis of the coin's value. Counterfeits before 1893 were profitable through the use of debased silver alloys, which often became discolored and revealed their base composition after minimal usage. Initially their differences were obscured, but eventually their debased metal was made visible.[50] After 1893, this problem disappeared because the circulating value of the rupee was so much higher than the cost of an identical weight of silver bullion. As one British police officer rather sympathetically explained:

> The hard times having deprived artisans of their usual means of earning an honest livelihood they were by necessity driven to cast about for some other means of occupation, and as about the same time silver in the shape of ornaments was being placed upon the markets at less than its weight value, this class of mechanic was not slow to perceive that a profit of over 50 per cent could be derived if this silver could be converted and floated on the market as coin of the realm. The actual value of silver in a rupee being but 10 ½ annas, a man who purchased it for less could well afford to manufacture rupees with their full weight of silver and if he could strike good specimens he had little to fear in the way of detection in the market.[51]

So with the colonial government maintaining a gap between the value of the rupee coin and its silver content, silversmiths could profit by producing rupees of exactly the same intrinsic value as government rupees. These were not counterfeits in the sense that they appeared to be something different than they actually were. In physical terms, these coins were identical to the production of British mints. These silversmiths were not deceiving the population but distorting the colonial government's calculations of money supply and depriving it of seigniorage revenues.

Counterfeiting was a particularly profitable venture when there was a change in currency. When a prince relinquished the right to mint his own currency, he also put out of business dozens of silversmiths employed in producing the state's coinage.[52] Who better to produce counterfeits than the artisans that had just been fired from producing the real thing! As we saw with East African florins, each demonetization involved a chaotic period of transition in which British treasuries gave rupees in exchange for the old coins. A huge mass of old currency would flood into British treasuries, making it particularly easy to pass off a counterfeit princely coin to treasury clerks.[53] Massive flows of currency, overworked clerks, and the intense desire to eliminate these alternative currencies came together to make counterfeits invisible. Large write-offs for counterfeit currency were an inevitable cost of unifying currency regimes.

Forms of paper currency introduced by colonial authorities in the late nineteenth century also proved to be profitable targets for counterfeiting. Monetary authorities were initially concerned that the inherent novelty of a paper currency might prevent the population from accepting these new monetary instruments. However, these fears proved unfounded. The wide acceptance of rupee notes did not indicate their acceptance as a replacement for coins; rather, rupee notes functioned more like *hundis*.[54] A *hundi* or *ḥawāla* (in Arab and East African areas) was a bill of exchange or simply a slip of paper that allowed the bearer to withdraw hard currency at the offices of a particular trading firm after a specified amount of time had elapsed. *Hundis* and *ḥawālas* could be designed in different ways with different rates of interest and contractual requirements. The rate of interest also depended on a customer's relationship with the *hundi* issuer, so terms were more generous to those obtaining *hundis* from merchants of the same family or community. But *hundis* were also negotiable instruments and were bought and sold at fluctuating discounts depending on location, due date, and the reputation of the firm.[55] *Hundis* could operate only through the existence of far-flung mercantile networks, but their value depended on one's physical location and social position within these networks. Currency notes were accepted within merchant networks that used *hundis* and *ḥawālas*, and they operated in similar ways. Currency notes did not function as the fiat currencies that colonial officials had intended; rather, they became simply a variation on a *hundi*.

So rather than relying on the government to ensure that counterfeits did not circulate, merchants paid close attention to how these notes flowed through their commercial networks. Many merchants even kept track of the currency notes that they received, noting down from whom these notes were received. This allowed them to identify the source of forged notes and avoid transactions with those firms or to accept notes from them only with a heavy discount.[56] Government treasuries had no similar system, so fear of forgery led them to forbid the encashment of rupee notes at district treasuries except when those notes were presented by Europeans.[57] So even colonial offices did not treat paper currency as a universal medium of exchange; rather, their reliability was premised on who presented them. Watermarks, security features, signatures, and all the apparatus of authentication were rendered meaningless against the canny ability of counterfeiters to make even the state suspicious of its own currency.

Currency notes could be converted into hard metallic cash only within a colony, at a government treasury, and only if you were a reputable individual, so there continued to be a broad demand for the surreptitious transfer of gold and silver across borders. Smugglers like Ganga Ram used the bodies and personal space of travelers to conceal currency from the gaze of the colonial bureaucracy. Smugglers traveling on steamers carried coins in special belts, secret pockets, and even specially designed sandals. Some of the more desperate degradations suffered by smugglers include descriptions of coins concealed between the thighs of passengers, or stowed "behind the private parts in a very clever manner."[58] Eventually, though, customs officers figured out the ruse. One sailor protested vigorously and challenged customs officials to search him, thinking he would never be discovered: "He was then made to squat on his haunches and prodded in the stomach. The result was that one packet containing 50 sovereigns which had been concealed in his rectum dropped on the deck."[59] Other smugglers swallowed small ingots of gold that were later recovered with laxatives and hot tea. Customs officials countered this practice by taking suspected smugglers to the hospital and having them undergo X-rays.[60] Gold smugglers and customs authorities were engaged in a constant back and forth as smugglers invented new ways to make their gold and silver invisible and customs found newer technologies to render them visible.

This protected personal space was more comfortably exploited in the case of Arab and Indian nobles, whose entourages were generally treated as immune from customs searches. One notorious smuggler, Muhammad Ismail, apparently co-opted the king of Saudi Arabia, the sultan of Muscat, and the emir of Kuwait, proposing to give them a cut of his smuggling profits if they helped him transport gold out of India during World War II. Ismail allegedly used the entourage of King Abdul Aziz ibn Saud to smuggle tens of thousands of gold sovereigns out of India on a single trip. This trip was only a small component of a massive operation that moved hundreds of thousands of gold sovereigns a week, charging three rupees for each smuggled sovereign.[61] These reports were probably exaggerated, but certainly an element of truth inheres in them, as royal entourages became infamous as conduits for the smuggling of commodities from diamonds to automobiles.[62]

Most contraband evaded the scrutiny of customs officers by being concealed among legally traded goods. Coins were smuggled in agricultural products that journeyed between the Gulf and India because customs officials could hardly scrutinize all of the agricultural goods that traveled between India and the Gulf.[63] Coins and bullion were similarly hidden in bottles of pickle, tins of ghee and halwa, large jackfruits, and packages of dates and sweetmeats.[64] One particularly inventive group of smugglers stuffed Maria Theresa thalers into surmai fish. Surmai is considered a delicacy in western India, and it was fished in large quantities in the Gulf and the Arabian Sea. Their entrails were removed and replaced with silver and gold coins. Sometimes these silver-laden fish would be dropped overboard and were then picked up when they washed on shore or were fished out by local fishermen who were coconspirators. Sailors and fishermen profited on the premiums demanded both for the fish and for the silver hidden in their bellies.[65] By hiding contraband capital in these mundane commodities, smugglers quite effectively moved gold and silver directly under the noses of customs officials.

Those British officials who weren't themselves profiting from the smuggling of gold always seemed one step behind the evolving methods of the smugglers. One British official, confronted with the elaborate machinations of World War II smugglers like Ganga Ram, summed up the situation in a rather sportsmanlike vein: "Now that the export of silver from Bahrain to Kuwait is restricted to the comparatively small amounts that can be smuggled through, new methods of 'playing the money market' will certainly be devised by Kuwaiti and Basrawi and Bahraini merchants and brokers, and we shall have to be on the look out for their next move. It is an interesting kind of game that we play with these gentlemen; their great skill in playing the game is balanced by the authority that we have to alter the rules!"[66] This quote captures perfectly the evolution of smuggling and monetary regulations in the Arabian Sea. As British administrators began to understand how trade and smuggling was occurring they initiated new regulations to control and limit their effect. Counterfeiters and smugglers all thrived by shrouding their contraband in other trade flows. The more adept they were at evading the gaze of customs authorities, the longer their methods would remain profitable. Authorities in turn enlisted new technologies and new regulations to unveil monetary flows. In setting up barriers through which monetary flows could be documented and controlled, colonial monetary authorities hoped to more efficiently manage monetary circulation. But these barriers also produced vast spaces beyond the border where monetary flows were invisible. Trafficking networks were keenly aware of what was visible to colonial authorities and continuously innovated to stay one step beyond the horizon of colonial vision.

THE MANY FACES OF MONEY

Perhaps if Ganga Ram had worn his gold as jewelry he might have escaped prosecution. Jewelry hidden in baggage was as much contraband as sovereign coins, but a person wearing heavy jewelry could argue that he or she was guilty of nothing more than conspicuous consumption. The very same object in different contexts could be contraband or couture. Therefore, an important avenue of trafficking gold was to have customs officers view and document this transportation as legitimate. Women were prominent as "mules" because it would be less out of place for a woman to travel bedecked in gold.[67] While this method never allowed the economies of scale afforded by the tens of thousands of pounds smuggled by Ganga Ram's operation, it also circumvented the risk of being prosecuted. It was thus possible to highlight and contextualize an object so that it was deemed legitimate by regulators. This kind of tactical visibility was a very effective method of trafficking in money. Traffickers more adept than Ganga Ram recognized that not just beauty but also money was in the eye of the beholder.

Money was not subject to regulations when it was handed out as charity. In western India small coins were often handed out as charity, and this was particularly the case at weddings where upper-class families customarily showered coins upon a gathered crowd to demonstrate their joy, wealth, and generosity. In one particularly auspicious marriage season in Gujarat, the demand for *pie* pieces was so high that it actually caused a spike in the exchange rate between *pies* and rupees.[68] Gujarati merchants in Muscat consequently realized that the local copper *baiza*s could have a profitable afterlife if they were imported into India. The sultan of Muscat minted the *baiza,* a copper coin similar to Indian *paisa,* which was one denomination higher than *pie* pieces. The sultans were more interested in the profits from seigniorage on these coins than in managing the money supply. So copper *baizas* were minted to excess and circulated at a significant discount against their intrinsic value.[69] Gujarati merchants made a tidy profit by exporting the discounted currency of Muscat and selling it at a premium in India. Upper-class Indians in Gujarat, Sindh, and Punjab bought such *baizas* at a significant discount and still maintained an appearance of extravagant largesse. The only losers in the transaction were the impoverished population who received coins that were not legal tender in India. Since Indian merchants imported *baizas* not as a currency but as charity, the colonial administration declined to interfere.[70]

Currency arbitrage was also disguised by declaring that coins were merely pieces of metal. In 1895, the princely state of Baroda (in Gujarat) had relinquished its minting rights and agreed to replace its local coinage with the British rupee. Baroda coinage circulated as currency across India and as far afield as the Gulf. So when colonial officials demonetized the currency, Baroda merchants got rid of their coins in the Gulf. They hoped to avoid the discounted rates that prevailed in Baroda, where everyone knew it was being demonetized. Much to their surprise, officials discovered that the British trading and shipping firm Killick and Nixon was also involved in this traffic. When asked to justify their actions, the firm explained that they were exporting the coin for use as copper bullion. Indeed, they planned to transport about one hundred tons of Baroda copper coins to England to be melted and sold as copper metal. Satisfied that these coins were to be used as bullion, monetary authorities granted a retrospective exemption to Killick and Nixon.[71] Simultaneously firms like Ratansi Purshottam were being prosecuted and fined for exporting the coin to other parts of India and to the Gulf.[72] By being made tactically visible as copper bullion, these coins were transformed from contraband into commodity.

Ironically, the claim that a coin was nothing more than bullion was even deployed by the British Empire to rebut claims that it was counterfeiting the Maria Theresa thaler. For centuries, governments along the Arabian Sea littoral respected Austria's sovereign monopoly on the minting of the Maria Theresa thaler. However, on the eve of his invasion of Ethiopia, Mussolini obtained the dies for the thaler from Vienna and began minting thalers to take with his invading army. Once the invasion was complete, the Italian government prohibited the import or export of thalers from occupied

Ethiopia. This threw financial circuits across the Red Sea region into turmoil. Mr. C. Collier, the British governor of the Bank of Ethiopia, who had been expelled by the Italians, convinced British authorities to mint thalers, which he then smuggled into Ethiopia to undermine the Italian administration. The Italian government protested that Britain was counterfeiting its coin, but the Treasury demurred, saying that Maria Theresa thalers were a "non-national medium of exchange based on their intrinsic value."[73] Having carefully defined the thaler as something other than money, the British government went on to mint tens of millions of thalers in the following decade and derived substantial seigniorage profits.[74]

Perhaps the main trafficker of thalers into Italian territory was the Aden-based French businessman Antonin Besse. Besse and his network of Indian, Arab, and Somali associates had little difficulty in trading across the battle lines. The fighting in East and North Africa during the Second World War had expanded the demand for hard currency, while trade restrictions, profiteering, and hoarding had only exacerbated the problem.[75] Silver was cheaper than thalers, and thalers in Aden were cheaper than thalers in Italian Ethiopia. As a result, an immensely profitable traffic brought a flood of semi-counterfeit thalers into the lands adjacent to the Red Sea and the Gulf of Aden. Antonin Besse made immense profits by recognizing that silver was worth substantially less than a coin made out of silver, and he bent the law by convincing Allied governments that these coins were not counterfeits but merely pieces of silver.[76] Besse was so successful that the king of England would subsequently sanctify some of these profits as the founding endowment for St. Anthony's College at Oxford University.

After the war, the value of the thaler had reached a nadir, and one keen mind spotted the arbitrage value of reversing Besse's traffic. A young Indian trader named Dhirubhai Ambani noticed that while thalers glutted the market in Aden and Yemen there was simultaneously a surge in the silver market in London. He put out a standing order to purchase Maria Theresa thalers in Yemen and then had them shipped from Aden to be sold at a large premium on the London silver market. But the export of vast quantities of thalers from Aden to London raised alarm bells with export controllers in Aden, who were concerned that it might undermine imperial currency reserves. Ambani seems to have recruited the aid of his employer, Antonin Besse, who reassured colonial officials that these coins in fact added to currency reserves.[77] Ambani sold hundreds of thousands of thalers on the London market and single-handedly contracted the monetary supply in Yemen. Ambani made a small fortune, but on recalling the incident he merely noted, "I don't believe in not taking opportunities."[78] Ambani went on to become the founder of Reliance Industries, now India's largest private-sector company. This company would be built on Ambani's skill in exploiting the ambiguities in labyrinthine government policies while framing these transactions to fit within the letter of the law.

Imperial monetary policies sought to propagate a unitary money, while Arabian Sea merchants exploited the opportunities that arose out of the multiple identities of money. Money was Janus-faced, sometimes appearing as metal, other times as a measure of value. Diasporic firms spread out across the Arabian Sea particularly to capitalize on these slippages in money. Many firms even established shops and sold textiles and other commodities below cost price in the hope that they could keep abreast of arbitrage opportunities in currency.[79] The abstract fiction of a unitary yet multipurpose money did not serve colonial authorities terribly well. Merchant networks focused official perceptions on the facets of their transactions that were legitimate, even as they exploited the multifaceted reality of money.

BANKS AND *BADLIS*

Had Ganga Ram succeeded in selling his gold in Bahrain, he would probably have walked into the local branch of the Eastern Bank and converted his profits into rupees to take back to India. Many smugglers took their gold as cargo on dhows directly to Iraqi ports like Basra. They sold their gold sovereigns and bullion to local purchasers for Iraqi dinars. However, Indian smugglers like Ganga Ram had little use for dinars; they needed rupees that they could spend back home. The Eastern Bank in Bahrain was the cheapest place in the Gulf where they could exchange their dinars for rupees. By agreement with the sheikh of Bahrain, the Eastern Bank provided competitive exchange rates in exchange for a monopoly on formal exchange operations.[80] The invisible flow of gold into Iraq became visible as a flow of silver rupees taken from the Eastern Bank in Bahrain to India. Colonial authorities in India, Bahrain, Kuwait, and Iraq were anxious to capture Ganga Ram trafficking gold out of India. Yet had he succeeded they would have been conveniently blind to the visible profits that the Eastern Bank garnered from organizing the repatriation of these ill-gotten gains.

The Eastern Bank's participation in the wider circuits of illicit exchange was simply a side effect of its monopoly over Bahrain's foreign exchange operations. The position of the Eastern Bank in Bahrain was not unique; in fact, variations on a similar arrangement existed all along the Arabian Sea littoral. British diplomats convinced the sheikhs of the Gulf and the sultan of Muscat to grant monopoly concessions to the Eastern Bank or to the Imperial Bank of Iran. In Aden and East Africa, the National Bank of India was granted similar privileges.[81] The Imperial Ottoman Bank and the Imperial Bank of Iran not only dominated foreign exchange but also acted as the central banks for the Ottoman and Qajar Empires. These banks instituted new coinage, paper currencies, and monetary regulations in much the same way that British mints were doing in India.[82] All of these banks worked closely with British officials to promote stable currencies and free trade.

These banks were particularly charged with maintaining a stable rate of exchange with the gold standard currencies of Europe. Officials were anxious to prevent a situation in which trade became merely a speculation on the rise and fall of currencies, and banks were essential to the effort to forestall such an eventuality.[83] By limiting these exchange operations to a limited number of trusted institutions, monetary authorities hoped to limit speculation and stabilize exchange. Legally and institutionally, these were independent corporate entities, yet until the middle of the twentieth century British banks were deeply intertwined with imperial power. Like shipping companies, banks were headed by gentlemanly capitalists who socialized in the same circles as imperial officials. These men were granted special privileges because British bureaucrats trusted them.[84] Their banks functioned as an arm of the monetary authority of the British Empire. They presented evidence at numerous hearings and served as "independent" members on governmental committees.[85] Informal persuasion and gentlemanly favors gave officials powerful influence over financial markets, even as they proclaimed their noninterference in the market.

They were known as *exchange* banks because in India they were organized under the Eastern Exchange Banks Association, which was essentially a cartel that set exchange rates between the pound and the rupee. The exchange banks were supposed to be closely regulated by their charters, but regulations were so loosely enforced that they were irrelevant.[86] The benefit of the exchange banks' cooperation with imperial officials was a guaranteed line of profit, as well as neglect from those parts of the imperial bureaucracy policing fraud, speculation, and anticompetitive behavior. The exchange banks were seen as an infrastructural component of the economy, a mechanism by which monetary policy could be implemented, and as such they were exempt from normal regulation. Of course, this attitude occasionally resulted in spectacular scandals and devastating bankruptcies with impacts across colonial economies.[87] The scandals exhibited the limitations of informal political influence over these banks and the limited awareness of aristocratic British managers about their subordinates' activities.

While imperial officials influenced bank policies, the banks' actual operations were influenced by alliances with diasporic merchants and local *shroffs*. The diasporic *bania* firm of Khimji Ramdas played a pivotal role in the competition between the Imperial Bank of Iran and an Iraqi-Indian firm to open a branch in Muscat in the 1940s. In the absence of a bank, Khimji Ramdas was the main provider of credit to smaller firms in Muscat.[88] When the Iraqi-Indian firm tried to open a bank, Khimji Ramdas thwarted their efforts. Eventually Khimji Ramdas helped the Imperial Bank of Iran take up an official banking monopoly with the sultan.[89] Since the Imperial Bank was run by aristocratic Britons, they would limit their operations to financing the Petrol Concession and leave local financing to Khimji Ramdas. There was a clear consonance of interest between the exchange banks and prominent diasporic firms operating around the Arabian Sea. Exchange banks profited from serving the financial demands of the empire, and diasporic firms could control financial arbitrage at the level below the imperial vision.

Colonial officials perceived the increasing penetration of rationalized European business practices, but appearances were deceiving. The gap between the official record and the everyday reality is perhaps best exhibited in the person of Dinshaw Manekjee Mapla. Dinshaw Mapla was a diligent employee for almost forty years in the Bombay branch of the Mercantile Bank of India. He first appears in newsprint as a clerk, corroborating the testimony of the European managers of the bank. Fifteen years later, Mapla had made his way up the hierarchy and executed the indemnities to become head *shroff*. Then he is listed as the high-scoring batsman on the Mercantile Bank's cricket team, partnering with the branch manager to lead the team against a prominent trading firm. Sadly, we hear that on the morning of September 26, 1927, Dinshaw Maneckjee Mapla passed away. The interesting detail in his story occurs a few days later, when the Mercantile Bank's post of head *shroff* was effectively inherited by his son, Jehangir Dinshaw Mapla.[90]

Dinshaw Maneckjee Mapla could be a stock figure in colonial history, the westernized elite Indian bending over backwards to assimilate into the culture of the colonizers. Yet upon further investigation he emerges as a rather more interesting person. While he was a mere clerk, Mapla was making large tenders to buy Government of India bonds and on his own capital competing with the likes of the National Bank of India and industrial tycoons like David Sassoon.[91] It is rather incongruous that someone with access to the capital necessary to make such large investments had any need for employment as a bank clerk. There was clearly more to Dinshaw Maneckjee Mapla than his employment at the Mercantile Bank. So the fact that the Mercantile Bank would sanction Jehangir Mapla's assumption of his father's duties suggests a power dynamic that was not nearly as one-sided as one might expect.

While ostensibly under the complete control of British management and subject to the cultural hierarchies of a colonial business, the position of head *shroff* reveals the hidden dependence of exchange banks on their local employees. The term *shroff* within an exchange bank was clearly taken from the merchant bankers that we have already discussed, and certainly the employees that would serve as *shroffs* were from those same families. A head *shroff* was the fulcrum of the exchange bank's employee hierarchy, mediating between the British management and the large local staff responsible to him alone. The head *shroff* had to indemnify the bank not only for his own actions but also against loss from fraud or incompetence by all of the "native" employees. Thus, in return for salaried employment, the head *shroff* had to put up his own assets in escrow with the bank and obtain a substantial guarantee from a friend or family member willing to stand surety; then an insurance policy was taken out to further buffer the bank from any chance of loss by the employment of non-European staff.[92] These large indemnities protecting the bank against its employees were a consequence of the fact that European managers had little understanding of local business practices and great difficulty distinguishing between what they saw as an amorphous mass of brown faces. Indeed, more than once exchange banks were swindled because they could not distinguish between "native" names and faces.[93] Any interaction between European managers and Indian, Arab, and African employees occurred through the *shroff*. The position of the *shroff* as the only broker between a European and a "native" establishment within the bank gave these men significant power to shape the practices of the bank as a whole.

The head *shroff* was technically an employee of the bank, but the men, or more accurately the merchant families, that took up these positions did not think of themselves as employees. The steep liabilities and meager salaries of these positions practically drove away potential employees. The only candidates left were connected to merchant families who could profit from the privileged access that the position of head *shroff* afforded.[94] A merchant family could gain early access to market information and deeper insights into investment opportunities and the creditworthiness of competitors. These opportunities led at least one family to obtain appointments as head *shroffs* at all the branches of a single colonial bank.[95] In such situations, it becomes difficult to assert that these were really "British" banks. In more remote ports of the Gulf or Africa, "one-man" branches were opened, in which one European manager stood as figurehead over the operations of a *shroff* and his local establishment.[96] Unsurprisingly, British managers complained that their *shroffs* were lazy and disobedient.[97] This was probably a result of their intention to do the minimal work possible in order to focus their attentions on their real job of collecting information for the family business. As a result, it is impossible to sustain the impression that modern rationalized practices displaced local traditions. Exchange banks displaced local merchants as the largest providers of credit and capital in colonial port cities, but the role of *shroffs* within these European institutions belied the pretense that financial institutions were becoming more transparent.

A central difficulty for many exchange banks was that they were more dependent on the bazaar economy than they would have liked. Managers of exchange banks were anxious to have greater contact with the bazaar, sending local employees regularly to the bazaar to attract business and even opening "bazaar branches" in order to be closer to the hub of business activity.[98] British managers were continually searching for ways to attract deposits from local businesses, but inevitably those deposits were attracted to the higher rates of return in the bazaar.[99] Indeed, exchange banks were providing low-interest loans to merchants, who then lent these sums at much higher rates in the bazaar. Bazaar discount rates on a firm's *hundis* served as a central method for banks to evaluate the creditworthiness of a firm. Banks also encashed the *hundis* of their clients, so instead of displacing this traditional mechanism of transmitting credit, banks were incorporated into *hundi* networks.[100] Rather than "rationalizing" and documenting opaque traffics, exchange banks were veiling them behind white faces and Savile Row suits.

Much to the dismay of headquarters in London, exchange bank branches in the region began to enter into the sort of speculative transactions that merchants were profiting from across the Arabian Sea. In Bombay, this took the form of something similar to a futures contract, called *badli*. *Badli* transactions usually involved a contract in which one party would purchase a good for delivery within ninety days at a specified price along with a premium. The purchaser bet that the price would rise and the seller that the price would fall, or more often that the price of the money itself would rise or fall. Only the premium would be paid up front, and usually the contract would be settled without the actual delivery of goods but merely payment of the difference. Exchange banks would lend to such speculators and hold their money in escrow for future payments, and as a result they could maintain a certain amount of their working capital. Exchange banks were deeply invested in all aspects of this market and even admitted that 99 percent of their business was speculation.[101] The sense of discomfort in having to deal with such speculators is evident in what is essentially an apology from the manager of the Eastern Bank to headquarters in London: "Fresh deposits are virtually impossible to obtain at the present time. Although crores [tens of millions] of Rupees have been made in the "black market" during the last few months . . . this money is invested in the bazaar; in any case to evade Income Tax, this money is not available for deposit in banks unless in fictitious names, which would be a dangerous and reprehensible practice."[102] *Badlis* were one of the few avenues by which banks could secure deposits from Indian merchants, and as discomfiting as they found the practice, British managers were forced to adopt it. Moreover, the ease with which merchants could ignore banks and evade imperial regulations rendered the banks complicit in the "black market."

Once on this slippery slope, exchange banks also directly engaged in *badli* transactions as a means of obtaining quick money. As one bank manager phrased it, they "pawned" assets, usually government securities, to merchants for a considerably smaller premium than one required for borrowing money from another bank.[103] The exchange banks started to realize that indigenous forms of financing like *badli*s were more flexible than European financial instruments. Certain *badli* transactions served another very useful purpose, which was reducing the value of the bank's taxable assets. When operating in reverse, exchange banks would buy securities in a *badli* transaction just before the end of the tax year. Since government promissory notes were issued tax-free, the bank obtained income tax exemptions for their securities at the year's end. In the new year, they returned the securities for their initial investment plus a premium, having already obtained the tax break of holding government securities.[104] *Badli* transactions provided cheap short-term financing and a means of reducing tax assessments. Thus as gentlemanly capitalism expanded into the Arabian Sea it was drawn into a number of highly ungentlemanly practices.

Exchange banks played a powerful role in implementing monetary policies around the Arabian Sea. Their privileged position within this financial world was clearly a result of operating as an extension of monetary authorities. They helped link the Indian rupee, the Qajar *kran*, and the East African shilling to the international gold standard and hence facilitated increasing trade, investment, and extraction by industrialized nations. Monetary policies could thus be pursued by colonial authorities under the cover of independent businesses. Even as exchange banks were concealing the penetration of the state into the economy, they were also concealing the penetration of Asian and African business practices into European financial institutions. *Shroffs* accepted underpaid employment to take advantage of increased access to European capital and commercial information.[105] Rather than turning *shroffs* into disciplined calculating employees, exchange banks became enmeshed in a web of currency speculation and arbitrage. Banks' dependence on these opaque networks was concealed within careful documentation and accounting practices, and monetary authorities were further blinded by their trust in aristocratic accents and old boys' clubs.

Over the course of the century of the international gold standard, the Indian rupee would play a prominent role in the development of the modern science of economics. Irving Fisher used the rupee as an important case study for his ideas about monetary theory.[106] J. M. Keynes famously cut his teeth as a monetary economist while at the India Office pondering the fluctuations of the rupee.[107] Indian nationalism was founded on an economic critique of British rule that employed colonial statistics to question various economic policies, including the management of the rupee.[108] The rupee has proved such rich fodder for economic debates because it simultaneously provided large data sets and highly erratic swings of monetary policy, and thus wide room for different interpretations. I would like to suggest that this is partly due to the invisibility of a wide swath of monetary flows to statistical collection. No economic analysis of the rupee problem that I have found even considers its wider circulation in East Africa and the Arabian Peninsula. Monetary statistics were collected at government mints and customs houses, so even if the numbers included this transregional circulation their view was sharply circumscribed by colonial borders.[109] Moreover, it was difficult to collect any statistics on the circulation of competing currencies like the Maria Theresa thaler, the coins of Indian princely states, or the commodity currencies of East Africa. Furthermore, it was virtually impossible to calculate the illicit traffics of gold and silver across colonial borders.

The everyday circulation of money within and across borders remained largely invisible to distant monetary authorities and even more distant economists. Meanwhile the solutions that these economists proffered could employ only the tools of a centrally administered monetary authority. Limitations of knowledge and action prevented actual intervention at a local level or even attempts to understand how monies were used in ordinary practice. Monetary authorities failed to recognize the multiple levels of intermediaries they employed to implement monetary policy along the Arabian Sea littoral. Yet moneylenders, regulators, and even dockworkers and pilgrims had a role in maintaining a fixed monetary regime. Each level of mediation opened up possibilities for subversion, so mercantile networks that straddled the boundaries between states, between state and market, and between licit and illicit benefited the most from attempts to establish a neutral standard of value.

From the 1870s, the monetary history of the Arabian Sea was a chaotic process of replacing the objects that people used as money, disciplining the circulation of these objects, and transforming how these objects measured value. New monetary theories posed a radically new conception of money as an abstract measure of value, which created new problems of hoarding, instability, and the opacity of monetary flows. In piercing the "veil of money," colonial officials failed to ask what were the material qualities of money. They had imagined perhaps a transparent veil of muslin but were confronted with an ever-expanding cataract in their vision. The final outcome of these efforts to stabilize and unify money was a disparate range of currency forms connected by networks of arbitrage. Only in economic statistics did these exchanges appear as circumscribed colonial currencies connected by exchange banks.

Money as a standard of value consequently had to be framed out of the market so that coins could flow through the market as an avatar of capital. Yet even with a universal standard of value, there remained the question of how the market determined the value of any particular commodity. Accordingly, we now turn to how states and markets—ostensibly constituted by free labor, secure property rights, and a stable monetary standard—transformed the divergent valuations of traders into a singular "real value."

FIVE

Valorizing Markets

Taḥāsabū kul youm takūnū khawā doum.

Settle accounts every day that you may always be brothers.

AN INVOICE SEEMS LIKE A rather boring object. It is a bill, a piece of paper that documents a transaction. A seller sends a specified quantity x of goods to a buyer and requests that the specified price y be remitted. Such documents are produced and transmitted millions of times each day across the world. Few documents are more mundane. But when is an invoice sent and when isn't it? For whom is this document written? What precisely is the relationship between the seller and the buyer? Were x goods really sent? Is price y the actual value of the goods? Does an invoice have anything to do with the transaction that it is purported to represent? The apparent ordinariness of the invoice conceals myriad possibilities for both subversion and hegemony.

An invoice is a commercial document, yet in most cases it hints at the interest of a third party: a state that levies taxes on this transaction. Invoices in the Arabian Sea were frequently transmitted only for the purposes of a state bureaucracy: their specific content, categories, printing, and even paper were the result of bureaucratic decisions. No matter what their content, invoices framed transactions to make them legible to a bureaucracy. Individuals, goods, and money were brought together into a very specific assemblage. Buyers were distinguished from sellers, and goods were exchanged for a specific currency at a specified price. Transactions were rendered uniform, prices were enumerated, and taxes were levied. Colonial bureaucracies could then aggregate, average, and determine economic policy on the basis of these statistical measures. Invoices, then, were the agents of bureaucratic desires to determine economic value and to tax it accordingly. They were disciplinary devices, but they could also be harnessed as a tool of subversion.

In the trading world of the Arabian Sea, invoices were always documents of translation. The particularities of an exchange were translated into the general paradigm of market exchange. This presented the possibility of an overly generous interpretation, a particularly convenient oversight, or an altogether fraudulent representation of the transaction. The intended recipient of these misrepresentations was not the consignee but more often the bureaucrat poking his nose into their business. Ambiguity, flexibility, and trust worked to the advantage of merchants in making out invoices, but they were an anathema to statistically minded bureaucrats. This seemingly negligible piece of paper is a useful place to start because it was the interface between merchant networks and imperial bureaucracies in the Arabian Sea.

Yet invoices were hardly the only tool for mercantile communication. Long before colonial efforts to standardize transactions, merchant networks had developed their own methods of conveying information, enforcing contracts, and resolving disputes. Personal trust, informal coalitions, and religious injunctions played a vital role in ordering commercial relationships.[1] All kinds of information were required to organize such transactions: about personal habits, spiritual beliefs, family affairs, and political connections. Prices and commercial intelligence were conveyed not by invoices but by letters, messengers, and meetings where fraternally inclined merchants could hash out differences and accommodate changing circumstances. This broad and deep range of communication built trust and placed value in relationships themselves.[2] It was such relationships rather than market prices that determined transactions. Value was not objective and was not determined by markets; rather, it was negotiated within the context of a particular commercial relationship. The epigraph to this chapter speaks to the importance of fraternal bonds in commercial transactions. It hints that transactions occurred within enduring relationships and that value was determined more by extensive negotiations within these relationships than by market prices.[3] Transactions across the Arabian Sea were accounted for within relationships that were diverse, complicated, and rarely commensurable.

Information in this context was scarce, precious, and protected. *Information* is perhaps too innocuous a term to capture what these merchants were seeking; *commercial intelligence* or even *espionage* might more accurately represent their activities. Private communications about familial conflict or impending political changes could be manipulated to reduce trading losses or maximize gains. As we saw in the previous chapter, arbitrage was the main occupation of traders in the Arabian Sea, and intelligence made arbitrage possible. Market prices certainly existed, but they did not determine transactions; rather, they were benchmarks that merchants hoped to exceed. Merchants devoted substantial resources to seeking out hidden information about buyers and crop conditions. Similarly, much effort was expended in concealing and protecting information about one's own business. These relationships were consequently a means of overcoming ignorance about quality and managing an information-poor trading environment.[4] An extraordinarily rich historical literature in medieval and early modern trade has emerged to explain the nuances of commercial information and the organization of trading networks.[5] This chapter builds on their insights but seeks to extend them into a world where capitalist categories were becoming hegemonic and where transactions that manipulated these categories were particularly profitable. For trafficking networks, concealing information could be as important as conveying it, and strong relationships were central to managing private information in public markets.

These secretive and personalized trading relationships contradict the neoclassical conception of markets as the mechanisms that determined value. While the virtues of free markets had been extolled by Adam Smith, only beginning in the 1860s did they come to be seen as the ultimate arbiters of value itself. In the late nineteenth century, political economy underwent what is known as the marginal revolution, in which the concept of marginal utility became the center of a statistically based science of economics. The founders of marginalist economics presumed, first, that individuals had a limited endowment, meaning a specified amount of wealth. Second, they assumed that individuals exchanged goods in their possession to maximize the utility that they obtained from this limited endowment of wealth. After individuals had provided for their basic needs and most intense desires, they were left with the more difficult decisions about the usefulness of one more gallon of water as compared to one more slice of bread or one more ounce of gold. *Margins* here refers to this space at the edge of one's ability to consume, where one's subjective desires and valuations interact with others' subjective valuations in market exchange. Marginal utility is the number of units of commodity y that one would give up in order to obtain one more unit of commodity x. So at the margins of one's resource endowment, qualitative judgments about use-value could be quantified through market exchange. Marginal utility was such a revolutionary concept because it allowed classical economics to reconcile use-value with exchange-value. The cumulative effect of myriad subjective decisions about marginal utility could be coordinated by the market to produce a quantified and collective (if not quite objective) measure of value. This chapter consequently interrogates this notion of "margins" as the border between the individual and the market where qualitative feelings of pleasure were transformed into quantities of utility.

However, the marginal revolution was a set of ideas that began in academic circles and filtered down into everyday market practice. Around the Arabian Sea, marginalism had a powerful impact in the calculation and calibration of tariff rates, but only through the preoccupations and heuristics of colonial officials. Colonial governments and international organizations needed an unbiased measurement of value in order to equitably tax trade. Marginalist economics suggested that markets could provide such a measure of value by coordinating supply and demand to produce market-clearing prices. Customs houses subsequently seized on the notion that market prices were the most effective means of measuring "real value." The difficulty they faced across the Arabian Sea was that most transactions did not occur in markets or at market prices. In attempting to translate the mercantile practice of the Arabian Sea into the abstract calculations of marginalist economics, customs officials found themselves deliberating on the minutiae of what constituted an ideal-typical market transaction. To find "real value," customs authorities had to standardize measurements, convert currencies, and conjure up arm's-length transactions. Equitable taxation required that the extraordinary complexity and diversity of trading relationships in the Arabian Sea be uniformly rendered as abstract market exchange.

Invoices consequently became the site where the everyday practice of trade was translated into the abstracted and quantified language of neoclassical economics. Around the Arabian Sea, market prices were produced not by the convergence of supply and demand curves but by an interminable struggle over values declared on invoices. Colonial bureaucrats insisted that merchants declare the "real value" of their goods. The difficulty was that it was not there to be discovered; it had to be produced by the surveillance and intervention of the colonial bureaucracy. Market prices were not a simple reflection of real value but prosthetic devices or artifacts of bureaucratic intervention.[6] Marginal utility was performed for the benefit of customs officials. So merchants contrived invoices that documented arm's-length transactions even though they occurred within preferential relationships. This chapter suggests that the cold, calculative logic of invoices, accounts, and statistics did not replace but supplemented the affective relationships of diasporas. As the epigraph to this chapter intimates, calculation was very much part of noncapitalist trade, but accounting was in the service of maintaining fraternal bonds. The following pages will detail how market price was produced through bureaucratic entanglement with personal networks.

This chapter explores the history of valuation across the Arabian Sea: from incommensurable negotiations within families to an objective measurement of market price. Merchant networks organized their transactions through enduring relationships. Values were negotiable, and prices were determined by bonds of family, friendship, and community. Customs bureaucracies inserted themselves into these relationships and demanded that exchanges be documented by invoices that assumed market exchange. Colonial statisticians standardized weights and currencies, graded qualities, configured documentation, and rendered prices commensurable across time and space. This reformatting of transactions permitted the construction of statistical tables, macroeconomic indicators, and colonial development planning. Yet these prices and statistics were built on shifting sand. Merchants were constantly engaged in misrepresenting their transactions and manipulating measurements. Every determinant of value was subverted to reduce tariffs and amplify profits. Trade in the Arabian Sea was channeled and mediated by these quantitative measures, but by the same token merchant networks contrived to use these measures to their own advantage. This was not a transition from diasporic trade to capitalist markets; rather, it was a continuous process of translation in which familial negotiations were expressed as market prices. Value was produced not as an objective determination of free markets but by the framing out of familial relationships from invoices and ambiguous standards from market statistics.

DIASPORIC INTELLIGENCE, NEGOTIATED VALUE

Few invoices, whether inside or outside colonial archives, have remained preserved for the historian. By design, they are disposable documents that almost invariably end up in the garbage after the transaction is completed. Moreover, outside bureaucratic demands, the merchant networks of the Arabian Sea did not rely on standardized written invoices. The relevant intelligence was conveyed by messengers, on little chits, or embedded in personal letters. The information conveyed in these diverse forms of communication was both broader and more limited than in invoices. Correspondence covered issues of politics, family, and religion as well as business; indeed, there was no division between these arenas of life. Yet these letters and messages often did not specify taxes and discounts or prices and values. Prices were certainly important, but they were negotiable even after commodities had been exchanged. Prices were not objective determinations of the market but were negotiated within and subordinate to enduring relationships.

At first glance, much of the correspondence of these trading diasporas seems to be only tangentially interested in trade and commerce. Most letters opened with lengthy expressions of greeting, blessings upon the recipients and their family, inquiries after their health, and wishes for their good fortune. These comments often occupied more than half of a letter, and in Arabic correspondence would be separated from the more commercially oriented information by the phrase 'āmā ba'd, which indicated that the writer was turning to the main substance of the correspondence.[7] In letters that are preserved only in translation, this whole component was shortened to a curt "Greetings &c" or elided altogether.[8] Yet what colonial bureaucrats interpreted as needless pleasantries served as a social and moral binding for a commercial relationship. Indeed, the encasing of commercial information in such sentiments made it possible to use the information more judiciously and with attention to the preservation of an enduring relationship. Sustaining a relationship was often more important to the long-term economic health of a trading concern than a good price on any particular transaction.[9] This was an investment in relational value, which could yield returns for a buyer or seller in future transactions.[10] The success of a business over the long term was deeply dependent on maintaining such conduits of information, transactional partners, and reputations. Thus the time, ink, and paper expended in conveying blessings, inquiring after family members, and sharing in personal joys and sorrows was invested in a broader framework of calculating value.

The correspondence of the prominent Gujarati Muslim merchant Tharia Topan illustrates this overlap between commercial value and family values. Topan had followed many other Gujarati merchants to find his fortune in Zanzibar in the middle of the nineteenth century. By the end of the century he had become one of the wealthiest and most influential merchants around the Arabian Sea. Late in life he remarried and lived primarily in Bombay, leaving the two eldest sons from his first marriage to handle his affairs in Zanzibar. He corresponded frequently with his two sons, chiding them for their disagreements and inquiring after their health, but also interrogating them regarding trading losses. Since their family was central to their business, it was essential that conflicts be minimized to protect the firm from personal discord and to protect the family from commercial competition.[11] Though Tharia Topan kept the peace while he was alive, on his death familial conflict would destroy the family business. A conflict emerged between Topan's sons and their stepmother, Bai Janbai, who transgressed her appointed gender role to take control of the firm after her husband's death. Patriarchy was normative both in the home and in the office, as Tharia Topan complained to his son: "Women do not at all know how to preserve wealth."[12] The firm did lose profits, but not necessarily because Janbai was incapable. Rather, her gender weakened the firm's social capital, disrupted homosocial bonds, and undermined her stepsons' masculinity.[13] Both Janbai and her stepsons were astute businesspeople, and the trading environment was conducive to profit, but the discord between stepmother and stepchildren dissipated the unity of the family and hence the profits of the firm.

One of the biggest hurdles that Janbai would have faced was her difficulty in receiving male visitors, attending personal meetings, and engaging in secret, unwritten communication. Certain communications were appropriate in written form and others were best handled in personal meetings or through verbal messages. Topan's son Jafferbhai had a brother-in-law who was employed by another merchant. Jafferbhai had written to this merchant requesting a raise for his brother-in-law. When word got to Tharia Topan that his son had made such a request he became incensed. He wrote: "To write such a thing is unbecoming of us. It is also not [suited] to our dignity to communicate such things in writing."[14] Topan's concern was not that Jafferbhai had requested a raise for his brother-in-law but that such a request was conveyed in writing. Such problems, with undoubtedly complex financial and personal stakes, should have been handled in a conversation where the medium would have allowed for both parties to avoid publicizing family conflicts as well as potentially saving face if the request could not be granted. Both the nuance and the deniability of verbal communications made them essential in maintaining trading relationships.

Moreover, messengers and personal meetings were particularly useful in arranging transactions that skirted or bent the law. A merchant named Alibhai Ababhai Jhaveri wrote to a potential customer that if he wished to deal in sugar, a highly taxed commodity, the transaction should be arranged in person.[15] Customs officials were anxious to cut down on evasions of sugar tariffs, and sugar merchants were conscious of postal censorship, so personal meetings arranged transactions without leaving a paper trail. While this letter seems to have brought Jhaveri under police suspicion, they did not prosecute him, most likely because he did not leave any written evidence. Personal meetings fostered the trust necessary to complete illicit transactions and reduced the risk of prosecution. Some letters included extensive greetings and inquiries about health, but after the 'āmā ba'd merely stated that the messenger would convey the relevant details.[16] There are numerous hints in court records, censors' files, and preserved correspondence that sensitive information was conveyed only verbally. One historian has perceptively shown how commercial intelligence was the "salt" in a merchant's letter, but when transactions tested the limits of the law it was safer on the tongue of a messenger.[17] The lack of merchant correspondence and its fragmentary nature are suggestive of the importance of verbal communications to business networks.

Written correspondence across these merchant networks was further limited to exchanges between correspondents who were already known to one another. The sultan of Zanzibar was shocked and confused when a merchant of the Imperial British East Africa Company wrote to him without any introduction.[18] The sultan took affront at the presumption of this man and instead of responding wrote to one of the company's employees with whom he was already acquainted. The sultan complained of this strange letter and insisted that he would never listen to requests from people whom he did not know. He stated, "It is not our custom that strangers should write to us on important matters direct" but added that he was always happy to hear from his "friends" at the Imperial British East Africa Company. Messengers similarly required the authentication of a known and trusted correspondent who vouched for the authority and reliability of the message.[19] So written correspondence did not replace personal contact but sustained personal relationships that were already established in some form. In this trading world, there was little space for impersonal arm's-length transactions; friendship and familial connections were what made long-distance transactions possible.

Since most diasporic firms spread across the Arabian Sea by sending out sons, nephews, and sons-in-law, less time and effort was necessary to monitor and instruct distant agents. This is not to suggest that family members were naturally trustworthy; rather, effort invested in building strong personal relationships reduced the costs of monitoring and enforcing contracts.[20] Familial agents were incentivized because in the long term they stood to inherit the firm's wealth and power. Such commercial relationships were managed through dense social and religious connections and ultimately a careful and measured belief that these ties and incentives would lead agents to act in the long-term interests of the family firm. Even where principals and agents were not tied by blood, commercial relationships were not contractually defined relationships between disinterested parties. These relationships tended to be lasting, embedded in wider social networks, and characterized by trust and fiduciary duty. The sultans of Zanzibar appointed agents who could buy, sell, and contract with the goods and the money of the sultan yet in their own name.[21] The property of the sultan was thus entrusted to his agents without any security of title, much to the confusion of European merchants. Indeed, the standard language of a *wakāla* (agency or power of attorney) contract involved the phrase *qad 'aqām maqām nafsihi*, which indicates that the agent might act as if the principal "was himself standing there." Unlike British common-law power of attorney, *wakāla* was by default unlimited or at least unspecified and provided little protection against misconduct or poor decisions on the part of the agent. The Islamic *muḍāraba* or agency partnerships tended to be open-ended in duration, while the European equivalent (*commenda*) was generally limited to a single journey.[22] Merchants did not simply trust friends and family; rather, they very carefully entered into commercial ties after having developed relationships of trust. In this trading world, the value of a strong relationship was far more important than any particular transaction.

The transactions that occurred within these long-term relationships were not discrete or well defined. The prices at which goods were exchanged were tied to many other transactions occurring simultaneously. Buyers and sellers could use profits from some transactions to subsidize other transactions with the same trading partner. As we saw in the previous chapter, shops were established and operated without any profits, merely as a means of obtaining intelligence for currency arbitrage.[23] Merchants who monopolized or just temporarily dominated the sales of one commodity in a market might withhold sales of that commodity in order to force counterparties to buy or sell other goods at preferential prices. For example, Antonin Besse in Aden refused to sell Standard Oil kerosene to merchants who would not trade with him in his other lines of business.[24] Other traders organized barter transactions, not because money transactions were not possible, but because monetary transactions involved losses from fluctuating exchange rates and the profits that accrued to merchants who could provide cash up front. Barter was consequently an alternative structure of transactions that allowed traders to bypass the inefficiencies and middlemen that characterized market transactions.[25] The basic unit of trade was an enduring relationship and not an impersonal market transaction. The conditions, counterparties, and prices at which transactions occurred were consequently specific to particular relationships and were difficult to abstract into objective values.

While the letters and notes that moved through trafficking networks were silent on many issues that invoices might have expressed, they were also more informative in other ways. Indeed, much correspondence was concerned less with prices or the state of the market than with how to circumvent market prices. Understanding the prices at which goods were selling on the market was important as a benchmark that successful merchants were continually hoping to exceed.[26] In fact, selling at the market rate was often an indication of failure, a desperate attempt to stanch further losses, or an admission that the firm could no longer obtain credit.[27] The reaction to a tough market was not to innovate and find further economies in production but to mobilize connections to find ways of circumventing the market. Traders comforted and cajoled their counterparties, called in favors, and cultivated relationships with credit.[28] Moreover, merchants looked not only to fellow merchants but also to officials and incorporated the efficacy of regulation or the presence of corruptible officials in their commercial decisions.[29] Traders did not seek to successfully compete within a single market; rather, they sought to expand their networks to bypass competitive markets.

Perhaps there is no better indication of this attitude than the Omani proverb that states, "It is better to have a good market than good merchandise" (*Ḥusn al-sūq wa la ḥusn al-biḍāʿa*).[30] Competitive markets prompted merchants to search for more profitable markets. Information even about market prices was hard to come by from a distance, so prices varied dramatically between locations. If little profit could be made at one market, a merchant would search out a better market.[31] Merchant letters were filled with information about which commodities could be sold at a healthy profit and which could not, and where good markets could be found.[32] These networks did not specialize in a single commodity; instead, they specialized in uncovering intelligence about arbitrage opportunities in any commodity. Diasporic networks and communications infrastructures allowed merchants to circumvent competitive pressures in any particular market. A good market was not defined by orderly governance, a wide variety of merchandise, or even a large volume of transactions. It was simply that place where a trader obtained good profits.[33]

Time presented another dimension through which merchant networks escaped market prices. If traders could not find more profitable markets or dispose of their commodities through preferential trading relationships, they simply waited for conditions to improve.[34] This even took the form of setting up a shop and slowly selling off wholesale quantities of goods directly to consumers.[35] Waiting out the market is of course a time-honored tactic of all traders, but the value of goods circulating through the Arabian Sea was not "marked to market." Rather, value was renegotiable, and contracts were often extended to allow for depressed conditions. Tharia Topan frequently negotiated for extended repayment schedules or confronted counterparties who had delayed their payments.[36] Similar renegotiations appear as a matter of course between merchants of the same community, between different diasporic communities, and between diasporic merchants and British firms.[37] Transactions, contracts, and prices were treated, not as rigid and intractable commitments, but as part of a relationship in which both parties had to operate flexibly, sacrificing the profits of particular transactions in order to maintain enduring commercial relationships.

Accounting practices are a particularly useful entry point into trade and calculations of value around the Arabian Sea. Indian accounting practices mirrored European practices of double-entry bookkeeping but also incorporated certain facets of caste and religion into their calculations.[38] For Arab merchants, regular accounting was also an important component of commercial practice. Omani folk wisdom warned, *Man yakharraj wa la yahsub, yaflis wa la yadrī*; that is, "He who spends and does not keep accounts becomes bankrupt and is not aware [of it]."[39] Yet despite the importance given to accounts in these proverbs, there does not appear to be a standardized method of accounting among the few examples of Arabic accounts that have survived from the Arabian Sea littoral.[40] Figure 5 appears to be more a working tally than a rigorously ordered set of accounts. Indeed, the Arabic word *ḥisāb* (like the English *account*) encompasses a much broader meaning of a set of records or reckonings. I'd like to argue that the purpose of these accounts was quite distinct from the purpose of accounts in contemporary Europe. Double-entry bookkeeping is a device that arranges and orders myriad transactions into a single visual interface. Double-entry accounts are legible to anyone trained to read them, and their purpose is precisely to render the business transparent to an abstract, external observer. The surviving Arabic accounts, on the other hand, are legible only through close knowledge of the relevant transactions. They provide a much more specific and descriptive account of commodity and financial flows. They indicate which ships arrived or left on which date and give descriptions of commodities, weights, and *ḥawālas* received. The word *ḥisāb* is also etymologically related

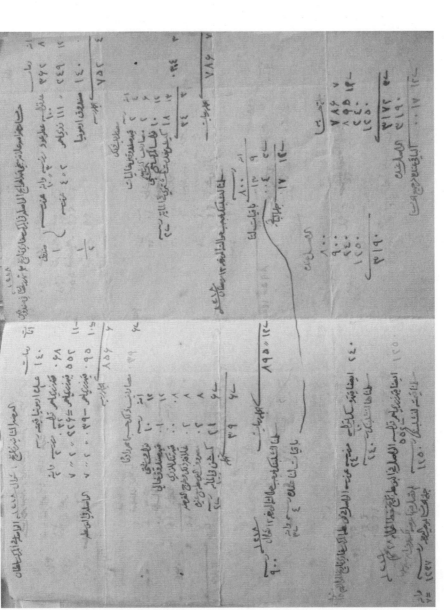

FIGURE 5. Page of accounts of the sultan of Zanzibar. Pages of Accounts (unsigned, ca. Muharram 1219 AH/April-May 1804), AM1/6, Zanzibar National Archives. Reproduced with the kind permission of the Zanzibar National Archives.

to the practice of *ḥisba,* discussed in the previous chapter. I don't want to overstate this connection, but it hints that keeping accounts was also a moral reckoning.[41] These Arabic accounts, like double-entry accounts, resulted in a tally of assets and liabilities and an awareness of the total financial position. But whereas double-entry accounts allow legibility, commensurability, and surveillance, the Arabic accounts created a more embodied and contingent knowledge.

These Arabic accounts were a means of maintaining a commercial relationship rather than an abstract and objective determination of asset values. In the proverb that begins this chapter ("Settle accounts every day, that you may always be brothers"), the verb *taḥāsabū* is the key to understanding this distinction. The direct translation of this term would be two people *mutually* settling an account. Accounting in English presumes an individual working alone, whose accounts can then be read, reproduced, and checked by any another individual with the proper knowledge of accounting methods. The injunction in the Omani proverb, on the other hand, refers not to an abstract or atomized activity but to something cooperative and reciprocal. Whereas European accounting should theoretically allow two separate individuals to come to an identical balance by the scrupulous application of abstract rules, this proverb indicates a collaborative process in which points of disagreement or confusion are resolved through compromise and conversation. This cooperative accounting then is not just a means of preventing disputes but the very work of building and maintaining a strong and "brotherly" relationship.

A. G. Jayakar's idiomatic translation of this phrase is the English proverb "Short reckonings make long friends," meaning one should quickly pay back debts in order to maintain friendships.[42] I would argue that this is a misreading because, in the mercantile context of the Arabian Sea, settling accounts was distinguished from clearing accounts. Settling an account was a process of negotiation and reckoning in which the status of debts and pending transactions was calculated but not necessarily paid off. It was vital for agents to keep careful records and to submit this information to their partners, but repayment of debt fell under clearing of accounts, an operation that was not as frequent and often indicated the termination of a trading relationship.[43] In Hindu family firms the partnership was not dissolved until the family itself was divided, and the investment capital belonged to the family as a whole rather than any particular individual.[44] In the *muḍāraba* contract, when the initial capital was repaid the principal was no longer contributing to the partnership, and thus the partnership was effectively dissolved.[45] The subtleties of this distinction were parsed and interrogated in a dispute between the Indian merchant Ahmed Najoo Khan and his trading partner the Somali merchant Ali Ibrahim Noor.

Their case hung on the question of whether a particular settlement between Ali Ibrahim Noor and an agent of Ahmed Najoo Khan was a clearing of accounts that terminated the trading relationship or simply a temporary settling of accounts that left the relationship open to further transactions, debts, and profits. Khan insisted that he had authorized his agent only to obtain an account of Ali Ibrahim Noor's business and that the agent did not have the power to clear accounts. Ali Ibrahim Noor contended that he had cleared his debts with Ahmed Najoo Khan and that consequently the relationship was terminated. Both agreed that if all debts had been repaid and balances cleared then the relationship was over. In the eyes of Noor and Khan, the dispute was whether Khan's agent had the power to clear accounts *and* terminate their relationship. The British judges split the difference. They imagined that the relationship was not terminated by the agent but that the debts were cleared, so that Ahmed Najoo Khan had no further claims on Ali Ibrahim Noor.[46] The imperial officials who began to penetrate this world imagined a commerce constituted out of discrete market transactions. But the world in which they intervened was constituted out of enduring relationships.

Tharia Topan also had extensive and varied dealings with the infamous Zanzibari slave trader Ḥamad bin Mohammed al-Murjebī, more commonly known as Tippu Tip. Their accounts with each other were not regularly cleared, so at his death Tharia Topan owed Tippu Tip over Rs. 67,000.[47] Their commercial relationship was so strong and so productive precisely because neither was required to provide cash on the spot for the transactions that they wanted to make; instead, both could assume that the debts would be settled in due time. Immediate cash payments were the exception rather than the rule around the littoral and indeed around the world. Transactions usually involved extensions of credit, transport costs, free warehousing, or currency exchange.[48] Indeed, cash only seemed to be necessary for European traders around the Arabian Sea. This was most likely because they had not built relationships of trust, and local merchants avoided such transactions except in hard cash.[49] While the ideal-typical market exchange involved an immediate transfer of cash, this was the exception in the trading world of the Arabian Sea.[50]

Merchant letters forged strong relationships embedded in debt, friendship, and constant renegotiation of value. Merchants expended much of their effort in obtaining intelligence and obfuscating intelligence, and in such an environment, relationships were more important than any particular transaction. So what scattered merchant letters remain in collections today can be understood only if we imagine them in the broader context of verbal and personal communication and try to interpret the silences in this documentation. The absences and illegibilities were evidence of the success of these networks in staying secure from the prying eyes of governments and competitors. Merchant letters mobilized relationships outside and across markets; the prices quoted in such letters were not public information but private intelligence. It was colonial intervention in these relationships that extracted prices and aggregated them into publicly available market information.[51]

FORMATTING FREE TRADE

The diasporic organization of traffics around verbal communications, personal networks, and bargaining bore little resemblance to the free trade imagined by classical political economists. Trade, in the writings of political economists like David Ricardo, occurred between states and was determined by tariff barriers and competitive advantages. Classical political economy presumed a mercantilist system that was standardized and ordered through state administrations. Marginalist political economy then required that state administrations quantify values and assess trade through ever more precise statistical measures of standardized transactions. Yet in an environment where information about transactions was fiercely protected, quantifying trade involved intensive surveillance and intervention in trade. Mercantile correspondence had to be converted into standard invoices, commercial relationships reimagined as arm's-length transactions, and diasporic networks reformatted as interstate trade.[52] Capitalist political economy has been so closely affiliated with limitations on state power that it is easy to miss the fact that in the Arabian Sea its prescriptions entailed a massive expansion of state surveillance and intervention in trade

In the second half of the nineteenth century, the "science" of statistics was being disseminated and standardized through a series of international congresses.[53] These statistical congresses attempted to establish common standards and measurements that could create commensurability across the globe.[54] Trade statistics were collected and standardized, and increasing pressure was brought to bear on individual states to provide the requisite statistics in the required formats. Statistical congresses were followed by various institutes, conventions, and international bureaus that enforced global standards.[55] However, these international efforts were implemented around the Arabian Sea primarily by the British Empire. Imperial officials brought regulations in line with international standards and marginalist formats of trade.[56] Standards were formulated by administrators and academics in European capitals and subsequently were implemented by colonial empires along the coasts of the Arabian Sea.

One of the mechanisms by which statistical standards were imposed on Arabian Sea trade was in fact a machine. The Hollerith machine was developed in the late nineteenth century to reduce the time required to process and calculate the results of the American census. By the early twentieth century, this predecessor of the computer was being employed in ports around the Arabian Sea to facilitate the aggregation and publication of commercial statistics.[57] The sheer quantity of numerical information and the speed demanded for the publication of trade reports meant that customs administrations were some of the earliest locations where computers were used in Asia and Africa. Hollerith machines used punch cards, so while the machines could process vast amounts of data, commercial intelligence first had to be reduced to a set of numbers that could be punched on a card. Customs officials were saddled with the laborious work of coding ambiguous trading relationships into a format readable by Hollerith machines.[58] The very architecture of customs houses was altered by the presence of these large devices, and clerks were spatially arranged to best fit the requirements of the Hollerith machine.[59] These tabulating devices framed the analytical work of customs officials and disciplined their calculations to the requirements of a machine.

Hollerith machines were only the final stage of a long process of appraising, translating, and documenting trade. Long before being converted into punch cards, documentation was employed for surveillance and control over merchants and clerks. Logbooks were used to monitor and control the movements of guards and maintain the consistency of patrols.[60] The circulation of documents through the customs house was delineated in minute detail and brought under the increasingly strict control of senior European officers.[61] The information provided by merchants in invoices and manifests was collated and reproduced in the standard format of a "Bill of Entry" for a particular merchant. As these slips of paper moved around the docks, warehouses, and customs houses, new copies were made and the quantities and values were aggregated and recalculated into different categories. Duplicates, triplicates, and even quadruplicates of forms were required on green, blue, violet, and "buff"-colored paper.[62] Detailed manuals were produced to ensure uniformity and standardization in the calculation of customs duties, and they were regularly updated to eliminate possibilities for discretion and diversity in the calculation of values.[63] Both merchants and customs officials had to be trained to read, write, and calculate in particular ways to render these complex itineraries of paper into a transparent and enumerated representation of a particular territorial economy.

The central aim of these elaborate documentary regimes was an accurate and objective measure of value. In Britain, tariffs were primarily administered at predetermined amounts known as *specific* duties, but its colonies around the Arabian Sea littoral collected tariffs on an *ad valorem* (percent of value) basis.[64] Furthermore, even those few imports and exports that were taxed at rates unrelated to their value had to have their value recorded for statistical purposes. Thus almost all customs work that was not routine was related to problems of valuation. Drawing on marginalist economics, "real value" was determined by the price of a commodity on the free market. Yet "free market" prices were as intangible in the Arabian Sea as "real value." Prices were distorted by monopolies, monopsonies, and information asymmetries; they varied between different types of transactions and different types of market participants; and often market prices did not seem to exist at all. Value was consequently determined by an ad hoc process in which customs officials translated transactions into formats that approximated free market prices.

DECEPTIVE DOCUMENTS

In March of 1939, as the clouds of war were gathering in Europe, a Goan clerk named Angelo Da Silva was patiently working in the audit department of the Mombasa customs house. As he was double-checking a set of invoices regarding goods sent from Bombay to Mombasa, he noticed something peculiar. The handwriting on the invoices from a number of different firms was strikingly similar. We can imagine his brow furrowed in confusion: with his curiosity piqued he began to go back through the invoices from these firms. He then happened upon another peculiar detail: the declarations of one of the Bombay exporters suddenly seemed to change handwriting without any obvious reason. Da Silva could not make out exactly what was going on, but he smelled something fishy. He took the invoices and declarations to

Mr. Bishop, the collector of customs, and explained his suspicions. It was certainly a worrisome coincidence, so Mr. Bishop ordered that the next consignment from this merchant be stopped and rigorously searched. When customs searched the consignment, their suspicions were confirmed. There was a substantially larger quantity of goods in the consignment than declared in the customs documents. The importer in Mombasa had forged the invoices to reflect smaller quantities than had actually been consigned.

This might have been a triumph of bureaucratic procedures and careful regulation, except that it was the tip of an iceberg of fraud, smuggling, and corruption in the Mombasa customs house. The fraud implicated Indian and Swahili traders, but also Italian, British, and Japanese companies. Colonial officials were stunned at just how pervasive, entrenched, and blatant these frauds were. They did not involve one firm or one corrupt official or even a single method of evasion. Rather, this was a routine component of trade in East Africa and across the diasporic networks in the Arabian Sea.[65] The material qualities of the paper, ink, and handwriting became a site of intense anxiety for officials. The very documents that were supposed to monitor transactions had become a tool for the subversion of regulations.[66]

Customs officials did not trust verbal declarations because they believed it was far too easy to lie and then modify or recant after the fact. So they assumed that written invoices were necessary for the promotion of honesty and accountability.[67] However, the invoices being submitted to customs authorities were diverse and of doubtful authenticity. Frequently importers purchased and transported goods without a formal invoice but rather a simple paper chit. Such chits were associated with the bazaar, its opacity to colonial officials, and an ostensible propensity for dishonest dealing. These chits were usually written in languages like Sindhi and Gujarati and hence were even more illegible to colonial officials.[68] The fact that these communications were not transparent to a British administrator made them suspicious.

Colonial customs across the Arabian Sea expended much effort in standardizing the forms, categories, and material artifacts that circulated through various offices. Specific requirements were made of the invoices that merchants submitted to customs. Invoices could not be copies or "mutilated," and they had to bear an original handwritten signature.[69] One can imagine that poor-quality or damaged paper often provided a convenient excuse for inscrutable or misleading documents. These invoices were the basis upon which a welter of other documents was produced both by firms and by governments. Banks granted financing documentation, insurance companies collected premiums, and shipping companies prepared manifests based on invoices. Ship captains also had to produce manifests on ruled paper of an approved quality. These documents were then copied, signed, countersigned, compared, reconciled, and filed in an elaborate dance choreographed to ensure the accuracy of statistics and the full collection of duties.[70] The material qualities of documentation and the mobilities of these documents were rigorously controlled but also a source of tremendous anxiety for bureaucracies.

For all the machines, ordinances, and international conventions, the collection of trade statistics ultimately came down to interactions between merchants and petty clerks. Whether the publication of commercial statistics helped or hindered trading firms, their cooperation was essential to the administration of customs. As distasteful as colonial officials found it, they could not escape the fact that for most cases they had to presume the truthfulness of merchants. The sheer volume of trade flows made it impossible to verify the truth of the vast majority of invoices.[71] Checks were made to ensure that forms were correctly filled, and valuations were often compared against other invoices and appraisals, but these checks were sporadic and better at catching mistakes in form rather than in substance.[72] Much information like countries of origin for imports or countries of destination for exports could never be cross-checked and simply had to be taken at the word of the merchant. Since they could not confirm or disprove this information, customs authorities were forced to coax the cooperation of merchants.[73] They vainly hoped that simplified documents and friendly treatment might elicit honesty where it was impossible to enforce it. British officials had constructed a vast bureaucratic infrastructure of valuation, but it was utterly dependent on the honesty and forthrightness of the merchants being regulated. Unsurprisingly, this self-regulating system was prone to contrivance and fraud.

QUANTIFIED VALUE

Value for the purposes of customs was accordingly determined by a number of different facets, which together defined an ideal-typical market transaction. Customs officials and merchant networks were therefore constantly struggling over how one could translate the corrupted reality of commercial practice into this ideal form in order to determine "real value." One important facet of this ideal was that it was a wholesale transaction. While its general meaning was understood by merchants and officials alike, the term *wholesale* resisted precise definition. Attempts to define *wholesale* inevitably became circular: transactions in wholesale quantities took place between wholesale dealers in wholesale markets. Officials imagined that in Europe trade operated through a "direct and business-like method" in which an importer sold to a wholesale dealer, who sold to a retailer, who finally sold to the consumer.[74] This sequence of transactions certainly occurred in markets around the Arabian Sea, but it was far from universal. Merchants did not specialize as consistently as regulators would have liked, so questions arose over which merchants should be characterized as wholesale dealers.[75] Similarly, wholesale markets existed, but many wholesale transactions occurred outside these physical spaces. The awkward resolution to this indeterminacy was to focus on *wholesale* as an expression of quantity. Wholesale transactions were apparently those that occurred in "large wholesale lots."[76]

Ascertaining the quantity of a good and hence the size of the lots was, of course, a convoluted affair. Length, volume, weight, number of commodities, and number of containers were all used in determining quantity. British officials hoped to standardize measures of quantity into a singular measure of weight. This would allow for easy comparison across countries and between commodities as well. Statistics were supposed to be reported in imperial weights across the British Empire.[77] Yet this was resisted by trades that had traditionally used different systems of measurement and had developed expertise in exploiting these measures. Even where weight was commonly used in trade, there were many different systems and units of weight. Traders employed the metric system, the imperial system, and various Asian and African units of measurement like the *maund,* the *frasila,* and the *batman.* Each of these in turn had variations in its practical application and measurement between different ports.[78] The weight of the *maund* in Bombay, Muscat, or Aden varied, just as the hundredweight (cwt) varied between London and New York. Into the second half of the twentieth century, the use of local units of measurements persisted and customs authorities had to rely on approximate conversions into imperial measures.[79] Statistical reports also fabricated a uniformity that was purely nominal by employing terms like *packages*, which was not a uniform measurement but just an umbrella term that referred to the usual measure for any particular commodity.[80] Thus different commodities appeared to be comparable in statistical returns, yet this was a façade that disguised a far more convoluted reality.

Merchant networks were quick to exploit this muddle of systems for measuring quantity. Declaring a lower quantity of goods was a routine infraction of customs regulation; indeed, it was the second most common fine imposed by customs.[81] Textiles were the largest item of trade in the Arabian Sea, and merchants regularly understated the length of their goods in the hope that they could reduce their costs.[82] Given the size of the trade in textiles and the vast extent of infractions, there is little doubt that a significant proportion of merchants got away with it.

Merchant networks were also particularly adept at manipulating the diversity of units of measurement. Regulators were often unfamiliar with local practices of measurement, so they were dependent on conversions into imperial units, but where a *maund* varied from port to port, merchants could choose the most advantageous rate of conversion. Moreover, conversion to imperial measures allowed merchants to simultaneously underpay their duties and to scam local consumers who did not understand imperial units.[83] Traffickers alternatively exploited local units of measurement like the *jotta*. A *jotta* referred to several bags or packages bundled together for transportation. Traffickers would declare ten packages of a commodity to customs and then ship ten *jotta*s, allowing the merchant to transport many times as many goods for the same duty.[84] The diversity of measurements around the Arabian Sea allowed diasporic merchant networks to extract greater profits from more parochially minded officials and consumers.

Trade Discounts

Calculations of real value included trade discounts, yet customs authorities continually confronted the problem of deciding which discounts could properly be considered "trade discounts." Their decisions turned on whether the discount was generally available or whether it was provided only to special trading partners. As bureaucrats struggled to classify the discounts employed in transactions across the Arabian Sea, they confronted the diversity of commercial practices and the prevalence of extramarket transactions and personalized prices. Nevertheless, customs officials deemed commercial relationships that privileged trusted partners as aberrant to the determination of real value, even if they were in fact the norm. Only discounts that were given to an abstract trader could be incorporated into customs valuations.[85] Generic trade discounts thus became the touchstone by which the colonial bureaucracy defined arm's-length transactions.

However, even as customs officials were attempting to extrapolate impersonal market exchange, they had to accommodate practices that privileged particular merchants. British firms frequently succeeded in in obtaining accommodation of their discounts, both because of racial biases and because they could more persuasively articulate their exchanges as generic arm's-length transactions. Colonial officials accepted shipping rebates or banking privileges as trade discounts, even though they were not available to all comers.[86] Customs officials even recognized a *shahi* discount, which applied to large, well-respected merchants (*shahs*), even though such a discount was obviously not available to less established traders.[87] Furthermore, as the processing of imports and exports through customs became increasingly complicated, firms started hiring clearing agents whose expertise was in managing customs formalities. These clearing agents, known as *dalal*s and *muqaddam*s, were not only able to expedite customs formalities but also well placed to reduce customs valuations. Consequently clearing agents themselves had to be limited, regulated, and in some cases replaced altogether by government employees.[88] The person who was presenting documents to customs had a pivotal impact on which transactions were interpreted as impersonal.

Like Kind and Quality

A single, unique transaction does not make a market. Market exchange involves multiple transactions in a class of fungible goods; hence, determining market price involved identifying "goods of like kind and quality." Most transactions across the Arabian Sea were in staple agricultural goods like dates, rice, cloves, and fish. Customs officials believed that these items of trade did not vary significantly in quality and hence were traded at market-clearing prices.[89] Yet a substantial amount of work had to be done to divide this diverse mass of goods into grades of like kind and quality. Distinctions based on geography, purity, and ultimately price itself filtered into the determination of tariff categories.[90]

Yet even as these categories were being consolidated, merchants were manipulating them to their advantage. Importers of branded goods deployed advertising to increase the retail price of their goods, but they were anxious to be included with cheap products in customs categories. Merchants could substantially reduce the tariffs on highly taxed goods like cigarettes, tea, and sugar by resisting gradations. So a merchant dealing in high-quality sugar would be taxed at only an average value of a broad range of sugars of different qualities.[91] When price controls and export restrictions severely curtailed the trade in a particular commodity, merchant networks renamed or even reprocessed their goods to evade restrictions. During World War II, sugar was brought under price controls across the British colonies of the Arabian Sea, and merchants were anxious to exploit the potential of the black market in what had become white gold. The most successful method of evading price controls in Zanzibar turned out to be selling sugar in the form of unrefined blocks of brown *jaggery*. Usually a cheaper product used by lower-class Indians and Africans, *jaggery* was suddenly selling well above the price of pure white sugar.[92] Customs categories did not recognize sugar and *jaggery* as goods of a like kind and quality, but trafficking networks recognized that for many consumers they were put to the same uses.

A League of Nations committee had created a global classification system that divided commodities by their stage of manufacture. So the categories ran from livestock to food stuffs to textiles to heavy machinery. Petroleum products and alcohol were taxed at different rates depending on how highly refined they were. This required increasingly sophisticated tests and expertise in gauging the potency of these different products. But it similarly allowed myriad opportunities for evasion, as gauging departments could only ever test a small proportion of imports, and liquors of different qualities were mixed to pass at lower tariff levels.[93] Conversely, automobile retailers imported partially assembled vehicles as automobile parts. By leaving the relatively simple final assembly to domestic workers, importers were able to vastly reduce their tariff payments, since the whole car was worth far more than the sum of its parts.[94] Defining classifications for customs purposes thus proved to be a slippery process, and merchant networks were constantly engaged in exploiting these slippages.

Yet perhaps the most successful method of discounting tariff valuations was to bypass markets altogether. Many firms found success in arguing that their products were one of a kind and hence did not have a market price. To benefit from such a monopoly, prices would reflect a premium that increased tariff duties. Yet many European and American firms took control of the retailing of their products in foreign countries and were able to manipulate calibrations of value to reduce their tariffs. Rather than sell to wholesale merchants, these firms set up subsidiaries to exclusively import their merchandise. Business historians have explored at length how firms like Singer used local subsidiaries to advertise, sell, and finance sewing machines to local consumers.[95] Yet one of the key benefits of this sales model was that it reduced the tariff valuations of these products. Singer sewing machines, Ford automobiles, and Mobil Oil all exported their products to subsidiaries or local affiliates in places like India, Aden, and Kenya. These local affiliates were sent invoices for goods valued at as little as 30 percent of their ultimate retail price. This drastically reduced their tax bill, and the corporations claimed that the additional value was created by the marketing and salesmanship of their local affiliates.[96] By selling directly to consumers, these manufacturers bypassed wholesale markets altogether and forced customs officials to accept these corporations' own conspicuously low valuations.

Geography

Reorganized customs administrations and new trade statistics reordered the geography of trade. As trade statistics of the Arabian Sea began to be published in the late nineteenth century, they were organized around ports and bodies of water. Trade reports presented a geography of trade more aligned with maritime distances than with the geopolitical divisions between nation-states. Yet over time trade figures that had been organized into categories like "the Persian Gulf" or "the Mediterranean" were dispensed with, and empires and nations came to be the organizing principles. The trade of particular ports was consolidated and listed under colonies and states, which were in turn organized within empires and continents.[97] This reflected a broader shift in the understanding of trade from transactions between individuals or firms to transactions between states. In this representation, the relationships of merchants themselves disappeared from view. By means of the publication of statistics, international treaties, and the coordination of customs procedures, free trade came to mean low tariff barriers and carefully documented transactions across state borders.

The British Empire had long prided itself as the paragon of free trade, but the sequential shocks of the First World War and the Great Depression had made protectionist policies palatable to imperial officials. Thus in 1932 imperial officials erected preferential tariff barriers as a means of protecting imperial industry and encouraging intraimperial trade. By claiming manufacture within the British Empire, importers could obtain lower tariffs and be subjected to less customs scrutiny. Consequently, the most common fraud against the Indian Merchandise Marks Act was the misstatement of geographic origins, which constituted between two-thirds and three-fourths of all offenses.[98] Companies like Ford seem to have organized their production lines, completing the assembly of cars across the border in Canada, at least in part to take advantage of these preferential rates for sales within the British Empire.[99] The operation of preferential tariff rates within the British Empire led to increasing efforts to pass foreign goods as British-made. Imperial customs administrations subsequently demanded additional certified invoices from all importers to confirm imperial origins.[100] Other states were anxious to overcome protectionist barriers and provided their own incentives to export industries. Some states provided bounties and grants to their exporters, while other states were even more directly involved in exporting their manufactures and "dumping" goods at below-cost price in order to build market share. Imperial customs regulations therefore attempted to compensate by increasing valuations and imposing penalties on such commodities. Indeed, colonial governments came to use these provisions as additional methods of protecting domestic industries.[101] The territorial conception of economic space was thus a deeply contested arena for the determination of value.

These territorial regulations were particularly challenged by the existence of princely states, semiautonomous rulers, and foreign colonies along the Arabian Sea littoral. These states were more than willing to overlook regulatory demands and reduce tariffs in order to attract trade to their ports. The coastal states of Gujarat were particularly problematic because merchant diasporas were based out of their ports and their intermingled domains made it virtually impossible to monitor trade flows through the region. These princes and their merchant clients became embroiled in intense competition to capture the trade in highly tariffed commodities like tea, silk, and sugar. Princely states like Junagadh, Bhavnagar, and Kutch provided various incentives from rebates of customs duty, to the elimination of landing charges, to simply turning a blind eye to smuggling. British authorities attempted to close off these territories through a customs cordon known as the Viramgam Line. This geographic cordon was particularly ineffective because it crossed through the Thar Desert and the Rann of Kutch (the world's largest salt marsh). Even for goods that came through the railway station in Viramgam, it was impossible to ascertain the itineraries and rebates applicable to commodities that could have passed through half a dozen jurisdictions.[102] Similar jurisdictional overlaps and ambiguities were present in southern Yemen and along the Shatt al-Arab.[103] The clear geographies articulated in statistical charts were possible only through the elision of such convoluted geopolitics.

Time

Market value is something that exists only at a specific time. Colonial customs confronted a great deal of difficulty in determining at what time an import or an export should be valued. Was it the time that the contract was signed, when the ship came into port, when the commodity was unloaded onto the docks, when it entered the customs house, when it cleared customs, or when it was actually sold by the importer to a wholesale dealer? There were compelling reasons to employ any one of these moments to determine the value of a commodity, and indeed in different times and in different circumstances value was calculated at all of these moments.[104] Yet transactions were rarely instantaneous and often lasted weeks or even years. Merchants often brought their documents to the customs house a week in advance to expedite the release of their goods. The clearance of these goods could then be delayed for weeks, or the goods could be warehoused for years, before customs formalities were actually completed.[105] Over this period, market prices could have changed dramatically, and merchants were anxious to claim the most advantageous moment for valuation.

Customs officials did not have the time or the resources to determine an objective time of importation, so they settled for a time that could be employed consistently for customs purposes.[106] Customs ascertained market value at the moment when "the bill of entry is first presented for index number in the Import Department."[107] This was a time documented by customs clerks and hence easily ascertained. It may have poorly reflected the complexities of any particular transaction, but this standard left little room for dispute. Merchant networks, of course, quickly found ways to circumvent this rule. Most frustrating for colonial officials were the huge surges in trade right before a change in policy. Even a rumor of policy changes produced oscillations of trade flows in anticipation of modifications.[108] However, the most cunning effort of merchant networks was to employ forward contracts to reduce their customs valuation. Colonial customs would not accept contract prices as a means of valuation if a market price existed, but publicized forward contracts affected market prices. Consequently, some merchants announced large forward contracts that would temporarily glut the market and reduce the valuation of their imports when they were registered in the customs house. Of course, they still got paid at the earlier contract prices they had negotiated, or they could wait out the market and sell when prices recovered. Other merchants merely sold off excess inventory or smuggled goods at bargain prices to depreciate market prices in preparation for their new imports. Consequently, regulations aiming to eliminate fraud merely opened up new avenues of manipulation.[109] Merchant networks could not control the time at which their goods were valued, but they could manipulate the market at the time of valuation.

Credit also skewed the ideal of a simultaneous exchange of commodity for cash. Most transactions across the Arabian Sea relied on credit, renegotiated payment plans, and long-term accounts. Determining the real value of a transaction consequently required customs administrations to approximate "cash price." The prices quoted by importers and exporters generally assumed a certain provision of credit, so some authorities attempted to compensate for credit in their valuations. They tried to ascertain local interest rates and identify in each port the discount that a merchant might provide for an immediate cash payment.[110] Yet frequently these were meaningless. Thus officials seem to have given up and simply deducted 3 percent off quoted prices.[111] The phrase *cash price* also assumed a single hard currency, but around the Arabian Sea transactions frequently involved multiple fluctuating currencies. So provisions had to be made to incorporate the cost of currency conversion into calculations of value. Exchange rates were determined from quotes by exchange banks, but given delays in delivery and payment many firms also made or lost money on the fluctuations in the exchange rate. As we have seen in the previous chapter, these bets on currency fluctuations were an integral part of transactions.[112] The prevalence of credit relations and exchange rate fluctuations also rendered "cash price" little more than a convenient fiction.

STATISTICS FABRICATE SMUGGLING

International statistical conventions dictated how local customs clerks should document trade and calculate value. In turn, statisticians aggregated and computed the information collected by clerks into public statistics. British colonies across the globe produced identically formatted "Blue Books." Blue Books were relatively thin publications between blue covers that enumerated basic statistical information about a colony, from population and health to shipping and trade. They were produced for a metropolitan audience with prices in sterling and measurements quoted in imperial units, and the book itself was kept as brief as possible in order to avoiding taxing overmuch the attentions of European readers. While the numerical information varied, the arrangement and formatting of this information were identical in order to facilitate easy comparisons between colonies.[113] Territories under India Office control produced slightly different "Reports on the Trade and Navigation" of a particular territory. While these reports did not have blue covers, they served virtually identical audiences and presented the same information in similar formats.[114] No matter how vastly different and internally diverse these places were, they were rendered into simple, uniform, and modular statistical units. In a certain sense, colonies had been rendered into commodities; they appeared to be units of like kind and quality that investors could distinguish through marginal comparisons of value.

Colonial statisticians produced orderly statistical tables and calculations for their territories, but in private they acknowledged that these were works of fiction. British officials in Iran did not trust the statistics produced by the Pahlavi state despite the increasing control asserted over trade. The Pahlavi state attempted to control its currency reserves and trade balance by allowing merchants to import only as much as they exported. Many merchants seem to have responded by exporting goods, even at a loss, but declaring high values in order to justify undervalued imports. The British commercial secretary believed that the total exports were overvalued by at least 30 percent and that imports were undervalued by at least 30 percent.[115] Colonial officials encountered similar distortions in Indian princely states. Customs officers pressured princely state officials toward the more accurate and timely collection of statistical data and ultimately demanded the ability to collect their own price data.[116] Yet these problems were far from limited to areas administered by non-Europeans. British-administered territories also published statistics that bore a tendentious relationship to actual conditions of trade. One statistician insisted that "colonial statistics are extremely bad; and that the superficial appearance of accuracy which that outrageous document, the Blue Book, lend to some of its contents is, with rare exceptions, a mere façade."[117] Statistical publications appeared accurate, but the slightest interrogation revealed little in the way of verisimilitude.

Colonial statistics were particularly skewed by the difficulties of comprehending multiple cultures, awkward territories, and mobile populations. Statistics collected at customs houses helped to produce markets that mapped onto colonial territories, but colonial territories rarely looked like ideal-typical nation-states. This was partially a consequence of colonialism itself, which created settler populations, investment flows, and extractive trades that distorted the stable borders of national markets. It was also a consequence of the littoral features of colonies and protectorates around the Arabian Sea. These colonies had populations that were not only racially heterogeneous but also diverse in their socioeconomic customs. Littoral populations were difficult to aggregate because they did not easily divide into per capita units.[118] Averages, medians, and per capita calculations were blunt and warped tools for understanding mobile and cosmopolitan populations. Colonial economies were inherently hard to quantify using statistical tools developed for ostensibly homogeneous European nation-states.

Nevertheless, statistics would come to be a key tool in the identification of smuggling and the calculation of its costs. Without statistics, smuggling could be discovered only on a one-off basis and its prevalence could be estimated only by rough guesswork. Much of the history recounted in this book emerges out of a period in which there was nothing more than anecdotal evidence and speculative estimates. Beginning roughly in the 1920s in British India, and quickly spreading around the coastline to colonies in Africa and Arabia, officials began to detect smuggling through statistics. It is likely that the experience of trade controls during World War I and increasingly entrenched statistical measures allowed officials to measure the total commodities required for a particular territory for the first time.[119] Large deviations that could not be explained otherwise were blamed on smugglers. Surges in the quantity of imports into free ports were interpreted as heading to illicit destinations, and large declines could now be explained as a diversion of regular trade into unrecorded smuggling.[120] Deviations in reported prices also started to stand in for physical evidence, and colonial authorities insisted that low prices were proof of smuggling. One official insisted on the "infallible criterion" that goods could not be sold at a price less than their true cost plus import expenses.[121] Therefore, goods that were too cheap had to be smuggled goods. Princely state officials pleaded that the need for hard cash or stanching of further losses often compelled merchants to sell at a loss.[122] It was to no avail, as the apparent objectivity of statistics was more convincing to colonial officials. Smuggling had become a useful tool for colonial statisticians because it accounted for deviations from statistical norms. The failings of statistical collection could now be glossed as quantitative evidence of smuggling.

The unknown was accordingly a central factor in the determination of prices and the infrastructure of transactions.[123] The deviations between market prices and "real values" were rationalized not as the inefficiencies of the market but as the consequence of corrupt and uncivilized traffickers. The impossibility of determining objective "real values" did not bring into question the basic tenets of capitalist political economy because smuggling provided a convenient scapegoat. Trafficking networks in this reading were not something internal and integral to the operation of free markets but an exogenous aberration. Meanwhile trafficking networks were making themselves tactically visible as well-governed capitalist enterprises. Truly panoptic surveillance of exchanges would have revealed this contrived performance of free market exchange. It was, however, enormously productive to be ignorant of how merchant networks perverted market prices. This strategic ignorance allowed colonial bureaucracies to neglect problems inherent in the model of free markets and to justify economic policies that facilitated colonial businesses and investments.

The diasporic traffics of the Arabian Sea were built to conceal information from producers, consumers, and competitors and to secretly exploit arbitrage opportunities. Carefully constructed networks of trusted friends and relatives allowed diasporic firms to keep transactions embedded in enduring relationships that facilitated searching for concealed information and keeping information concealed. Over the course of a century of bureaucratic intervention, trade regulation, and statistical collection, the unknown became a proxy for the illegal. Trade was monitored and documented so that price became a public measure of value. Colonial documentation and statistical calculations produced market prices and equated these bureaucratic artifacts with "real value." Merchant networks recognized the power of the documents that they were required to produce and responded with various contrivances. They performed compliance even as they undermined categories, manipulated geographical boundaries, and distorted timings. The ambiguities in documentation allowed colonial bureaucracies to produce objective market prices even as merchant networks continued to obscure their determinations of value.

Conclusion

In the late 1940s, Mastan Mirza, a dockworker on the Bombay waterfront, was approached by an Arab who called himself Sheikh Mohammed al-Ghalib. Al-Ghalib asked the dockworker to assist him in smuggling a few watches and gold biscuits past customs. Mastan agreed, and when the appointed time arrived he surreptitiously slipped some watches and gold into the folds of his clothes and turban. At a convenient moment he then passed them on to al-Ghalib on the other side of the customs cordon. For his efforts, Mastan was amply rewarded and became a regular conduit for the smuggling of various goods. Soon after, Mastan was being approached by other smugglers requiring similar services, as well as countless sailors, travelers, and pilgrims arriving on the Bombay docks with contraband.[1] By the 1960s, this demand for contraband had made this humble porter, Mastan Mirza, into the fabulously wealthy and notorious smuggler Haji Mastan. Or at least, so goes the general consensus of rumors and speculations that have surrounded his life and fashioned his larger-than-life reputation.[2]

Haji Mastan's extraordinary career was in large part a consequence of the infamous "License Raj" set up by Jawaharlal Nehru in the years after Indian independence. Inspired by Keynesian economics and the success of Soviet industrialization, Nehru hoped to accelerate India's development into a self-sufficient industrial power. Customs houses were the front lines of this battle to create a self-sufficient economy. The License Raj aimed to channel imports toward those sectors deemed a national priority by the postcolonial state. Haji Mastan, on the other hand, served the vast Indian population who resented the state's attempt to deprive them of watches, radios, and polyester shirts, as well as gold, which they used as a hedge against inflation. Haji Mastan was an outlaw in the eyes of the state bureaucracy but a Robin Hood figure in the streets of Bombay. He was the photogenic face of a vast network of businesses who connected virtually every Indian consumer to the unregulated souqs of Dubai. Haji Mastan's thriving business was so successful that it contributed to the devaluation of the rupee in 1966. Yet he lived to a ripe old age in a mansion overlooking the Arabian Sea, dabbling in politics, Bollywood, and even Bollywood starlets.[3] Bollywood in turn has eulogized his life in no less than three films: he is India's own Don Corleone.

Haji Mastan may seem like an exceptional figure, but I would suggest that his life marks the culmination of practices that we have traced throughout this book. Haji Mastan's enormous success as a trafficker was a direct consequence of his ability to tap into the diasporic networks of the Arabian Sea. As a coolie on the Bombay docks, Haji Mastan understood the space of the port and the materiality of gold biscuits and turbans better than any customs official. He could see and feel in ways inaccessible to office-bound authorities in New Delhi. Yet Haji Mastan was merely one of thousands of dockworkers; it was Sheikh al-Ghalib who facilitated the essential connection to gold and consumer goods in Dubai. From this initial link Mastan built a vast network of allies, including underworld figures as well as officials who were willing to turn a blind eye to his activities. Moreover, his connection to Bollywood was not merely for the glamour: it constituted a pioneering effort to launder black money through the underfunded film industry.[4] The stock character of the crook with a heart of gold in the golden age of Bollywood cinema is probably an effect of Haji Mastan's bankrolling of the industry. This pervasive network, which spread its tentacles both inside the Indian bureaucracy and out into the markets of Dubai, was what turned a small-time crook into a trafficking kingpin.

Haji Mastan's network was also possible because it capitalized on the ambitions of Nehruvian planning to produce a self-sufficient national economy. These postcolonial policies were unquestionably a continuation of colonial efforts to impose territorial sovereignty and foster a free market within this territory. The liminal space of the Arabian Sea was an important terrain across which colonial efforts were pursued. The British Empire invested substantial time, resources, and intellectual energy into monitoring the borders and coastlines of all its colonies and protectorates around the Arabian Sea littoral. The violence, interference, and surveillance of the Royal Navy in the Arabian Sea made it possible to sustain laissez-faire policies and a posture of noninterference within territorial markets. I have referred to this process as framing out, in that intensive action at the border and in the international space of the sea helped structure the freedoms within territorial borders.

Framing out is not merely a geographical metaphor; it also applies to the conceptual space of the market. In the capitalist worldview, the market is a distinct sphere of human activity that excludes familial relationships, cultural practices, and political power. Yet human bodies, rifles, and metal coins constantly trespassed across the boundaries of the market. They were intermediaries: physical objects that framed the market and yet in doing so also bridged this conceptual divide. So framing out the market was a Sisyphean task: a never-ending process of eliminating slaves, violence, and counterfeits in order to produce labor, property, and money. Most scholarship on smuggling has taken the view that the illicit is always a response to governmental action: laws create their other in crime.[5] I think there is much to recommend in this vision of smuggling and the state, yet when we focus on trafficking and the market the reverse appears to be true. In the Arabian Sea, colonial regimes fostered capitalist markets by excluding and suppressing existing practices of exchange. The preceding chapters have shown that trafficking networks preceded the free market and that only by framing out illicit traffics could the free market come into existence.

However, this was not simply a top-down process of colonial bureaucracies outlawing certain forms of exchange. Merchants, sailors, and travelers were all essential participants in this new regime of capitalism. Classical and then marginalist political economists abhorred intervention in free markets, yet in order to test their theories and develop their models they required data and documentation. It was the much-reviled customs house that produced data through increasing surveillance and intervention in trade. Commercial regulations thus required merchant networks to document their transactions within the conceptual framework of capitalism. Some merchants resisted these impositions, but resistance was futile. Successful trading networks found contrivances around these new regulations. Trafficking networks performed the principles of capitalist political economy to the extent that they produced invoices and filled out forms that represented their activities as free market exchanges. Officials then aggregated and computed these representations to determine prices and market conditions. The result was not a transformation of exchange relations but a tactical performance that framed diverse transactions as capitalist exchange.

Institutional economists have long argued that strong institutional structures are necessary for the successful operation of free markets and the growth that this entails.[6] This book has argued that free markets are just as often a contrived performance. Self-regulating markets depend upon the honest and forthright reporting of transactions, but there are innumerable incentives for traders to generously interpret the rules or misrepresent their transactions to the wider market. As we have seen, merchant networks in the Arabian Sea sought out ambiguities, loopholes, and blind spots in the documentation of trade. They could maintain the diversity and opacity of their traffics by carefully framing them to conform to bureaucratic categories. Moreover, merchants designed many transactions specifically to exploit ambiguities and slippages in these categories. Trafficking networks structured whole lines of business to evade the regulation of the free market. Merchants—and the conniving officials who facilitated their transactions—were thus essential to performing the free market as efficient and self-regulating.

Trade looks homogeneous and flat when viewed from a page of customs statistics, but what becomes apparent from the deck of a dhow is the unevenness of capitalist development. Around the Arabian Sea littoral were numerous polities, political economies, and economic practices. Not only was their incorporation into objective and commensurable data sets about wage labor, capital flows, and military budgets incomplete, but the incorporation of each was incomplete in its own peculiar way. By traversing the sea, trafficking networks could scrutinize these gaps and exploit the arbitrage opportunities that followed from them. Merchants encountered different interpretations of abstract categories: in some ports a slave became an adopted child, an offensive weapon became sporting equipment, or a counterfeit coin became a souvenir. Trafficking networks reorganized themselves to best exploit these slippages. Capitalist categories formatted trade across the Arabian Sea, but trafficking networks exploited the slippages between these categories.

The histories of free trade and trafficking are therefore inextricably entangled. The emergence of capitalist markets is a consequence of an elaborate dance between bureaucracies and merchants. Colonial bureaucracies introduced regulations that merchant networks then found ways to circumvent. Laws were revised and new methods of surveillance were instituted, but merchants again identified the gaps in surveillance and loopholes in the law. Over time commercial regulation evolved in response to trafficking, and trade evolved to exploit slippages in regulation. The particular history of capitalism in the Arabian Sea is in large part the history of this interplay. It was not the teleological unfolding of natural propensities toward the division of labor or self-interested accumulation. Rather, it was and continues to be a profoundly contingent struggle between bureaucratic efforts to format the free market and mercantile efforts to evade the competitive pressures of the market.

Therefore, this was particularly a struggle over perceptions. Many of the terms I have been using—*framing, surveillance, elision, opacity*—hint at the importance of visibility and modes of seeing the market. This does not suggest a separation of representation and reality but rather that practices of exchange were shaped by the interplay between devices of perception and methods of evading this perception. For transactions across the Arabian Sea to become visible to "the market," bureaucrats had to collect, aggregate, and distribute this information. Invoices, Hollerith machines, and trade reports were devices that became essential to perceiving the free market in the Arabian Sea. Without these aids, it would be impossible for individual traders to visualize themselves and their exchanges as being determined by the market. This method of perceiving the market consequently framed out certain types of information that could not be easily conveyed in prices. Personal communications expressed family relationships, personal biases, and subtle inflections, but invoices could not. Moreover, misleading documentation was easily employed to obscure the transparency assumed by free market ideology. Colonial bureaucrats perceived an objective market through a regime of documentation; traffickers were able to perceive the gaps in the market by arbitraging between bureaucratic regimes of perception.

While these difficulties of perception were present in all markets, they were exacerbated in the shifting terrain of the sea. The Arabian Sea was not a territory that could be possessed and bounded but a network through which transactions were routed. I have tried to account for the Arabian Sea in the previous chapters as a network that used dhows, monsoons, and families to slip through the increasingly rigid boundaries of states and markets. European maps depicted the Arabian Sea as an empty homogeneous space between bounded territories of unitary sovereignty. While the sea did develop toward this image over a century of British hegemony and European cooperation, this bounded homogeneous geography always overlaid a more complex and shifting topography of trafficking networks. There were multiple, overlapping, and interlinked geographies of the Arabian Sea. Where the historiography has struggled to determine whether the Indian Ocean was a unified space, this book traces the evolution of divergent yet densely interconnected spaces. I hope these previous chapters have portrayed not just the abstract perspective of modern cartography but also the mobile and tactical perspectives of trafficking networks.

This study is grounded in specificities of the Arabian Sea and the political and cultural dynamics that were in operation during the roughly one hundred years when it was dominated by the British Empire. Yet the conclusions I have drawn hopefully have some utility beyond this specific time and space. The Bay of Bengal, the South China Sea, the Caribbean, and of course the Mediterranean could all be studied as littoral zones with similar characteristics and histories. Each of these littoral zones encompasses a variety of political and cultural groupings that interact with each other across the sea. There are intensive connections and exchanges across these seas, but no single polity is capable of bounding and controlling these spaces. I am confident that similar studies could be made of these regions, which would improve the analysis presented here. Yet trafficking is hardly limited to these regions; it clearly affects every corner of the globe. These entangled histories of trafficking and capitalism convey an aspect of free markets that is less visible in other parts of the globe but is no less present. Capitalism as a lived reality is different for every location and evolves in every moment, yet there is a common reference point in the abstraction of political economic categories. The constant reframing of capitalism through the interplay of regulators and traffickers is occurring globally but is easiest to trace in these maritime spaces.

A history of dhows, slaves, and gold coins seems to have little relevance to the contemporary world, but contemporary neoliberal capitalism may have more in common with colonial capitalism than is at first apparent. The prevalence of informality in our contemporary economy undoubtedly has roots in this deeper history of trafficking and capitalism.[7] Only a few of the diasporic firms traced in this book still survive, but the tactics they employed are only too familiar. Diasporic networks evaded regulation, mobilized personal relationships, and capitalized on flexibility to carve out profitable niches within Arabian Sea commerce. Informally organized firms today are similarly structured to be small, flexible, and lightly regulated. Furthermore, these small firms tend to be subcontractors that cooperate with and feed into larger firms just as dhows fed into steamship lines and *shroffs* fed into exchange banks. Exchanges continue to be organized outside the market, and they still turn out to be essential to what occurs inside the market. Indeed, businesses seem to gravitate to the margins of the market, and profits appear to proliferate from trafficking across these boundaries. The performance of free markets is not just an interesting facet of the history of capitalism; it continues to characterize capitalist exchange today.

The problem of human trafficking continues to plague governments across the globe precisely because it continues to be such an effective means of keeping labor docile and disorganized. Vegetables are harvested in America, skyscrapers are constructed in Dubai, houses are cleaned in Hong Kong, and libidos are serviced in Germany at competitive prices only because free labor continues to be disingenuously performed. Banks, hedge funds, and university endowments continue to grow at unprecedented rates because they can arbitrage currencies, manipulate interest rate benchmarks, obscure transactions in dark pools, and simply launder money. The financialization of the global economy proceeds apace at least in part because money itself continues to beguile and mystify. Violence is still an inescapable facet of modern economies: pirates stalk the ocean, private contractors prosecute wars, and terrorists target the World Trade Center in New York, malls in Nairobi, and chic hotels in Mumbai. The regular destruction and extortion of private property across the globe produces high risks but also high yields for the roving hoards of global capital. So the fact that the fundamental prerequisites of capitalism are still only partially realized is perhaps responsible for the failure of the rate of profit to decline and the sedate quality of class struggle. The surprising ability of capitalism to weather crises and suspend its contradictions could be attributed this continuing incompleteness of free labor, private property, and money.

Incorporating trafficking into the analysis of capitalism questions not so much Marxist analyses of capital as their more teleological strains. Similarly, it does not reject neoclassical analyses of economic history but asks that such analyses address the ways that traders subvert the conceptual foundations of econometric analysis. Whether you believe in the inevitability of capitalist crisis or in the inevitability of free markets, I hope it is evident from the preceding pages that it is impossible to document the history of capitalism without understanding how documentation itself is central to that history. Moreover, it is impossible to understand how markets work without understanding what is framed out of those markets. The ubiquity of fraud, insider trading, currency manipulation, and trafficking in the global economy should be indicative of how easy it is to fool a statistic. While economists and statisticians have developed ingenious proxies for measuring illicit and informal activities, they have shown relatively less interest in how metrics themselves are susceptible to manipulation. As statistics and econometrics become increasingly performative in the global economy, we need to be more conscious of how these measurements are the result of contrived performance. The margins of the market are not amenable to quantification, but they are nevertheless essential to the framework of capitalism.

ABBREVIATIONS USED IN NOTES

AT	Abdullah al-Ṭābūr Archive, Jumʿa al-Mājid Library, Dubai, UAE
BT	Papers of Bertram Thomas, Faculty of Middle East and Asian Studies, Cambridge University
CBR	Central Board of Revenue
CUST	Customs Department
FO	Foreign Office
GL	Guildhall Library (Now held at London Metropolitan Archives), London
GoB	Government of Bombay
GoI	Government of India
GoZ	Government of Zanzibar
HSBC	Hongkong and Shanghai Banking Corporation Archive, London
IO	India Office
IOR	India Office Records, British Library, London
MSA	Maharashtra State Archives, Mumbai, India
NAI	National Archives of India, New Delhi, India
NAUK	National Archives of the United Kingdom, Kew, UK
NMM	Caird Library, National Maritime Museum, Greenwich, UK
PA	Political Agent
PRPG	Political Resident in the Persian Gulf
RG	Registrar General

RP	Ratansi Purshottam Archive, in possession of Vimal Purecha, Muscat, Oman
SNO	Senior Naval Officer
SSFA	Secretary of State for Foreign Affairs
SSI	Secretary of State for India
SSC	Secretary of State for the Colonies
UKPC	United Kingdom Privy Council—Proceedings of Cases before the Judicial Committee of the Privy Council (British Empire)
ZNA	Zanzibar National Archives

NOTES

INTRODUCTION

1. Marx, *Grundrisse*, 410, 524; Harvey, *Enigma of Capital*, 47. Marx and Harvey suggest that capital turns limits into barriers that can then be circumvented. I find this argument persuasive but suggest that it operates distinctly with regard to the definitional constraints of capitalism itself that I discuss below.

2. Karras, *Smuggling*, 7.

3. Smith, *Inquiry* bk. 5, chap. 2, 209.

4. Marx, *Grundrisse*, 415. Marx also suggests that there are inherent limits to capitalist production in the form of necessary labor, surplus value, money, and so on, but he is concerned with limits produced *by* capitalism rather than the conceptual limits that produce capitalism.

5. See the insightful analysis of maps and movement in Winichakul, *Siam Mapped;* de Certeau, *Practice of Everyday Life,* ch. 7; Schwartzberg, "Nautical Maps."

6. Pearson, "Littoral Society."

7. Regarding the concept of "itinerary," see de Certeau, *Practice of Everyday Life,* 116–20.

8. I cannot cite all of them, but there are myriad histories that follow the model of Braudel, *Mediterranean;* Chaudhuri, *Trade and Civilisation.* My use of the term *Arabian Sea* derives in part from Barendse, though I am not interested in the same structural and systemic questions. Barendse, *Arabian Seas.*

9. Regarding the distinction between history *of* the sea and *in* the sea, see Horden and Purcell, *Corrupting Sea,* 2, 9.

10. See Simpson, *Muslim Society,* Conclusion; Horden and Purcell, *Corrupting Sea;* Trivellato, *Familiarity of Strangers,* chaps. 4 and 8; Chaudhuri, *Asia before Europe,* chaps. 1 and 5.

11. This follows the knottiness and entanglement of History 1 and History 2 as formulated in Chakrabarty, *Provincializing Europe,* chap. 2.

12. *OED Online,* www.oed.com.silk.library.umass.edu/view/Entry/204334, s.v. "traffic, verb."

13. See Wallerstein, *World-Systems Analysis;* Hopkins, *Globalization in World History;* Pearson, *Indian Ocean.*

14. Pearson, *Indian Ocean,* 16–19, 197–99; Prange, "Trade of No Dishonor"; Chaudhuri, *Trade and Civilisation;* Barendse, "Trade and State," 211–18.

15. See Aslanian, *From the Indian Ocean;* Greif, *Institutions;* Trivellato, "From Livorno to Goa"; Markovits, *Global World.*

16. See Abdullah, *Merchants;* Onley, *Arabian Frontier.*

17. Smith, *Inquiry,* especially bk. 2, chap. 3.

18. Marx, *Capital,* especially vol. 3, chap. 48.

19. Polanyi, *Great Transformation,* 72–73.

20. The sea is not what de Certeau calls a "place" and is not subject to the panoptic orderings that he describes for cities. De Certeau, *Practice of Everyday Life.*

21. Callon, "Essay on Framing"; also see Goffman, *Frame Analysis;* Mitchell, *Colonising Egypt,* chap. 2; and the discussion of frontiers in de Certeau, *Practice of Everyday Life,* 127.

22. Foucault, *Security,* 346; Foucault, *Birth of Biopolitics,* 63–69; Mitchell, "Limits of the State"; Kalpagam, "Colonial Governmentality"; Roitman, *Fiscal Disobedience,* 2–3, 6–7.

23. See Callon, *Laws of the Markets;* MacKenzie, Muniesa, and Siu, *Do Economists Make Markets?*

24. Friedman, *Essays in Positive Economics;* McCloskey, *Rhetoric of Economics.*

25. Porter, *Rise of Statistical Thinking;* Desrosières, *Politics of Large Numbers.*

26. The quantitative emphasis of Jevons and Walras had broad impacts in the discipline eventually leading to the development of national income accounting by Fisher and eventually Kuznets in the early twentieth century. See Mitchell, "Fixing the Economy"; Mitchell, "Economentality"; Kalpagam, "Colonial Governmentality."

27. Gibson-Graham, *End of Capitalism;* Parthasarathi, "Was There Capitalism"; Mitchell, *Rule of Experts,* chap. 1.

28. Butler, *Gender Trouble;* Butler, "Performative Agency." My approach also builds on what Janet Roitman (*Fiscal Disobedience,* 2–3) calls the "historical inscription" of economic concepts.

29. See Mitchell, "Properties of Markets."

30. de Certeau, *Practice of Everyday Life,* xiv–xviii, 32–38; Scott, *Seeing Like a State,* 6–7, Ch. 9.

31. See Foucault, *Power/Knowledge;* Tsing, *Friction;* Gibson-Graham, *End of Capitalism;* Prestholdt, *Domesticating the World.*

32. Horii, "Reconsideration of Legal Devices"; Schacht, "Problems."

33. Hacking, "Looping Effect"; de Certeau, *Practice of Everyday Life,* 35, 107.

34. See Beunza, Hardie, and MacKenzie, "Price"; also see Benton, "Colonial Law"; Benton, *Law and Colonial Cultures,* 3, 13, 164.

35. For similar practices in Africa, see Guyer, "Niches"; Guyer, *Marginal Gains,* 37–47; Roitman, *Fiscal Disobedience.*

36. Guyer, *Marginal Gains,* 15, 155–56.

37. See Goodhart, "Problems of Monetary Management"; D. Campbell, "Assessing the Impact."

38. Sālimī, *Jawābāt al-Imām al-Sālimī*, 4:230.

39. Regarding the genre of the fatwa, see Masud, Messick, and Powers, *Islamic Legal Interpretation*.

40. See discussion of "measuring silences" in Spivak, "Can the Subaltern Speak?," 81–83; Trouillot, *Silencing the Past*.

41. Bhagwati and Hansen, "Theoretical Analysis of Smuggling"; M. Sheikh, "Theory of Risk."

42. McGoey, "Strategic Unknowns."

43. Trivellato, *Familiarity of Strangers*, chap. 6; Aslanian, "Salt."

44. Vimal Purecha, interview by author, June 22, 2008.

45. See Bahadur, *Coolie Woman*, 32.

46. See Morris, *Unknown Known*.

1. COMMODITIZING TRANSPORT

The proverb in the chapter's epigraph is taken from Jayakar, *Omani Proverbs*, 70.

1. Agius, *In the Wake*, 33–35; Gilbert, *Dhows*, 37; Sheriff, *Dhow Cultures*, 79–80.

2. Phillips-Birt, *Fore and Aft*, 58 n. 11.

3. See generally Leur, *Indonesian Trade and Society;* Meilink-Roelofsz, *Asian Trade;* Geertz, *Peddlers and Princes;* Steensgaard, *Carracks;* Subrahmanyam and Bayly, "Portfolio Capitalists."

4. See generally Gilbert, *Dhows;* Sheriff, *Dhow Cultures.*

5. NAUK: FO367/16, Ordinance Regarding the Registration of Sea-Going Dhows, East African Protectorate, 1906; IOR: R/20/B939, Legal Supplement to the Official Gazette No. 34 of July 12, 1941, Colony of Aden.

6. Government of Great Britain, *Muscat Dhows Arbitration*, Appendix 34, General Act of the Brussels Conference.

7. Ibid., Appendix 34, General Act of the Brussels Conference, Article 39.

8. NAUK: ADM127/40, Commander Columb, Reporting on the Slave Trade on the S.E. Coast of Arabia, H.M.S. "Dryad," June 30, 1869; NAUK: ADM127/40, Mājid bin Saʿīd, Sultan of Zanzibar, to H. A. Churchill, PA Zanzibar, December 1868; NAUK: FO881/1703, Memorandum by Mr. Churchill on Slave Trade on the East Coast of Africa, October 24, 1869; NAUK: HCA36/5, Decision of Vice-Admiralty Court, January 12, 1871.

9. IOR: R/20/C/1119, Imam of Yemen to Mr. Ingrams, Acting Governor, Aden, 17 Dhu al-Qaʾda 1359 (December 16, 1940).

10. Monfreid, *Pearls*, 92–105; Villiers, *Sons of Sinbad*, 110–52.

11. Government of Great Britain, *Muscat Dhows Arbitration*, Appendix 34, General Act of the Brussels Conference, Article 31.

12. NAUK: MT9/5400, The Aden Merchant Shipping Ordinance, 1943.

13. Villiers, *Sons of Sinbad*, 14.

14. MSA: Political Department, 1905, Vol. 137, No. 1428 (Henceforth P1905–137/1428), J. Sladen, Acting Secretary GoB, Marine, to Secretary GoI, DCI, No. 115-G, March 16, 1905.

15. NAI: Department of Revenue, Agriculture and Commerce, Commerce and Trade Series, Proceedings 7–26 (Henceforth RA&C/CT7–26), Government of Bombay Diary, September 8, 1876; NAI: DCI/MS6–7, January 1908, Report by Principal Surveyor for Tonnage, John T. Wilkins, to Asst. Secretary Board of Trade, Marine Dept., March 4, 1907; MSA: R1894–63C/888, Collector of Salt Revenue, Bombay, to Commissioner of Customs, December 20, 1894; MSA: R1894–63C/888, Gopal Dhoudba Musurkar to Under-Secretary GoB Revenue, January 18, 1895, and May 30, 1895.

16. NAUK: FO367/16, Ordinance Regarding the Registration of Sea-Going Dhows, East African Protectorate, 1906; IOR: R/20/B939, Legal Supplement to the Official Gazette No. 34 of July 12, 1941, Colony of Aden.

17. NAUK: ADM127/40, Return of Vessels Captured for the Slave Trade or Piracy, December 31, 1869; Villiers, *Sons of Sinbad*, 59.

18. IOR: R/20/B/938, Governor of Aden to Chief Secretary Government of Aden, November 15, 1940—Table of Dhows Which Sailed for Mukalla and Shihr between October 24, 1940, and November 13, 1940; IOR: R/20/B/1084, Statement Showing the Dhows Which Have Entered Shoqra, Nasir Ahmed, 7 Sha'ban 1358 (July 21, 1939); IOR: R/15/2/1373, Details of Dhow Accidents, Second Secretary PRPG, n.d. (June 1950).

19. Villiers, *Sons of Sinbad*, 14, 281.

20. Chaudhuri, *Trade and Civilisation*, 59–60, 108.

21. Villiers, *Sons of Sinbad*, 301.

22. IOR: R/15/5/45, PA Kuwait to First Asst. PRPG, December 29, 1909; IOR: R/15/5/45, Shakespear, PA Kuwait, to PRPG, December 20, 1910; NAUK: DO174/4, Note by E. H. C. Eyers, Commercial Officer, n.d. (July 1962).

23. Schwartzberg, "Nautical Maps"; S. Sheikh, "Gujarati Map."

24. IOR: R/20/B/939, Note on Dhows Built in Aden, Captain Wadison, n.d. (September 1940).

25. IOR: R/15/5/45, PA Kuwait, to First Asst. PRPG, December 29, 1909; IOR: R/15/5/45, Shakespear, PA Kuwait, to PRPG, December 20, 1910; IOR: R/15/2/359, Political Officer Trucial Coast, Sharjah, to PA Bahrain, March 15, 1942; IOR: R/15/2/1376, A. M. Green, Collector of Customs, Bombay, to PRPG, February 23, 1924; IOR: R/15/2/1376, N. R. Pillai, Collector of Customs, Bombay, to PA Muscat, April 7, 1937; IOR: R/15/2/1376, P. N. Chandavarkar, Collector of Customs, Bombay, to PRPG, October 28, 1938.

26. IOR: R/20/B/939, Legal Supplement to the Official Gazette of the Colony of Aden, No. 34, July 12, 1941.

27. MSA: P1880–217/820, Kirk, PA Zanzibar, to Earl Granville, November 30, 1880; MSA: P1880–217/820, Report of Port Officer Bombay, May 31, 1881; NAUK: FO371/82004, British Residency Bahrain to G. W. Furlonge, FO, May 4, 1950; NAUK: DO174/4, Note by E. H. C. Eyers, Commercial Officer, n.d. (July 1962);

NAUK: DO174/4, H. C. Jakins, PA Kuwait, to H. J. Evans, PRPG, May 5, 1951; also see Çalışkan, *Market Threads,* chap. 2.

28. MSA: P/1905–25/583, R. P. Schneider, Asst. Resident, Perim, to F. B. Hancock, First Asst. PR Aden, September 21, 1905; MSA: P/1907–24/277, Edmund S. Poe, Commander-in-Chief East Indies to Admiralty, January 29, 1906; NAUK: FO248/1612, H. F. Bartlett, Consulate Khorramshahr, to B. H. C. Sykes, British Embassy Tehran, September 8, 1965.

29. NAUK: FO248/1612, H. F. Bartlett, Consulate Khorramshahr, to B. H. C. Sykes, British Embassy Tehran, September 8, 1965.

30. IOR: R/20/A/2932, C. Crawfurd, HMS *Minto,* to SNO Southern Red Sea, October 31, 1915.

31. Schaefer, "'Selling at a Wash'"; Villiers, *Sons of Sinbad,* 253; Villiers, "Some Aspects." Also see the concept of "relational value" in Elyachar, *Markets of Dispossession,* 7, 189–90.

32. Villiers, "Some Aspects"; Gilbert, *Dhows,* 97–99; Geertz, "Bazaar Economy"; Geertz, *Peddlers and Princes,* 40.

33. Rispler-Chaim, "Insurance and Semi-insurance Transactions"; Mankabady, "Insurance and Islamic Law."

34. GL: EB39, 010/20, M. Gunn, Bahrain, to Golder, London, December 10, 1947; NAUK: CO852/1245/2, Convention on the Valuation of Goods for Customs Purposes, 1950–51, Part II, p. 40.

35. Villiers, *Sons of Sinbad,* 253.

36. NAI: RA&C/CT7–26, 12/1877, Rules for the Measurement of Tonnage of Native Craft; IOR: R/15/1/130, Insurance Agents to Charles Allen, Secretary GoI Calcutta, June 23, 1852; IOR: R/15/2/1373, Manager, Paramount Tea Company, Bombay, to PA Kuwait, January 14, 1947; NAUK: CAB37/99/63, Marine Insurance (Gambling Policies), April 20, 1909.

37. NAUK: FO539/79, H. M. Hozier, Lloyd's, to FO, April 15, 1898; NAUK: FO539/79, extracts from the *Times* regarding Fracis Times & Co. v. The Sea Insurance Co., June 25, 1898, May 30, 1898, and July 5, 1898.

38. IOR: R/20/A/2960, W. Baddeley, Admiralty, to Under-SSFA, September 22, 1919; IOR: R/20/A/2960, Aden Residency Note, November 15, 1919; IOR: R/20/A/2960, James Stewart, PR Aden, to High Commissioner, Cairo, December 2, 1919; IOR: R/20/A/2960, Cowasjee Dinshaw to C. C. J. Barrett, First Asst. PR Aden, July 12, 1921.

39. Villiers, *Sons of Sinbad,* 308.

40. This of course does not apply to shipwrecks, which could be relatively frequent; see Mathew, "Moral Economies of Violence."

41. Furuseth, *Safety of Life,* 7.

42. MSA: M1904–80/26, Statement of Hamad bin Hamad, *Nākhodā* of Baghla Fath al-Khair, May 3, 1904; MSA: M1904–80/26, Report of P. J. Maitland, Vice Admiralty Judge, May 6, 1904; MSA: P1907–95/1525, Commissioner of Sind, Memo. No. 2679, November 28, 1894.

43. MSA: P1907–95/1525, Commissioner of Sind, Memo. No. 1595, October 10, 1907; Villiers, *Sons of Sinbad,* 214.

44. MSA: M1904–80/26, Report of P. J. Maitland, Vice Admiralty Judge, May 6, 1904; MSA: P1907–95/1525, Commissioner of Sind, Memo. No. 2679, November 28, 1894; IOR: L/PS/20/C229, Report of Shipping Casualties, September 21, 1891.

45. IOR: R/15/2/1373, Manager, Gray Mackenzie, Bahrain, to PA Bahrain, April 21, 1945; IOR: R/15/2/1369, Statements Taken by PA Bahrain after Collision on August 12, 1929; IOR: R/15/2/1369, PA Bahrain to Secretary to PRPG, April 18, 1930.

46. NMM: BIS/7/46 [MS77/081], R. J. Rickford, Commander S.S. "Pachumba," to Mackinnon Mackenzie & Co., BISN Agents, August 3, 1901; NMM: BIS/8/6, Lord Inchcape, Chairman of BISN, to J. S. Henderson, BISN Calcutta, May 18, 1932; IOR: R/15/6/331, Ext. 8529/47, E. P. Donaldson, IO, to Secretary GoI External Affairs, March 4, 1947.

47. C. Davies, *Blood-Red Arab Flag*, 294; Midura, "Flags."

48. Benton, "Legal Spaces of Empire," 702–4.

49. NAUK: FO84/1120, W. M. Coghlan, Muscat-Zanzibar Commission, to H. L. Anderson, Chief Secretary GoB, November 1, 1860; NAUK: HCA 36/5, J. Kirk, Acting PA Zanzibar, to Chief Secretary GoB, April 10, 1869.

50. NAUK: FO27/3489, Memorandum by John Kirk, PA Zanzibar, March 9, 1898.

51. Miers, *Britain*, 293.

52. NAUK: FO27/3489, Saqar ibn Khalid, Sheikh of Sharjah, to PRPG, 19 Muharram 1310 (September 1892); NAUK: FO27/3489, J. Hayes Sadler, PA Muscat, to PRPG, September 26, 1894.

53. NAUK: FO27/3489, F. A. Wilson, PRPG to Secretary GoI, Foreign Dept., October 6, 1894.

54. NAUK: FO27/3489, C. J. Baker, SNO Persian Gulf, to E. C. Drummond, Commander-in-Chief East Indies, October 1, 1896.

55. NAUK: FO27/3489, Arthur Hardinge to Marquess of Salisbury, SSFA, April 26, 1897; NAUK: FO27/3489, C. J. Baker, SNO Persian Gulf, to E. C. Drummond, Commander-in-Chief East Indies, October 8, 1896.

56. NAUK: FO27/3489, H. F., Foreign Office to India Office, September 2, 1897.

57. NAUK: FO27/3489, Col. E. V. Stace, PA Somali Coast, to PR Aden, March 17, 1892; NAUK: FO27/3489, Arthur Hardinge to Marquess of Salisbury, SSFA, April 26, 1897.

58. NAUK: ADM127/30, Capt. H. Boyes, SNO Persian Gulf, to Commander-in-Chief East Indies, August 17, 1928.

59. NAI: F1937/583-N, Notes from Intelligence Bureau, M. Mazhar, September 9, 1937; NAI: F1937/583-N, PA Kuwait to Secretary to PRPG, December 20, 1937; IOR: R/15/2/1376, Residency Agent, Sharjah, to PA Bahrain, February 9, 1939; NAUK: ADM1/20627, W. R. Hay, PRPG, to Ernest Bevin, FO, January 13, 1949.

60. IOR: R/15/6/160, Note by T. C. Fowle, PRPG, April 6, 1937.

61. NMM: CAY/85/10, Statement of W. P. Orr, n.d.; NMM: CAY/85/5, Statement of E. C. Gould, n.d.

62. NAUK: MT9/5400, Note by G. V. Cameron, Legal Advisor on Aden Merchant Shipping Ordinance, October 23, 1937; NAUK: MT9/5400, Aden Merchant Shipping Ordinance 1943.

63. *Bandar* (also *bunder*) is the Persian word for port but was used across the Indian Ocean especially to refer to areas where *dhows* landed.

64. NAUK: MT9/5400, File M6360/1938, Rules under Section 12(1)(c) of the Aden Merchant Shipping Ordinance.

65. NAI: DCI/MS28, 1/1918, Statement Showing Sailing Vessels That Left Karachi for Foreign Countries, 1915–16 and 1916–17; IOR: R/20/B/1084, Letter from Nasir Ahmed, 7 Sha'ban 1358, Enclosing Statement of Dhows Entering Shuqra, October 4–10, 1939; IOR: R/20/B/938, Statements Showing Dhows Proceeding to Mokalla and Shehr, August 24, 1940, and November 13, 1940; IOR: R/20/C/2537, Dhow Traffic to Yemen, October 28, 1939, to January 30, 1940.

66. IOR: R/20/B/1438, Chairman, Port Trust Aden, to Chief Secretary to Govt. of Aden, July 13, 1942.

67. MSA: P1907–24/277, Edmund Poe, Commander-in-Chief East Indies, to Admiralty, No. 68/49, January 29, 1906; IOR: R/15/5/45, First Asst. PRPG to PA Kuwait, February 22, 1910; NAUK: ADM 127/38, Declaration of Blockade, November 29, 1888.

68. NAUK: MT9/5400, Blockade Rules under Section 12(1)(c) of the Aden Merchant Shipping Ordinance, 1938.

69. NAUK: T161/90, Memo by W. M. P. Wood, First Asst. Resident Aden, September 6, 1917.

70. IOR: R/20/A/2960, W. Baddeley, Admiralty, to Under-SSFA, September 22, 1919; IOR: R/20/A/2960, W. R. W. Kettlewell, HMS Espiegle, to Rear Admiral, Egypt, July 15, 1919.

71. IOR: R/20/A/3994, Shipping Bond of Munasir bin Ali et al., September 30, 1916.

72. IOR: R/15/2/1376, N. R. Pillai, Collector of Customs, Bombay, to PA Muscat, April 7, 1937; IOR: R/15/2/1376, P. N. Chandavarkar, Collector of Customs, Bombay, to PRPG, October 28, 1938.

73. IOR: R/15/2/1376, A. M. Green, Collector of Customs, Bombay, to PRPG, February 23, 1924; IOR: R/15/2/1376, P. N. Chandavarkar, Collector of Customs, Bombay, to PRPG, October 28, 1938.

74. IOR: R/15/2/1376, PA Bahrain to PRPG, February 21, 1939.

75. IOR: R/15/2/1376, N. R. Pillai, Collector of Customs, Bombay, to PA Muscat, April 7, 1937.

76. IOR: R/15/2/1376, Residency Agent, Sharjah, to PA Bahrain, February 9, 1939; IOR: R/15/2/1376, PA Bahrain to PRPG, February 21, 1939; IOR: R/15/2/1376, M. E. Rahman, Collector of Customs, Bombay, to PA Bahrain, May 17, 1937.

77. See the discussion of documentary circulation in Çalışkan, *Market Threads*, 71–75.

78. Thompson and Adloff, *Djibouti*, 15–22.

79. IOR: R/20/B/1860, Port Officer, Aden to Officer of the Crown Court of Admiralty in Prize, Aden, November 29, 1940; IOR: R/20/C/1119, Acting Chief Secretary to Govt. of Aden to Resident Advisor, Mukalla, October 2, 1940.

80. IOR: R/20/C/1119, Asst. Frontier Officer to Chief Secy. to Govt. of Aden, December 14, 1940, and December 23, 1940; IOR: R/20/C/1119, Idris F. Baxamusa, Hodeidah, to Governor of Aden, December 25, 1940.

81. IOR: R/20/C/1119, Controller of Civil Supplies to Chief Secretary Govt. of Aden, January 2, 1941; R/20/B/1324, War Trade Reporting Officer, Khartoum to Ministry of Economic Warfare, London, December 18, 1939.

82. Thompson and Adloff, *Djibouti,* 15–22.

83. IOR: R/15/2/359, Baluchistan Intelligence Bureau, Quetta, to K. B. M. Mazhar, Asst. Director Intelligence, Govt. of India, November 26, 1936; IOR: R/15/2/359, Residency Agent, Sharjah, to PA Bahrain, January 5, 1943; Monfreid, *Pearls,* 93–97; also see Monfreid, *Secrets.*

84. NAUK: FO/1016/92, PA Gwadar to F. C. L. Chauncy, PA Muscat, May 20, 1950.

85. IOR: R/15/6/60, Khimji Ramdas, Sur, to PA Muscat, July 28, 1925; IOR: R/15/2/359, Diary of Dhow Searching Patrol 8, May 13, 1944.

86. Villiers, *Sons of Sinbad,* 117–18, 146; Government of Great Britain, *Muscat Dhows Arbitration,* Appendix 29, Annex 1, Statement of British Subject at Sur Regarding the Slave Season of 1901.

87. MSA: P1902–157/371, PA Muscat, to Govt. of Bombay, No. 495, December 27, 1901; IOR: R/20/C1119, Note by E. A. S., October 28, 1940; IOR: R/20/B/1309, Confidential Report re: Yemen-Aden Border, November 11, 1939.

88. Monfreid, *Pearls,* 230–31.

89. NAUK: DO 174/4, P. H. C. Eyers, Commercial Officer, n.d. (07/1962).

90. A similar vision of market formation is modeled in White, *Markets from Networks.*

91. See Munro, *Maritime Enterprise and Empire;* Cain and Hopkins, "Gentlemanly Capitalism"; Podolny and Scott Morton, "Social Status."

92. IOR: R/15/6/34, Memorandum by PA Muscat on the British Position on the Arabian Littoral of the Persian Gulf, 1921.

93. NAI: DCI/CT1–4, 9/1905, File 23—Indian Daily News, April 20, 1905; IOR: L/PS/20/C247, Précis of Correspondence on International Rivalry and British Policy in the Persian Gulf, 1872–1905.

94. MSA: R1907–341/1777, C. H. Armstrong and C. F. Michael, Chamber of Commerce, Bombay, to Under-Secretary Govt. of Bombay, April 25, 1907; MSA: R1907–341/1777, J. B. Leslie-Rogers to Under-Secretary Govt. of Bombay, May 24, 1907; IOR: R/15/2/1379, Dhamanmal Isardas to PA Bahrain, January 3, 1934; NAUK: FO371/4938, Intel. Summary of PA Muscat for August 1949; NAI: DCI/CT11–23, 9/1905, File 19—Major P. Z. Cox, PA Muscat, to PRPG, August 5, 1903.

95. IOR: R/20/B/1829, Cowasjee Dinshaw & Bros to Chief Secretary to Govt. of Aden, November 11, 1940; IOR: R/20/B/1829, Controller of Civil Supplies to Acting Chief Secretary to Govt. of Aden, December 4, 1940.

96. IOR: R/20/A/2960, W. Baddeley, Admiralty, to Under-SSFA, September 22, 1919.

97. MSA: P1880–159/1670, Gray Paul & Co., Bushire to Gray Dawes & Co., London, No. 1038, December 3, 1880; NAI: DCI/MS24–35(A), October 1907, File 7—R. P. Barrow, Acting Chief Secretary to GoB, to Secretary GoI, DCI, June 15, 1907.

98. GL: ICG 27/639, Working of Bombay and Karachi Conference Lines, January 1930.

99. NMM: CAY/174, Britain-India Conference Agreements; NMM: CAY/85/1, Reminiscences of Fred Bedford, n.d.; Mehta, *Indian Shipping.*

100. NAI: DCI/MS24–35(A), 10/1907, File 7—R. P. Barrow, Acting Chief Secretary to GoB, to Secretary GoI, DC&I, June 15, 1907; Cohen, Bateman, and Barbour, *Report;* Mehta, *Indian Shipping.*

101. NAUK: FO371/4938, PRPG to B. A. B. Burrows, FO, October 6, 1949.

102. GL: ICG27/605, Memo by D. Black on Persian Gulf Steam Navigation Co.; Blake, *B. I. Centenary.*

103. GL: ICG27/605, D. Black to Mackinnon Mackenzie & Co., Calcutta, September 16, 1924.

104. NMM: SRI/17/1, Frank Strick to Louis Mallet, FO, October 5, 1909; NMM: CAY/85/1, Reminiscences of Fred Bedford, n.d.; GL: ICG27/639, Working of Bombay and Karachi Conference Lines, January 1930.

105. IOR: R/20/A/2960, W. Baddeley, Admiralty, to Under-SSFA, September 22, 1919; IOR: R/20/A/2960, Major General James Stewart, PR Aden, to High Commissioner, Cairo, December 2, 1919; IOR: R/20/A/2960, Captain M. Fazluddin, Indian Medical Service, Loheiya, to Major Barrett, January 7, 1920; IOR: R/20/A/2960, Note of First Asst. PR Aden, February 10, 1920.

106. NMM: BIS/8/6, Earl Inchcape, Chairman of BISN, to J.H. Fyfe, BISN Calcutta, February 19, 1930, and February 18, 1930; NMM: BIS/8/6, L. C. Harris, February 17, 1930.

107. See Patel, *Alibhai Mulla Jeevanjee;* Patel, *Challenge to Colonialism.*

108. NMM: BIS/8/2, Memo of Meeting between BISN and A. M. Jeevanjee & Co., October 23, 1909.

109. NMM: BIS/8/1, Ruthven G. Monteath, Mackinnon Mackenzie & Co., Bombay, to Alick Monteath, Mackinnon Mackenzie, Calcutta, June 23, 1909; NMM: BIS/8/1, A. M. Monteath, Mackinnon Mackenzie, Calcutta, to James Lyle Mackay, Earl Inchcape, July 1, 1909; NMM: BIS/8/2, Memo of Meeting between BISN and A.M. Jeevanjee & Co., October 23, 1909; NMM: BIS/8/2, Mackinnon Mackenzie, Calcutta, to Mackinnon Mackenzie, Bombay, January 10, 1910.

110. Villiers, *Sons of Sinbad,* 78–79, 189, 253.

111. NMM: BIS/2/1 BISN, Memoranda, 1914, pp. 38–39; NMM: SRI/16/3, Contract between Frank C. Strick & Co. and Haji Ali Akbar, April 30, 1914.

112. GL: ICG 27/639, Working of Bombay and Karachi Conference Lines, January 1930; NMM: BIS/7/46, A. M. Monteath to Turner, August 15, 1901.

113. IOR: R/20/A/2960, Aden Residency Memorandum, n.d. (June 1920).

114. Statements of Persons Who Broke Out of Quarantine, Taken by Capt. Percy Z. Cox, Political Agent at Muscat, on April 11, 1903, Appendix No. 32 to Government of Great Britain, *Muscat Dhows Arbitration*, 80–86.

2. TRAFFICKING LABOR

1. MSA: P1879–129/239. This account is built from various pieces of correspondence collected in this file. Also see Chatterjeee, "Abolition by Denial."

2. Miers, "Slave Resistance and Rebellion"; see generally Toledano, *As If Silent*.

3. See generally Cooper, *Plantation Slavery;* Cooper, *From Slaves to Squatters;* Chatterjee, *Gender;* Campbell, *Abolition and Its Aftermath;* Harms, Freamon, and Blight, *Indian Ocean Slavery;* Hopper, *Slaves of One Master*.

4. Concerning the illicit slave trade, see Hopper, *Slaves of One Master;* Miers, *Britain;* Clarence-Smith, "Economics"; Austen, "19th Century Islamic Slave Trade"; Ricks, "Slaves and Slave Traders"; Carter and Gerbeau, "Covert Slaves"; Pankhurst, "Ethiopian Slave Trade."

5. See Tinker, *New System of Slavery;* R. Allen, *Slaves;* Carter, *Servants;* Anderson, *Convicts*.

6. NAUK: FO84/692, Treaty Concluded between the Imam of Muscat and Captain Moresby, August 29, 1822. Slave trading was permitted only west of the lines in Map 1; the Royal Navy was permitted to seize dhows carrying slaves for sale at any point east.

7. NAUK: FO93/65/2, Agreement for the Termination of the Export of Slaves, February 10, 1845.

8. IOR: R/15/6/4, Treaty for the Further Suppression of the Slave Trade with the Sultan of Muscat, December 4, 1873.

9. Seccombe and Lawless, "Foreign Worker Dependence."

10. MSA: P1878–135/877, S. Miles, PA Muscat, to E. C. Ross, PRPG, July 3, 1878; NAUK: ADM127/40, Commander Columb to Commodore L. G. Heath, June 30, 1869; G. Campbell, *Structure of Slavery,* 6–7, 89–91; G. Campbell and Alpers, "Introduction"; Vink, "'World's Oldest Trade,'" 142–43.

11. NAUK: ADM127/38, Admiral E. R. Freemantle to G. H. Portal, Acting PA Zanzibar, October 18, 1889; also see generally Alpers, *Ivory and Slaves;* Sheriff, *Slaves*.

12. MSA: P1873–114/64, Memorandum of Conversation between H. B. E. Frere and Khedive of Egypt, December 17, 1872; NAUK: HCA36/5, Report by the Committee on the East African Slave Trade, January 24, 1870; Edward Alpers, "Story of Swema."

13. NAUK: FO881/1703, Memo re: Slave Trade on the East Coast of Africa, Churchill, PA Zanzibar, October 24, 1869; Villiers, *Sons of Sinbad,* 117–18.

14. NAUK: HCA36/5, Moosa ibn Mohammed Hakeem to Mahomed ibn Harjee, October 28, 1868.

15. NAUK: ADM127/42, Slave Trade Report by Commander Foot to Rear Admiral Macdonald, October 10, 1875; Villiers, *Sons of Sinbad,* 117–18.

16. NAUK: FO84/1146, Lt. Col. C. P. Rigby, PA Zanzibar, to H. L. Anderson, Chief Secy. to Govt. of Bombay, May 14, 1861; NAUK: HCA36/5, Lt. Col. C. P. Rigby, PA Zanzibar, to A. K. Forbes, Acting Secy. to Govt. of Bombay, July 12, 1861; NAUK: ADM 127/40, Commander Columb Reporting on the Slave Trade in the Persian Gulf, June 30, 1869; Vianello and Kassim, *Servants of the Sharia*, Register Nos. 29.1, 338.1, 386.1, 561.1–562.5, 566.1, 759.1, 780.1, 824.2, and 930.1. Also see generally Machado, *Ocean of Trade,* chap. 5; G. Campbell, introduction to *Structure of Slavery.*

17. NAUK: ADM127/40, Majid ibn Sa'īd, Sultan of Zanzibar, to H. A. Churchill, PA Zanzibar, December 1868.

18. MSA: P1873–114/63, Memorandum re: Slave Market at Zanzibar, Clement Hill, January 17, 1873; MSA: P1873–114/63, H. B. E. Frere to Earl Granville, February 17, 1873.

19. IOR: R/15/6/4, Lt. Col. E. C. Ross, Acting PRPG, to H. B. E. Frere, November 18, 1872; NAUK: FO84/692, Remarks of J. B. Kemball, Asst. PRPG, on Treaty of 1822, n.d. (ca. 1847).

20. MSA: P1879–129/239, Statements of Accused Slave Traders, December 19, 1878; IOR: R/15/6/5, Examination of *Nākhudā* of Slave Dhow "Yasmeen," September 12, 1872; NAUK: ADM127/40, Extracts from Letters Found in Dhow No. 5, August 30, 1868, to October 28, 1868.

21. NAUK: FO881/1703, Report from Mr. Rothery Respecting the Dhows Lately Captured, September 6, 1869; NAUK: ADM127/41, PR Aden to Secy. Govt. of Bombay, June 3, 1873.

22. NAUK: FO84/692, H. Rawlinson, Consul General, Baghdad, to Lt. Col. Shiel, Envoy to Tehran, November 8, 1849; NAUK: FO84/692, Remarks of J. B. Kemball, Asst. PRPG, on Treaty of 1822, n.d. (ca. 1847); NAUK: FO84/815, Atkins Hamerton, PA Muscat, to Lord Palmerston, SSFA, August 20, 1850.

23. ZNA: AL1/13, German Consul to Sultan Majid of Zanzibar, 26 Muharram 1279H, p47; ZNA: AM1/6, Contract between Mohammed bin Saif al-Daramki and Rashid bin Salim al-Harithi, 15 Shawwal 1311H, p. 168; see generally Vianello and Kassim, *Servants of the Sharia.*

24. Cooper, *Plantation Slavery,* 135.

25. NAUK: FO84/1000, Captain Christopher to Admiral Josceline Percy, May 5, 1843.

26. NAUK: HCA36/5, Admiralty Memorandum on Mr. Seward's (PA Zanzibar) Despatch, September 9, 1866.

27. NAUK: HCA36/5, Memorandum by Kazi Shahabuddin, February 14, 1870.

28. NAUK: FO84/815, Commander B. H. Bunce to Commodore Wyville, Commander-in-Chief East Indies, May 27, 1850.

29. It is not clear which river Bunce was referring to, but it is probably the Mozambique channel.

30. NAUK: FO84/815, Commander B. H. Bunce to Commodore Wyville, Commander-in-Chief East Indies, June 8, 1850.

31. MSA: P1873–114/63, H. B. E. Frere to Earl Granville, May 29, 1873.

32. MSA: P1873–114/63, Memorandum of conversation between H. B. E. Frere and the Khedive of Egypt, December 17, 1872.

33. MSA: P1873–114/63, H. B. E. Frere to Earl Granville, May 29, 1873.

34. NAUK: ADM127/40, Commander Columb, Reporting on the Slave Trade, June 30, 1869.

35. NAUK: HCA36/5, Commodore L. Heath to Secy. to Admiralty, September 2, 1868.

36. NAUK: HCA36/5, Foreign Office Memorandum on Mr. Seward's Despatch, December 8, 1868.

37. NAUK: FO84/1204, R. L. Playfair, Acting PA Zanzibar, to H. L. Anderson, Chief Secy. Govt. of Bombay, May 23, 1863; NAUK: HCA36/5, Certificate of Liberation, n.d.; NAUK: HCA36/5, Foreign Office Memo on Mr. Seward's Despatch, December 8, 1868.

38. NAUK: ADM127/38, Blockade Memo 14 from Rear Admiral E. R. Freemantle, March 25, 1889.

39. NAUK: ADM127/40, Moosa ibn Mohamed Hakeem to Mohamed ibn Harjee, October 28, 1868.

40. NAUK: FO881/1703, Commodore L. G. Heath to Secy. of the Admiralty, March 1, 1869.

41. NAUK: FO84/1146, Lt. Col. C. P. Rigby, PA Zanzibar, to H. L. Anderson, Chief Secy. to Govt. of Bombay, May 14, 1861.

42. Ibid.; NAUK: FO84/1261, Edwin Seward, PA Zanzibar, to C. Gonne, Chief Secy. to Govt. of Bombay, September 10, 1866.

43. IOR: R/15/6/4, Political Dept. Govt. of Bombay, to Acting PA Kutch, December 31, 1872; NAUK: HCA36/5, Notice to British Subjects in Zanzibar, C. P. Rigby, PA Zanzibar, February 15, 1860.

44. NAUK: HCA36/5, Rigby, PA Zanzibar, to Anderson, Secy. Govt. of Bombay, February 11, 1860, March 21, 1860, and March 28, 1860.

45. NAUK: HCA36/5, Lt. Col. Pelly, Acting PA Zanzibar, to Bombay Govt., February 2, 1862.

46. NAUK: FO84/1146, C. P. Rigby, PA Zanzibar, to H. L. Anderson, Chief Secy. to Govt. of Bombay, May 14, 1861.

47. Cooper, *Plantation Slavery,* 128–29.

48. NAUK: FO84/1120, Brigadier General W. M. Coghlan to H. L. Anderson, Chief Secy. Govt. of Bombay, November 1, 1860 (quoting Col. Rigby).

49. NAUK: HCA36/5, Report by the Committee on the East African Slave Trade, January 24, 1870.

50. NAUK: ADM127/40, H. A. Churchill to Sayyid Majid, Sultan of Zanzibar, December 10, 1868.

51. NAUK: HCA36/5, Report by the Committee on the East African Slave Trade, January 24, 1870; NAUK: ADM127/38, Admiral E. R. Freemantle to G. H. Portal, Acting PA Zanzibar, October 18, 1889.

52. NAUK: FO84/1261, E. Seward, PA Zanzibar, to C. Gonne, Secy. Govt. of Bombay, September 10, 1866.

53. NAUK: FO881/1703, L. Heath to Secy. Admiralty, March 1, 1869.

54. NAUK: FO84/1120, Brigadier General W. M. Coghlan to H. L. Anderson, Chief Secy. GoB, November 1, 1860; NAUK: FO 84/1204, R. L. Playfair, Acting PA Zanzibar, to H. L. Anderson, Chief Secy. GoB, May 23, 1863.

55. NAUK: FO84/1245, R. L. Playfair, PA Zanzibar, to Earl Russell, Foreign Minister, May 30, 1865; NAUK: ADM 127/27, Decision in re: Dhows "Jameela" and "Fath al Karim," E. V. Stace, Asst. PR Aden, September 19, 1892.

56. ZNA: AA5/19, Letter to Sultan of Zanzibar, May 13, 1890; NAUK: HCA36/5, Commodore L. Heath to Secy. Admiralty, April 7, 1868.

57. NAUK: ADM127/41, Capt. L. Wood to Rear Admiral Charles Shadwell, October 24, 1873; NAUK: HCA36/5, Decision of Vice-Admiralty Court, January 12, 1871.

58. Colomb, *Slave-Catching*, 33.

59. NAUK: ADM 127/42, Commander Foot, SNO Persian Gulf, to Rear Admiral R. J. Macdonald, Commander-in-Chief, October 10, 1875.

60. IOR: R/15/6/415, R. W. Bullard, British Legation Jedda, to Viscount Halifax, FO, November 14, 1939.

61. IOR: R/15/6/417, Statements of Liberated Slaves.

62. NAUK: FO84/1120, Brigadier General W. M. Coghlan to H. L. Anderson, Chief Secy. Govt. of Bombay, November 1, 1860.

63. NAUK: ADM 127/42, Commander Foot, SNO Persian Gulf, to Rear Admiral R. J. Macdonald, Commander-in-Chief East Indies, October 10, 1875.

64. NAUK: ADM127/42, Commander Foot, SNO Persian Gulf, to R. J. Macdonald, Commander-in-Chief East Indies, October 10, 1875.

65. NAUK: ADM127/27, Henry Dyke, SNO, to Frederick Robinson, Commander-in-Chief East Indies, July 1, 1891, and January 1, 1892; NAUK: ADM127/27, Henry Dyke, SNO, to William Kennedy, Commander-in-Chief East Indies, January 1, 1893.

66. Sheriff, *Afro-Arab Interaction*, 11–12.

67. Sheriff, *Slaves*. This is disputed in part by Matthew Hopper, but his analysis does not dispute the predominance of children in the slave traffic to the Gulf. Hopper, "African Presence in Arabia," 198.

68. NAUK: ADM127/44, Slave Trade Report of Commander Charles Anson, January 22, 1885; NAUK: ADM127/40, Extracts from Blue Books re: Slave Trade, January 1, 1866, to December 31, 1866; NAUK: ADM127/40, Commodore L. G. Heath to Secy. of the Admiralty, April 9, 1869; NAUK: FO881/1703, Report of Mr. Rothery, August 21, 1869; NAUK: ADM 127/44, Commander Hubert Dowding to Capt Robert Boyle, May 21, 1883; etc.

69. IOR: R/15/6/5, Extracts of Letters from the Slave Dhow "Yasmeen," September 1872.

70. IOR: R/15/6/414, George Maxwell, British Representative on Commission on Slavery, to Under-SSFA, April 22, 1935.

71. MSA: P1878–135/877, Consul G. Beyts to Earl of Derby, SSFA, June 20, 1877.

72. MSA: P1878–135/877, Vice Admiral R. MacDonald to Secy. Admiralty, April 1, 1877; MSA: P1878–135/877, Nixon, Consul-General Baghdad to SSFA, March 26, 1877; P1889–294/1454, Commander Gissing to Admiral Freemantle, January 1, 1889; A. Powell, "Indian Muslim Modernists."

73. MSA: P1871–65/96, Haji Mahomed Jaffer, Merchant of Bushire, to Mirza Mahomed Khan, Slave Commission (Iran), November 3, 1870. For a fascinating discussion of "aggressive" forms of charity as acts of enslavement, see Indrani Chatterjee, "Slavery," 294–97.

74. MSA: P1878–135/877, S. B. Miles, PA Muscat, to E. C. Ross, PRPG, March 7, 1878. For an excellent discussion of manumission in East Africa, see McDow, "Deeds of Free Slaves."

75. MSA: P1873–114/63, Memorandum re: Slave Market at Zanzibar, Clement Hill, January 17, 1873.

76. MSA: P1889–220/440, Petition of Naz al-Bustan to the Commissioner of Police, Bombay, February 11, 1889 (It is unclear from the documents whether Khalifa was a member of the ruling family of Bahrain).

77. MSA: P1878–135/877, E. C. Ross, PRPG, to Secy. Govt. of India, Foreign Dept., March 13, 1878.

78. IOR: R/15/6/4, Lt. Col. E. C. Ross, Acting PRPG, to H. B. E. Frere, November 18, 1872; also see Brunschvig, "'Abd."

79. NAUK: ADM127/42, Commander Foot, SNO Persian Gulf, to R. J. Macdonald, Commander-in-Chief East Indies, October 10, 1875.

80. IOR: R/15/6/415, R. W. Bullard, British Legation Jedda, to Viscount Halifax, FO, November 14, 1939.

81. Sheriff, *Afro-Arab Interaction,* 10.

82. MSA: P1878–135/877, E. C. Ross, PRPG, to Secy. Govt. of India, Foreign Dept., April 20, 1878.

83. MSA: P1878–135/877, E. C. Ross, PRPG, to Secy. Govt. of India, Foreign Dept., March 13, 1878.

84. MSA: P1879–129/239, Bombay Police Commissioner to J. Nugent, Acting Secy. Govt. of Bombay, April 25, 1879.

85. NAUK: FO84/1261, Edwin Seward, PA Zanzibar, to C. Gonne, Secy. Govt. of Bombay, October 25, 1866.

86. NAUK: ADM127/40, E. L. Russell, PR Aden, to Secy. Govt. of Bombay, December 24, 1868.

87. NAUK: ADM127/27, Decision in re: Dhows *"Jameela"* and *"Fath al Karim,"* E. V. Stace, Asst. PR Aden, September 19, 1892. See also E. Powell, *Different Shade of Colonialism.*

88. IOR: L/PS/18/B408, "Slave Trade in the Persian Gulf," by J. G. Lorimer, September 29, 1928; IOR: R/15/2/143, Report by A. Razzaq, Residency Agent, Sharjah, November 12, 1944; IOR: R/15/6/415–417, Slave Statements, described in Sheriff, "Social Mobility"; Hopper, "Imperialism."

89. MSA: P1873–114/63, H. B. E. Frere to Earl Granville, February 17, 1873.

90. ZNA: AM7/1, Various labor contracts with former slaves as servants.

91. MSA: P1873–114/63, H.B.E. Frere to Dr. Kirk, PA Zanzibar, April 1, 1873.

92. NAUK: ADM127/40, Commander L.G. Heath to Lord Fitzgerald, Governor of Bombay, January 19, 1869; NAUK: HCA36/5, Report by the Committee on the East African Slave Trade, January 24, 1870.

93. NAUK: HCA36/5, Secy. Church Missionary Society to SSFA, November 30, 1869.

94. NAUK: FO881/1703, Civil Commissioner of Seychelles to H. Barkly, Mauritius, May 6, 1869.

95. MSA: P1890–222/241, Govt. of Bombay to Colonial Secy. to Govt. of Fiji, January 16, 1890; MSA: P1897–149/276, Govt. of India, Foreign Department, to SSI, January 13, 1897.

96. NAUK: FO84/1261, Dr. Seward, Acting PA Zanzibar, to C. Gonne, Secy. Govt. of Bombay, July 14, 1866.

97. NAUK: FO84/1261, Dr. Seward, Acting PA Zanzibar, to C. Gonne, Secy. Govt. of Bombay, October 25, 1866.

98. ZNA: AB69/3, Zanzibar Christian Natives to PR Zanzibar, April 20, 1922; ZNA: AB69/3, Letter (possibly from missionary) to PR Zanzibar, July 21, 1922.

99. See Nwulia, *Britain and Slavery,* 30–34; G. Campbell, "Madagascar," 212; Carter and Gerbeau, "Covert Slaves"; Machado, *Ocean of Trade,* 263; Stanziani, "Beyond Colonialism."

100. NAUK: FO84/857, Lyle Welch, American Merchant, to Major Hamerton, PA Muscat & Zanzibar, August 18, 1851.

101. NAUK: FO84/857, S. de Belligny, French Consul Zanzibar, to Sayyid Saʿīd, Sultan of Zanzibar, August 15, 1852.

102. NAUK: FO84/1120, W.M. Coghlan to H.L. Anderson, Secy. Govt. of Bombay, November 1, 1860.

103. MSA: P1879–129/239, S.B. Miles, PA Muscat, to E.C. Ross, PRPG, December 19, 1878. Regarding sources of indentured labor, see generally Tinker, *New System of Slavery;* Metcalf, *Imperial Connections,* 197–201.

104. MSA: P1885–120A/1995, Commissioner of Police to GoB, October 29, 1885.

105. MSA: P1885–120A/1995, Commissioner of Police to GoB, November 2, 1885.

106. MSA: P1873–114/63, Memorandum on Disposal of Liberated Slaves, n.d. (ca. April 1873). See L. Jones, "Bombay Africans."

107. MSA: P1898–160/276, Political Dept. Note—W., October 20, 1898.

108. MSA: P1889–294/21, Govt. of Bombay to Secy. Govt. of India Foreign Dept. No. 880, February 2, 1889.

109. MSA: P1878–135/877, Ross to Govt. of India, Foreign Dept. No. 71, April 20, 1878.

110. MSA: P1869–105/1387, Statement of Liberated Georgian Slave Girl, October 18, 1869; MSA: P1872–135/1285, H. Souter, Commissioner of Police, Bombay, to Govt. of Bombay, July 12, 1872.

111. MSA: P1869–105/1612, Commissioner of Police to Secy. GoB, November 12, 1869; MSA: P1891–169/115, GoB, Political Dept. No. 7271, October 5, 1891; MSA:

P1900–162/276, Commissioner of Police, Bombay, No. 10371–9, September 14, 1900. See the discussion of Sidis in Green, *Bombay Islam,* 59–61.

112. Green, *Bombay Islam,* 59–61; Jayasuriya and Angenot, *Uncovering the History,* 23; Catlin-Jairazbhoy and Alpers, *Sidis and Scholars.*

113. MSA: P1902–169/1157, Statement of Abdullah bin Nasib, June 17, 1902; also see Ewald, "Bondsmen."

114. MSA: P1894–175/33, Asst. PA Basra to Secy. Govt. of Bombay, December 12, 1894. For a similar case of freed slave networks in Istanbul, see Erdem, *Slavery,* 173–76; Toledano, *As If Silent,* chap. 5. Regarding the importance of labor recruiters, see Roy, "Sardars."

115. ZNA: HC4/2, Regina v. Abdulla Remtulla, May 9, 1890.

3. DISARMING COMMERCE

1. NAUK: FO539/79, Frederick W. Chaplin, Customs, to Home Office, November 30, 1897; NAUK: FO539/79, C. Hardinge to Marquess of Salisbury, FO, December 23, 1897; NAUK: FO539/79, Marquess of Salisbury, FO, to C. Hardinge, January 1, 1898; NAUK: FO539/79, R. T. Prowse, Customs, to FO, January 5, 1898; NAUK: FO539/79, Lt. Commander G. S. Q. Carr to Commander Fraser, January 25, 1898; NAUK: FO539/79, Report on the Traffic in Arms, M. J. Meade, PRPG, March 21, 1898.

2. Interview with Vimal Purecha, descendant and current head of the firm of Ratansi Purshottam, June 22, 2008, Muscat, Oman; see also C. Allen, "Sayyids," chaps. 5–6.

3. RP: Arms Trade correspondence, generally; IOR: R/15/6/67, Memo by P. Z. Cox, PA Muscat, July 30, 1900; NAUK: ADM 127/23, Horace Walpole, IO, to Under-SSFA, December 1, 1897.

4. Gallagher and Robinson, "Imperialism of Free Trade"; Cain and Hopkins, *British Imperialism;* Cain and Hopkins, "Gentlemanly Capitalism."

5. Prange, "Trade of No Dishonor"; Prange, "Contested Sea"; Subramanian, "Of Pirates and Potentates"; Layton, "'Moghul's Admiral.'"

6. See Chew, *Arming the Periphery;* Crews, "Trafficking in Evil?"; Grant, *Rulers.*

7. See Alchian and Demsetz, "Property Right Paradigm."

8. Foucault, *Security,* 349–57; Foucault, *Birth of Biopolitics,* 77, 116–18; Mitchell, "Limits of the State."

9. For a longer history of this process in North India, see Bayly, *Rulers.*

10. Vimal Purecha, interview by author, Muscat, Oman, June 22, 2008; IOR: R/15/6/4, Sayyid Salim, Sultan of Muscat, to H. B. E. Frere, Governor of Bombay, 19 Shawwal 1282 (March 7, 1866); IOR: R/15/6/7, Deposition of Sumdoo Isundass before S. B. Miles, PA Muscat, June 24, 1874; IOR: R/15/6/7, S. B. Miles, PA Muscat, to E. C. Ross, PRPG, December 22, 1875; IOR: R/15/6/14, Political Diary of the Muscat Political Agency, August 5, 1885.

11. Prange, "Trade of No Dishonor"; Prange, "Contested Sea"; Dua, "Sea of Trade"; Chaudhuri, *Trade and Civilisation;* Pearson, *Indian Ocean.* Regarding piracy, see al-Qasimi, *Myth of Arab Piracy;* C. Davies, *Blood-Red Arab Flag.*

12. See Steensgaard, *Carracks;* Lane, *Profits from Power.*

13. See Ibn Ruzaiq, *History of the Imams,* 44:320–25.

14. Aitchison and Government of India, *Collection of Treaties,* 10:127.

15. Ibid., 10:135–36.

16. Elias, *Precis of Papers,* 1–2.

17. MSA: P1877–99/34, Magistrate, Vingorla, to Commissioner of Customs, Bombay, January 6, 1877.

18. NAUK: ADM127/27, Lt. Commander Walter Hose to SNO Persian Gulf, September 10, 1906.

19. NAUK: FO539/79, Lt. Colonel Lock to GoI, January 26, 1898.

20. Churchill, *Story,* 5.

21. Ibid., 111–13. Churchill saw this as an anachronism in which primitive peoples were given access to modern technologies of violence. He blamed the loss of British soldiers on this smuggling of precision rifles.

22. See Jardine, *Mad Mullah of Somaliland;* Lewis, *Modern History.*

23. IOR: L/PS/18/B175, "The Arms Traffic in the Persian Gulf," by J. E. Shuckburgh, June 10, 1910, 14–15.

24. NAUK: FO539/79, "Report on the Traffic in Arms and the Steps Recently Taken for Its Suppression," by M. J. Meade, PRPG, March 21, 1898.

25. Government of India, *Indian Arms Act, 1878,* First Schedule.

26. IOR: L/P&S/18/B175, Persian Minister of Foreign Affairs to the British Legation, July 3, 1881, quoted in "The Arms Traffic in the Persian Gulf," by J. E. Shuckburgh, June 10, 19101.

27. MSA: P1910–27A/1787, GoB Political Notes, September 12, 1910; Miers, *Britain,* 261–70.

28. NAUK: FO539/79, Proclamation of Esa bin Ali al-Khalifah, 13 Ramadan 1315 (February 6, 1898), pp. 228–29; IOR: L/P&S/18/B175, "The Arms Traffic in the Persian Gulf," by J. E. Shuckburgh, June 10, 1910, pp. 4–5.

29. RP: Arms Trade, Schwarte & Hammer to Ratansi Purshottam, April 16, 1908.

30. MSA: J1876–18/138, Commissioner of Sind No. 380, May 26, 1876; MSA: P1876–47/1130, GoB No. 3415 to Commissioner of Sind, June 13, 1876.

31. MSA: P1890–144/219, PA Southeast Baluchistan, November 26, 1888.

32. BT: C/7, Thomas to PRPG, June 13, 1927; NAI: F1934/488-N, PRPG to Foreign Secretary GoI et al., May 13, 1935; IOR: R/15/2/359, Residency Agent Sharjah to PA Bahrain, January 26, 1942; IOR: L/PS/11/139 No. 4449, Bill, Consul in Shiraz to Political Commissioner, Baghdad, September 7, 1919.

33. MSA: P1899–24/976, S. W. Edgerley, Secretary GoB, to Secretary GoI Home, No. 2438, April 5, 1899.

34. MSA: P1895–130/250, GoB Judicial No. 5162, July 24, 1895.

35. MSA: R1902–46/425, GoI Home to Secretary GoB Revenue, No. 1105, April 9, 1902.

36. MSA: J1874–12/940, Police Commissioner Northern District, to Secretary GoB Judicial, No. 1082, June 23, 1873.

37. MSA: J1881–24/50, Acting Under-Secretary GoB Judicial No. 1149, February 22, 1881; MSA: J1874–35/681, A.C. Lyall Secretary GoI to Secretary GoB No. 66/3813, December 19, 1873.

38. MSA: P1905–25/583, Capt. J.B. Eustace, SNO Aden, to George Atkinson-Willes, Commander-in-Chief East Indies, September 1, 1905; MSA: P1905–25/583, S.W. Edgerley, Secretary GoB, to R.I. Scallon, Acting PR Aden, No. 5023, August 11, 1905.

39. MSA: P1905–25/583, Major R.P. Schneider, Asst. Resident, Perim, to Capt. F. De B. Hancock, First Asst. Resident, Aden, September 21, 1905; MSA: P1894–27/387, Wali of Basrah, to British Consul, Basrah, No. 487, September 23, 1893; IOR: L/PS/11/44—P2800, Report by Major Craufurd, No. 68, September 1, 1912; IOR: L/PS/11/44—P2800, C.M. Lefroy, SNO Persian Gulf, September 25, 1912.

40. MSA: P1894–27/388, GoI Foreign Dept. Letter No. 1728, November 25, 1879.

41. MSA: P1907–24/277, GoI Foreign to John Morley, SSI, February 21, 1907.

42. NAUK: WO106/6322, Arms Warehouse Regulations Notice by Sultan of Muscat, September 1, 1912.

43. IOR: R/15/6/46, Hamaid bin Sa'id al Falaiti to PA Muscat, 5 Sha'ban 1333 (June 19, 1915); IOR: R/15/6/46, Abdulla bin Rashid al Hashim, Qadi of Imam, to PA Muscat, 5 Sha'ban 1333 (June 19, 1915) and 14 Ramadan 1333 (July 27, 1915); IOR: R/15/6/34, PA Muscat to Civil Commissioner, Baghdad, May 25, 1920; IOR: R/15/6/34, PA Muscat to PRPG, July 7, 1913, pp. 8–9.

44. NAUK: FO608/116, Note by Political Dept., IO, December 4, 1918; IOR: L/PS/12/4094, No. 34, File 7, Extract from Muscat Intelligence Summary No. 11 for June 1–15, 1944.

45. IOR: R/15/5/49, Shakespear, PA Kuwait, to Cox, PRPG, November 7, 1912, and July 31, 1911.

46. IOR: R/15/2/359, PRPG to PA Kuwait, October 22, 1944, p. 238.

47. NAUK: FO539/79, Francis Bertie, FO, to Messrs. Waltons, Johnson, Bubb and Whatton, September 14, 1898; NAUK: FO539/79, H.J. Tweedy, Persian Gulf Trading Company, to Colonel Picot, June 23, 1898.

48. MSA: P1912–36/184, GoI Commerce and Industry, No. 7216–7220–88, September 28, 1911; NAUK: FO539/79, A. Godley, IO, to FO, August 9, 1898, p. 223; F.B. Prideaux, First Asst. PRPG, to IO, June 27, 1898, p. 238.

49. NAUK: FO539/79, Decision by Sa'id bin Muhammad, Wazir of Sultan of Muscat, regarding the Seizure of Arms in Muscat Territorial Waters, 23 Dhul Qa'dah 1215 (April 15, 1898); NAUK: FO539/79, Memorandum by W. Lee-Warner, IO, June 3, 1898.

50. MSA: J1881–24/50, H. Souter, Commissioner of Police, to Secretary GoB Judicial, April 20, 1880.

51. MSA: P1890–144/219, PA Kutch to Secretary GoB Political, December 29, 1888.

52. RP: Arms Trade, Schwarte & Hammer to Ratansi Purshottam, November 2, 1906, March 22, 1907, March 28, 1907, April 12, 1907, and May 3, 1907.

53. MSA: J1874–14/914, Political Dept. No. 4078, July 18, 1874; MSA: J1874–14/914, Police Commissioner Northern Districts No. 1311, July 17, 1874; MSA: J1875–31/723, Secretary GoB Political Dept. No. 2249, April 2, 1874; MSA: J1877–22/816, Arthur Howell Officiating Secretary GoI to Secretary GoB, June 28, 1877; MSA: P1904–24/681, P. J. Maitland, PR Aden, to Secretary GoB, April 16, 1904.

54. MSA: P1890–144/219, Memorandum by J. A. Crawford, April 17, 1889.

55. MSA: P1904–24/681, P. J. Maitland, PR Aden, to Secretary GoB Political, April 16, 1904; MSA: P1904–24/1535, Cox, PRPG, to C. H. A. Hill, Acting Secretary GoB Political, September 3, 1904.

56. MSA: J1910–38/1606, M. K. Nemazie, Hyderabad Deccan, to Secretary GoB Political, July 14, 1910.

57. See, for example, Robert Ludlum's *The Janson Directive* and Ian Fleming's *Goldfinger* (Cape, 1959), 29.

58. Churchill, *Story,* 155.

59. MSA: P1894–27/126, Collector of Land Revenue, Customs & Opium, to PRPG, January 11, 1894; MSA: P1895–133/484, GoB Revenue No. 133, January 8, 1895.

60. NAUK: FO539/79, Anglo-Arabian Steam Navigation Company to the Marquess of Salisbury, SSFA, May 6, 1898; NAUK: FO539/79, W. Lee Warner, IO, to C. G. F. Fagan, PA Muscat, December 23, 1897; NAUK: FO539/79, Lt. Commander G. S. Q. Carr to Commander Fraser, January 25, 1898; NAUK: FO539/79, Memorandum by H. C. Dixon & Company, March 7, 1898.

61. See generally Hughes, *Animal Kingdoms.*

62. RP: Arms Trade, Schwarte & Hammer to Ratansi Purshottam, February 15, 1907; RP: Arms Trade, Joseph Winterhoff to Ratansi Purshottam, July 5, 1907; RP: Arms Trade, Auguste Francotte & Co to Ratansi Purshottam, June 10, 1907.

63. MSA: R1895–62/607, Deputy Secretary GoI Home Dept. No. 39, January 14, 1895; MSA: R1895–62/607, Collector of Customs, No. C1068, January 19, 1895.

64. MSA: J1873–23/193, Note by Asst. Undersecretary of State Vincent, March 26, 1872 (emphasis in original); also see *Popular Introduction,* 87.

65. BT: C/7, Bertram Thomas to PRPG, June 13, 1927.

66. NAUK: FO539/79, Frederick W. Chaplin, Customs to Home Office, November 30, 1897.

67. Middle East Centre Archive, Papers of Percy Z. Cox: Richmond Ritchie, IO, to Cox, April 29, 1904; NAUK: WO106/6322, Report on the Arms Traffic, July 1, 1911, to June 30, 1913, Appendix C.

68. RP: Arms Trade, Schwarte & Hammer to Ratansi Purshottam, April 12, 1907, May 3, 1907, May 24, 1907, July 5, 1907, August 23, 1907, and September 6, 1907.

69. RP: Arms Trade, Joseph Winterhoff to Ratansi Purshottam, July 5, 1907; RP: Arms Trade, Schwarte & Hammer to Ratansi Purshottam, August 30, 1907;

NAUK: FO60/603, R.P. Menzies, Vice Consul, Liege, Belgium, to G.R. Perry, Antwerp, November 18, 1897.

70. MSA: P1904–24/681, S.W. Edgerley, Acting Secretary GoB, to L.W. Dane Secretary GoI, Foreign, March 11, 1904; MSA: P1904–24/1535, P.Z. Cox, PRPG, to C.H.A. Hill, Acting Secretary GoB, September 3, 1904; MSA: P1905–25/583, J.B. Eustace, SNO Aden, to R.I. Scallon, Acting PR Aden, August 21, 1905.

71. MSA: P1910–27a/1787, GoB Political Dept. Notes, April 9, 1910; also see Willis, *Unmaking North and South,* chap. 2.

72. MSA: P1904–24/681, H.M. Mason, PR Aden, to C.H.A. Hill, Acting Secretary GoB, October 31, 1904; MSA: P1905–25/583, J.B. Eustace, SNO Aden, to George Atkinson-Willes, Commander-in-Chief East Indies, September 1, 1905; MSA: P1905–25/583, S.W. Edgerley, Secretary GoB, to R.I. Scallon, Acting PR Aden, August 11, 1905.

73. Crews, "Trafficking in Evil?"; Cassanelli, *Shaping of Somali Society,* 241, 248; Lewis, *Modern History,* 50–51, 58, 71, 75–76.

74. MSA: P1890–144/219, Memorandum by J.A. Crawford, April 17, 1889; NAUK: FO539/79, F. Plunkett, Ambassador to Belgium, to Salisbury, SSFA, December 25, 1897; NAUK: FO539/79, Memorandum by W. Lee Warner, "The Trade in Arms with the Persian Gulf," June 3, 1898; IOR: L/PS/12/4094, No. 34, File 7, Extract from Muscat Intelligence Summary No. 11 for June 1–15, 1944 (both .303 caliber and .450/.577 caliber ammunition was widely available).

75. MSA: P1890–144/219, Memorandum by J.A. Crawford, April 17, 1889; IOR: R/15/2/359, Diary of H.M.S. "Oksoy," pp. 219–20, May 12, 1944; IOR: L/PS/12/4094, No. 34, File 7, Extract from Muscat Intelligence Summary No. 11 for June 1–15, 1944.

76. NAUK: FO 539/79, Memorandum by W. Lee Warner, "The Trade in Arms with the Persian Gulf," June 3, 1898; NAUK: FO 539/79, F. Plunkett, Ambassador to Belgium, to Salisbury, SSFA, December 25, 1897.

77. IOR: R/15/5/45, PA Kuwait to First Asst. PRPG, December 29, 1909.

78. BT: C/7, Bertram Thomas to PRPG, June 13, 1927.

79. In Arabic *wilayati* could mean literally "from the states," but a very small proportion of ammunition imported into Muscat came from America and the vast majority from England and Belgium. The Urdu word is a Mughal-era semantic shift from the Persian/Arabic *vilayat/wilayat* for province or state.

80. MSA: P1890–145/143, GoB Judicial No. 262, January 16, 1890.

81. NAUK: FO539/79, J. Calcott Gaskin, Vice-Consul, Bushire, to C.J. Zeytoon, November 30, 1897, p. 258.

82. IOR: R/15/5/45, PA Kuwait to First Asst. PRPG, December 29, 1909.

83. NAUK: ADM127/23, Horace Walpole, IO, to Under-SSFA, December 1, 1897; NAUK: FO60/603, J. Sadler, PA Muscat, to F.A. Wilson, PRPG, February 5, 1895.

84. See generally Kolsky, *Colonial Justice.*

85. See Mitchell, "Limits of the State."

86. MSA: J1873–23/193, John Nugent, Acting Under-Secretary GoB, to Secretary GoI Home Dept., n.d. (ca. August 1873).

87. Ibid.; MSA: J1873–23/193, Resolution of GoB Judicial Dept., No. 2091, May 8, 1872; MSA: J1878–31/642, Proceeding of the GoI Home Dept., June 21, 1878.

88. MSA: J1873–23/193, Henry Souter, Commissioner of Police to Under-Secretary GoB Judicial, April 26, 1872; MSA: J1873–23/193, Resolution of GoB Judicial No. 68, January 4, 1872; MSA: J1873–23/193, Resolution of GoB Judicial No. 2091, May 8, 1872; MSA: J1873–14/1140, Customs to Chief Secretary to GoB, August 14, 1874; MSA: J1875–31/723, W. Lee Warner, Secretary to GoB Judicial, June 15, 1875; MSA: J1877–22/816, Commissioner of Police, Bombay, to Under-Secretary GoB Judicial, August 24, 1877.

89. MSA: J1874–14/981, District Magistrate, Poona, No. 165, January 30, 1874; MSA: J1874–14/1140, Customs to Chief Secretary to GoB, August 14, 1874; MSA: J1873–23/193, Resolution of GoB Judicial Dept., No. 2091, May 8, 1872.

90. MSA: J1875–31/723, Henry Souter, Commissioner of Police, to Under-Secretary GoB Judicial, December 2, 1872, and whole file of applications for licenses.

91. MSA: J1873–23/193, District Superintendent Police, Shikarpur, to Commissioner of Police, Sind, April 6, 1873; MSA: P1893–40/1934, P. S. V. Fitzgerald, Acting Political Superintendent Savantvadi, to Secretary GoB, October 16, 1893.

92. MSA: J1909–29/1871, Walter Locke and Company to District Magistrate, Jullundur, March 24, 1909.

93. MSA: P1890–144/219, Memorandum by J. A. Crawford, April 17, 1889; MSA: R1895–62/607, Chief Secretary Government of Madras, Judicial No. 2909, November 30, 1894.

94. IOR: R/2/723/70, G. E. Hyde-Cates, Asst. PA Sorath Prant, to Charles Olivant, PA Kathiawar, February 15, 1895; IOR: R/2/723/70, C. H. A. Hill, Under-Secretary GoB Judicial, Circular No. 7657, November 15, 1894; IOR: R/2/728/141, Under-Secretary to GoB Judicial to Commissioner in Sind et al., August 15, 1901.

95. NAUK: FO60/603, Horace Walpole, IO, to Under-SSFA, December 1, 1897.

96. MSA: J1873–23/193, Resolution of GoB Judicial No. 68, January 4, 1872, and No. 2091, May 8, 1872; MSA: J1877–22/816, Commissioner of Police, Bombay, to Under-Secretary GoB Judicial, August 24, 1877.

97. NAUK: FO539/79, M. J. Meade, PRPG, to GoI, May 16, 1898, p. 232.

98. IOR: R/15/5/45, Note on Firearms by PA Kuwait, December 31, 1909; IOR: R/15/5/45, W. Shakespear, PA Kuwait, to PRPG, April 28, 1910, May 4, 1910, and May 16, 1910; MSA: J1912–36/184, Cox, PRPG, to Henry McMahon, Secretary GoI Foreign, September 30, 1911.

99. NAUK: FO371/88, pp. 293–94, Major Grey, PA Muscat, to P. Z. Cox, PRPG, February 5, 1906, and February 12, 1906.

100. NAUK: ADM127/23, G. S. Q. Carr, SNO Persian Gulf, to Edmund Drummond, Commander-in-Chief East Indies, January 15, 1898.

101. NAUK: FO539/79, Messrs. Livingstone, Muir & Co. to M. J. Meade, PRPG, October 30, 1896; see also Avery et al., *Cambridge History of Iran*, 200.

102. Garretson, "Naggadras."

103. MSA: J1877–22/134, S. C. Bayley, Secretary Government of Bengal, to Secretary GoI Home Dept., July 3, 1877; MSA: P1890–144/219, Memorandum by

J. A. Crawford, April 17, 1889; MSA: J1874–14/981, District Magistrate, Poona, No. 165, January 30, 1874.

104. MSA: P1890–144/219, Memorandum by J. A. Crawford, April 17, 1889; MSA: P1895–130/250, GoB Judicial No. 7959, November 14, 1895.

105. IOR: R/15/5/49, Sheikh Mubarak as-Sabah to P. Z. Cox, PRPG, September 29, 1911.

106. Abal, *Al-hawā ʿalā niyyatnā*. Thanks to Lindsey Stephenson for drawing my attention to this video.

107. IOR: L/PJ/12/78 (whole file); L/PJ/12/81, Deputy Commissioner of Police, Calcutta, to Asst. to Director Intelligence Bureau, Delhi, January 22, 1926; IOR: L /PJ/12/79, Report of a Special Branch Officer Regarding Arms Smuggling, July 27, 1925.

108. MSA: J1910–41/1606, Commissioner of Police, Bombay, to J. H. DuBoulay, Secretary GoB Judicial, August 3, 1910.

109. IOR: L/PJ/12/77 J. E. Ferard, to Under-SSFA, June 29, 1922; IOR: L/PJ/12/79, Letter from Trieste to an Officer of the General Staff Branch, Simla, January 1924.

110. IOR: L/PS/11/139, No. 4449, Political Baghdad to SSI, October 8, 1918, enclosure from H. St. John Philby, September 22, 1918; IOR: L/PS/11/139, Note by A. U., November 19, 1919; IOR: L/PS/11/139, Col. C. E. Wilson to Director Arab Bureau, December 8, 1918.

111. IOR: R/15/2/359, R. Hay, PRPG, to British Legation, Jedda, April 5, 1942, p. 84.

112. NAI: F1934/488-N, Hoare, Tehran, to SSFA, November 3, 1934; NAI: F1934/488-N, PRPG to Foreign Secretary GoI, May 13, 1935; IOR: R/15/6/70, Statement of Ahmad bin Mohammad to Commander of H. M. S. Fowey, December 11, 1934.

113. MSA: P1907–24/277, GoI Foreign Dept. to John Morley, SSI, February 21, 1907.

114. IOR: L/PS/11/139 No. 4449, Col. C. E. Wilson to Director Arab Bureau, December 8, 1918.

115. NAUK: ADM 127/23, F. Rich, SNO Aden, to C. E. Cunningham, PR Aden, January 18, 1898.

116. IOR: R/15/6/67, Memo by P. Z. Cox, PA Muscat, July 30, 1900.

4. NEUTRALIZING MONEY

1. IOR: R/15/2/351, G. C. L. de Grenier, Bahrain Customs Director, to PA Bahrain, September 21, 1940.

2. Shayzarī, *Nihāyat al-rutba;* Ibn ʿAbdūn, *Risālah fī al-qaḍāʾ wa-al-Ḥisbah.* The office of *muḥtasib* was incorporated into the Khedival bureaucracy in the middle of the nineteenth century in Egypt; see Hunter, *Egypt under the Khedives,* 43. It lasted as late as the twentieth century in Iran; see Floor, "Marketpolice in Qājār Persia"; Floor, "Office of Muhtasib."

3. Sālimī, *Jawābāt al-Imām al-Sālimī,* 367, 562.

4. See Bishara, "Sea of Debt," 1488–58; Lydon, *On Trans-Saharan Trails,* 311, 316; Ray, "Asian Capital"; Boxberger, "Avoiding Ribā."

5. Polanyi, *Great Transformation* chaps. 6 and 16.

6. Regarding the problems with barter as the origin of exchange, see Graeber, *Debt,* chap. 2.

7. Regarding the "veil of money," see Patinkin and Steiger, "In Search"; Schabas, "Temporal Dimension."

8. Hume did consider the material qualities of money in his more empirical moments, though they don't seem to have played into his broader ideas on monetary theory, and this is even less the case with later political economists; see Schabas and Wennerlind, "Retrospectives."

9. Regarding the persistence of asymmetrical exchange and the usefulness of volatility to colonial governments, see Guyer, *Marginal Gains,* chaps. 2, 10.

10. Shayzarī, *Nihāyat Al-Rutba.*

11. See Ray, "Asian Capital." For a nuanced consideration of arbitrage in the late twentieth century, see chap. 8 of MacKenzie, *Engine.*

12. IOR: R/15/2/351, G.C.L. de Grenier, Bahrain Customs Director, to PA Bahrain, September 21, 1940.

13. Daniell, *Gold Treasure of India;* "Hoarding."

14. MSA: F1891–100/664, Gerald Martin, Assay Master, to Secretary GoI Financial and Commercial Dept., December 5, 1890; Chandavarkar, "Nature and Effects."

15. MSA: F1879–19/516, GoB Financial Dept. Memo. 3133, September 15, 1879.

16. Thurston, *History of the Coinage,* 66.

17. Government of India, *Indian Penal Code,* Section 230.

18. MSA: F1870–4/217, L.C. Probyn, Accountant General Punjab, to Financial Commissioner Punjab, No. 752, April 19, 1870; MSA: F1870–4/217, Revenue Commissioner Northern Districts to Financial Dept. No. 5709, October 27, 1870.

19. MSA: F1870–4/217, Revenue Commissioner Northern Districts Financial Dept. No. 5709, October 27, 1870.

20. MSA: F1870–4/217, J.A.E. Miller, Secretary to Financial Commissioner Punjab, to Secretary Government of Punjab, April 28, 1870.

21. *Bombay High Court Reports,* vol. 11, Regina v. Ba'pu Ya'dav and Ra'ma Tulsira'm (October 9, 1874), 172–74.

22. MSA: P1891–145/270, Donald Robertson, PA Bagelkhand, to First Asst. to Agent to Governor-General for Central India, July 12, 1890. For an excellent discussion of the division between charity and economy, see Birla, *Stages of Capital,* especially chaps. 2 and 3.

23. MSA: P1892–146/476, Lee-Warner, Secretary GoB, to Secretary GoI, July 7, 1891.

24. Kuroda, "Maria Theresa Dollar"; Pankhurst, "Perpetuation."

25. Officer, "Gold Standard."

26. The Ottoman Empire had shifted to the gold standard by 1881, but the Qajar monetary system was primarily based on silver *krans,* though gold *tomans* were also coined. Pamuk, *Monetary History,* 214–21; Soucek, "Coinage of the Qajars."

27. MSA: F1881–12A/522, Memorandum from Accountant General No. R-1794, April 30, 1881.

28. The term *sarraf* was probably introduced to South Asia by Arab merchants in the early Islamic period. Haider, "Precious Metal Flows."

29. This was not dissimilar to government practices of countermarking foreign coins for local circulation. See Soucek, "Coinage of the Qajars."

30. MSA: F1878–14/356, GoI Financial Memorandum No. 2776, September 5, 1878.

31. MSA: F1880–22/689, GoI Financial Memorandum No. 2326, August 14, 1880.

32. Government of India, *Reports of Currency Committees*, Herschell Committee Report 1893, 1–58.

33. Keynes, *Indian Currency and Finance;* Ambedkar, *Problem of the Rupee.*

34. Government of India, *Reports of Currency Committees,* 43.

35. MSA: F1870–6/266, GoI Foreign Dept. Memorandum 273, October 6, 1870.

36. MSA: R1900–72/298, Revenue Dept. Notes, November 15, 1899.

37. MSA: F1869–3/301, C. E. Chapman, Officiating Accountant General, to Secretary Govt. of Bombay, November 26, 1869; MSA: F1869–3/301, T. C. Hope, Collector of Surat, to Accountant General, September 4, 1869.

38. MSA: F1871–86/120, GoI Financial Dept. Memorandum 1858, March 31, 1871.

39. NAI: DCI/CT11–23, September 1905, File 19, Report of H. W. Maclean on the Conditions of British Trade in Persia in SSI to GoI, July 22, 1904.

40. GL: EB39–010/20, M. Gunn, Bahrain Branch, to N. S. Golder, General Manager, London, November 12, 1947, and December 10, 1947.

41. MSA: P1886–152/145, John Kirk, PA Zanzibar, to Secretary GoB, May 11, 1886; NAUK: FO2/956, Resident Uganda to SSFA, May 18, 1906; Mwangi, "Of Coins and Conquest."

42. Mwangi, "Of Coins and Conquest"; Mwangi, "Order of Money," chap. 2; Metcalf, *Imperial Connections,* 206.

43. IOR: R/20/B/1665, Minutes of Meeting of Standing Finance Committee November 19, 1951; Seshadri, *From Crisis to Convertability,* 51.

44. IOR: R/15/2/351, G. C. L. de Grenier, Bahrain Customs Director, to PA Bahrain, September 21, 1940.

45. MSA: P1901–147/1574, Memorandum by H. N. Alexander, Superintendent Police, to Secretariat, December 9, 1901.

46. Ibid.

47. MSA: J1880–82/27, J. W. Walker, Remembrancer of Legal Affairs, to Secretary GoB Judicial, February 10, 1880.

48. MSA: P1895–20/138, R. H. Vincent, Commissioner of Police, to Secretary GoB Judicial, June 6, 1895; MSA: P1896–25/196, Turkish Consul General M. Kadri to Commissioner of Police, October 8, 1895; MSA: P1896–25/196, Commissioner of Police to Under-Secretary GoB Judicial, March 4, 1896; MSA: P1897–38/196, British Ambassador, Istanbul, to Secretary GoI, Foreign Dept., December 8, 1896.

49. League of Nations, "International Convention for the Suppression of Counterfeiting Currency and Protocol," April 20, 1929 [1931], League of Nations Treaty Series 45, 112 LNTS 371.

50. MSA: P1900–141/1066, GoB Financial Memorandum 4501/139, October 4, 1900.

51. MSA: P1902–136/1305, Asst. Inspector-General Police to Inspector-General Police, Bombay Presidency, March 26, 1902.

52. MSA: F1870–6/266, E. H. Percival, Acting Under-Secretary to GoB, to Secretary GoI, Foreign Dept., January 17, 1870; MSA: P1902–111/892, GoI, Foreign Dept. to GoB, February 19, 1904.

53. MSA: P1902–136/1305, Asst. Inspector-General Police to Inspector-General Police, Bombay Presidency, March 26, 1902.

54. MSA: F1878–29/482, Officiating Commissioner of Issue, Bombay, to Head Commissioner of Issue, Calcutta, August 15, 1878.

55. MSA: F1893–28/563, F. M. Hunter, PA Kutch, to Secretary GoB, December 28, 1892; Rudner, "Banker's Trust"; Ray, "Asian Capital"; Ballard, "Coalitions of Reciprocity."

56. MSA: J1877–69/32, Frank Souter, Commissioner of Police, Bombay, to C. Gonne, Secretary GoB, May 5, 1877; MSA: P1891–145/270, Col. H. L. Nutt, Police Superintendent Sawantwadi, to W. Lee Warner, Secretary GoB, February 10, 1891.

57. MSA: F1893–30/434, Kazi Shabudin to G. Vidal, Secretary GoB, April 1893.

58. IOR: R/15/2/351, GoI to PRPG, May 9, 1940; MSA: P1901–147/1574, Memorandum by H. N. Alexander, Superintendent of Police, to Secretariat, December 9, 1901.

59. IOR: R/15/5/309, V. G. Matthews, Collector of Customs Bombay, to M. Slade, Central Board of Revenue, April 21, 1944.

60. IOR: MSS Eur. C446, "Anecdotes of Smuggling in Bombay in the 1930s" (unsigned and undated in the collection of Patrick Sweeney, Customs Officer, Bombay, Berbera, and Aden).

61. IOR: R/15/2/351, Special Report by A. B., March 4, 1941, 217.

62. IOR: R/1/1/4795, Note by D. F. Keegan, July 30, 1937; IOR: R/1/1/4795, W. R. G. Smith, Commissioner Police Bombay, to Chief Secretary GoB, September 10, 1937; IOR: R/1/1/4800, Circular from Under-Secretary GoI, External Affairs, to Residents in Princely States, December 14, 1938.

63. IOR: R/15/2/351, Special Report by A. B., March 4, 1941, 217; IOR: R/15/2/352, Conclusions of a Conference Regarding Gold and Silver Smuggling in Bahrain, February 28, 1942, pp. 200–202.

64. IOR: R/15/2/351, G. C. L. de Grenier, Bahrain Customs Director, to PA Bahrain, September 21, 1940; IOR: R/15/2/351, GoI to PRPG, May 9, 1940.

65. IOR: MSS Eur. C446, "Anecdotes of Smuggling in Bombay in the 1930s."

66. IOR: R/15/2/352, PA Bahrain to Hickinbotham, PA Kuwait, May 11, 1942, p. 25.

67. Sweeney, "Game Warden's Permit," 155.

68. MSA: F1881–12/522, J. B. Richey, Collector Ahmedabad, to G. F. Sheppard, Acting Commissioner Northern Districts, May 20, 1881.

69. MSA: F1902-33/601 Specimens of Foreign copper coins, T.J. Thatcher, Karachi Police; MSA: F1905-44/601, GoB Memorandum No. 347 January 26, 1905.

70. MSA: R1902–40/601, Extract from Bombay Police Abstract of Intelligence No. 26, June 28, 1902.

71. MSA: P1904–111/944, Political Resident, Baroda, to Secretary GoI, Foreign, April 5, 1904.

72. MSA: R1895–313/854, Secretary GoB, Public Works, to Secretary GoI, Public Works, August 22, 1895.

73. IOR: R/20/B/1621, "History of MT Dollars," by Mr. Duncan of Aden Museum, January 1939; IOR: R/20/B/1623, Note from A. Besse, October 10, 1955.

74. Kuroda, "Maria Theresa Dollar."

75. IOR: R/20/B/1621, A. Besse & Co to Finance Officer, Aden, May 5, 1943; IOR: R/20/B/1621, Philip Mitchell, Political Branch, East Africa Command, Nairobi, to John Hathorn Hall, Government House, Aden, April 17, 1942; IOR: R/20/B/1621, National Bank of India to Finance Officer, Aden, February 5, 1941.

76. IOR: R/20/B/1309, Controller of Civil Supplies to Civil Secretary, Aden, November 24, 1939; IOR: R/20/B/1309, Asst. Frontier Officer, Hodeidah, to Political Secretary, Aden, November 10, 1939.

77. IOR: R/20/B/1622, Governor of Aden to SSC, July 24, 1948; IOR: R/20/B/1622, SSC to Governor of Aden, October 12, 1948; IOR: R/20/B/1623, Note from A. Besse, October 10, 1955.

78. McDonald, *Polyester Prince,* 15.

79. Schaefer, "'Selling at a Wash.'"

80. IOR: R/15/2/351, PA Bahrain Memorandum 148, May 21, 1940; IOR: R/15/2/352, Capt. J. B. Howes to PA Kuwait, August 16, 1941, 58.

81. NAI: DCI/CT11–23, 9/1905, File 19, Report of H. W. Maclean, July 22, 1904; IOR: R/15/6/444, PA Muscat Aide Memoire re: Muscat Bank May 4, 1948; NAUK: FO2/956, Francis Mowatt, Treasury to Under-SSC, September 21, 1894.

82. See Pamuk, *Monetary History;* G. Jones et al., *History.*

83. See Government of India, *Reports of Currency Committees;* Keynes, *Indian Currency and Finance.*

84. Cain and Hopkins, *British Imperialism;* McGuire, "Exchange Banks."

85. Government of India, *Report of a Commission;* Government of India, *Reports of Currency Committees.*

86. McGuire, "Exchange Banks," 146.

87. Ibid., 151–55; "Law and Police."

88. NAI: DCI/CT11–23, 9/1905, File 19, J. Calcott Gaskin, Asst. PA Bahrain, to First Asst. to PRPG, September 21, 1903; NAI: DCI/CT11–23, 9/1905, File 19, Report of H. W. Maclean, July 22, 1904; IOR: R/15/6/444, Geoffrey Prior, PRPG, to H. Weightman, Secretary GoI, External Affairs, April 21, 1946.

89. GL: EB39–010/20, M. Gunn, Manager, Bahrain, to N. S. Golder, General Manager Eastern Bank, London, February 25/1948; GL: EB39–010/20, N. S. Golder, London, to M. Gunn, Bahrain, April 9, 1948; GL: EB39–010/20, Report by Mr. Findlay, January 10, 1947.

90. HSBC: MBI-1604/019, Indenture between Jehangir Dinshaw Mapla and Mercantile Bank of India, October 3, 1927; "Law and Police"; "Bombay Cricket"; "Death."

91. "3 1/2 per Cent. Loan"; "3 per Cent. Loan."

92. HSBC: MBI-1604/019, Indenture between Jehangir Dinshaw Mapla and Mercantile Bank of India, October 3, 1927.

93. HSBC: MBI-1604/28, Decision of Bombay High Court in Capt. Vincent L. DeSilva et al. v. C. F. X. Fernandes et al., April 14, 1927; "Law and Police:."

94. Bagchi, *Presidency Banks,* 247–49.

95. Ibid., 243–60; GL: EB 39/087, P. W. Wilson, Manager Calcutta Branch, to N. S. Golder, London, March 15, 1951; GL: EB 39/087, N. S. Golder, London, to P. W. Wilson, Manager Calcutta Branch, February 23, 1951.

96. GL: EB39–010/20, Manager, Bahrain, to N. S. Golder, General Manager, London, November 12, 1947.

97. HSBC: MBI/BOM007, Edmonston, Hong Kong, to G. A. Todrick, Calcutta, July 13, 1937.

98. GL: EB39–106/44, Inspector's Report on Bombay Branch, August 28, 1939.

99. GL: EB39–087, P. W. Wilson, Manager Calcutta Branch, to N. S. Golder, London, March 15, 1951; GL: EB39–106/44, Inspector's Report on Bombay Branch, August 28, 1939.

100. GL: EB39–106/82, Report on Karachi Bank, October 29, 1927; GL: EB39–106/83, Report on Karachi Bank, September 21, 1939; GL: EB39–010/20, Manager, Bahrain, to N. S. Golder, General Manager, London, November 12, 1947. Also see Rudner, "Banker's Trust."

101. "Law and Police."

102. GL: EB39–087, P. W. Wilson, Manager Calcutta, to N. S. Golder, London, March 15, 1951.

103. HSBC: MBI/BOM-002.3, R. Drane, Bombay, to Barr, London, July 2, 1937.

104. HSBC: MBI/BOM-002.3, R. Drane, Bombay, to Barr, London, July 2, 1937 (second letter).

105. IOR: R/15/6/189, Said bin Taimur to Hickinbotham, October 10, 1939, p. 208; IOR: R/15/6/189, GoI Foreign to Secretary of State for the Commonwealth, May 28, 1948, 120; GL: EB39–010/20, N. S. Golder, London, to M. Gunn, Bahrain, April 9, 1948; GL: EB39–010/20, Report by Mr. Findlay, October 1, 1947.

106. Fisher, *Purchasing Power of Money,* chaps. 6–7.

107. Keynes, *Indian Currency and Finance;* Goswami, *Producing India,* chap. 2.

108. See Naoroji, *Poverty and Un-British Rule;* Naoroji, *Poverty of India;* Dutt, *Economic History of India;* Ambedkar, *History of Indian Currency.*

109. Keynes's correspondence while at the India Office does not indicate any thought about this wider circulation; see J. M. Keynes Papers: IA and IC series.

The chapter's epigraph is taken from Jayakar, *Omani Proverbs,* 29. In this phrasing, *khawā* is a colloquial form of *ikhwān.*

1. See generally Trivellato, *Familiarity of Strangers;* Aslanian, *From the Indian Ocean;* Greif, "Contract Enforceability"; Greif, "Reputation and Coalitions"; Bayly, *Rulers,* chap. 11; Subrahmanyam and Bayly, "Portfolio Capitalists."

2. See the notion of "relational value" developed in Elyachar, *Markets of Dispossession,* chap. 5; also see Lydon, *On Trans-Saharan Trails,* 336–37.

3. Kirman and Vriend, "Learning to Be Loyal." For the notion of "extensive negotiability," see Birla, *Stages of Capital,* 21, 59–63.

4. See Geertz, "Bazaar Economy."

5. Goitein, *Mediterranean Society;* Greif, *Institutions;* Aslanian, *From the Indian Ocean;* Trivellato, *Familiarity of Strangers;* Goldberg, *Trade and Institutions;* Markovits, *Global World;* Sood, "Informational Fabric."

6. For price as a prosthetic device, see Çalışkan, *Market Threads,* chap. 1.

7. See the Arabic correspondence preserved in ZNA: AA5/14 and in AT collection generally; also see Sood, "Correspondence."

8. See the translations of correspondence preserved in the UKPC's proceedings concerning the estate of Tharia Topan (1897 UKPC 17, Sala Mohommed Jafferbhoy et al. v. Dame Janbai) and the dispute between Ali Ibrahim Noor and Ahmed Najoo Khan (1924 UKPC 72).

9. Aslanian, "Salt"; Trivellato, *Familiarity of Strangers,* 159.

10. Elyachar, *Markets of Dispossession,* 7; European firms employed "goodwill" as a somewhat similar concept, though this was clearly distinct from normal value and quantifiable only as a remainder or excess. See GL: ICG-27/689, T.H. Carson, K.C., to Gray, Mackenzie & Co, May 31, 1904.

11. 1897 UKPC 17, Sala Mohommed Jafferbhoy et al. v. Dame Janbai, Tharia Topan to Moosabhai and Jafferbhai, August 10, 1890, p. 178.

12. 1897 UKPC 17, Sala Mohommed Jafferbhoy et al. v. Dame Janbai, Tharia Topan to Musabhai, November 5, 1890, p. 187.

13. 1897 UKPC 17, Sala Mohommed Jafferbhoy et al. v. Dame Janbai, Mehta Fulchand Panachand to Musabhai and Jafferbhai, n.d., p. 188.

14. 1897 UKPC 17, Sala Mohommed Jafferbhoy et al. v. Dame Janbai, Tharia Topan to Moosabhai and Jafferbhai August 10, 1890, p. 173; see also Lydon, *On Trans-Saharan Trails,* 35.

15. IOR: R/1/1/4781, R. Chhaganlal, Jamnagar, to Seth Ambalal Jugabhai, Patri, June 28, 1935; IOR: R/1/1/4781, Seth Alibhai Ababhai Jhaveri, Sugar Merchant Jamnagar, to Patel Ambalal Jugabhai, Patri, June 29/1935; IOR: R/2/597/12, Correspondence from Ratanchand Dipchand, September 7, 1941.

16. AT: Mohammed Nassīf to Mubārak bin Seif al-Nākhī, 4 Rajab 1343 AH; IOR: R/15/5/309, Collector of Central Excises and Salt Revenue, Madras, Order D351, May 28/1943.

17. Aslanian, "Salt."

18. ZNA: AA5/19, Sultan of Zanzibar to F. de Winton, Imperial British East Africa Company, February 27, 1891.

19. IOR: R/15/5/309, Collector of Central Excises and Salt Revenue, Madras, Order D351, May 28, 1943.

20. See Aslanian, "Social Capital"; Trivellato, *Familiarity of Strangers,* chap. 6; Leonard, "Family Firms in Hyderabad."

21. ZNA: AA5/18, Sultan of Zanzibar, to G. H. Portal, PA Zanzibar, 5 Shawwal 1306 (June 4, 1889).

22. Sālimī, *Jawābāt,* vol. 4, 539–49; 1924 UKPC 72, Ahmed Najoo Khan v. Ali Ibrahim Noor, 101–11. Also see Trivellato, *Familiarity of Strangers,* 159–61, 168; Udovitch, *Partnership and Profit,* 204–15.

23. 1924 UKPC 72, Ahmed Najoo Khan v. Ali Ibrahim Noor; Schaefer, "'Selling at a Wash.'"

24. NAUK: CO725/83/1, Note by Reilly, July 29, 1941.

25. IOR: R/15/2/143, Sheikh Abdulla bin Qasim al-Thani to PA Bahrain, December 19, 1944.

26. AT, 'Abd al-Rahmān Madfa' to Sheikh Jum'a Muhammad al Mutawa', 22 Sha'ban 1356; AT: Yusuf 'Abd al-Rahmān Mutawa' to Sheikh Ahmed bin 'Abd al-Rahmān bin Hadid, August 26, 1930 (2/1349 AH); AT: Muhammad Nassīf to Mubārak bin Seif al-Nākhī, 4 Rajab 1343 AH; AT: 1924 UKPC 72, Ahmed Najoo Khan v. Ali Ibrahim Noor, Letters from Ali Ibrahim Noor to Ahmed Najoo Khan, pp. 98–111.

27. 1897 UKPC 17, Sala Mohommed Jafferbhoy et al. v. Dame Janbai, Letters from Tharia Topan to Moosabhai and Jafferbhai, pp. 178–83.

28. IOR: R/20/B/1621, J. Premjee Aden to J. Premjee & Co., Addis Ababa, March 22, 1945, extracts from censor's files.

29. IOR: R/2/597/14, Akbarali, Abadan, to Ghulamali Mohamadali, Rajkot, May 31, 1942.

30. Jayakar, *Omani Proverbs,* 29.

31. 1924 UKPC 72, Ahmed Najoo Khan v. Ali Ibrahim Noor, Letters from Ali Ibrahim Noor in Jizan and then Meidi to Ahmed Najoo Khan, December 16, 1916 (20 Safar 1335) and November 16, 1916 (6 Dhu al-Hijjah 1334) (Common Era and Hijri dates are conflated in these translations), p. 12; Villiers, *Sons of Sinbad,* 298.

32. AT, 'Abd al-Rahmān bin Hassan al-Midfa' to Juma'a Muhammad al-Mutawa', 22 Shawwal 1356 AH; AT: Yusuf 'Abd al-Rahmān al-Mutawa' to Sheikh 'Ahmed bin 'Abd al-Rahmān bin Hadīd, August 26, 1930 (2 Rabī'a 1349 AH); 1893 UKPC 17, Sala Mohommed Jafferbhoy et al. v. Dame Janbai, letters from Tharia Topan to Moosabhai and Jafferbhai, pp. 178–83; IOR: R/2/597/12, Letter from Ratanshand Dipchand, September 7, 1941.

33. Jayakar, *Omani Proverbs,* 53 (*kul yamdaḥ sūqan ribḥ fihi*). For diasporic communications infrastructures, see Aslanian, "Salt"; Trivellato, *Familiarity of Strangers,* chap. 7.

34. ZNA: AA5/19, Sultan of Zanzibar to G. H. Portal, IBEAC, n.d.; IOR: R/2/597/12, Letter from Ratanchand Dipchand, September 7, 1941.

35. 1924 UKPC 72, Ali Ibrahim Noor to Ahmed Najoo Khan, September 16, 1916, p. 102.

36. 1897 UKPC 17, Sala Mohommed Jafferbhoy et al. v. Dame Janbai, Tharia Topan to Moosabhai and Jafferbhai, October 8, 1890, pp. 178–83.

37. RP: General Correspondence, Goguyer to Ratansi Purshotam, invoice, July 28, 1902; 1897 UKPC 17, Sala Mohommed Jafferbhoy et al. v. Dame Janbai, Tharia Topan to Moosabhai and Jafferbhai, August 10, 1890, pp. 178–83; ZNA: HC3/1236, Statement of Frederick Horton, Partner, MacKinlay & Co. December 9, 1924; 1929 UKPC 87 and 88, Julio Fernandes et al. v. Mercantile Bank of India, C. F. X. Fernandes to Julio Mascarenhas, March 8, 1924, p. 100; Villiers, *Sons of Sinbad,* 145–46.

38. Rudner, "Banker's Trust"; Rudner, *Caste and Capitalism;* Ray, "Asian Capital."

39. Jayakar, *Omani Proverbs,* 65; Lydon, *On Trans-Saharan Trails,* 248.

40. AT, ʿAbdallah Ṣaliḥ al-Muṭawaʿ to Ahmed bin ʿAbd al-Raḥmān bin Hadid, 28 Shawal 1346 AH; ZNA: AM1/6, Pages of Accounts (unsigned, ca. Muharram 1219 AH).

41. Gambling and Karim, *Business and Accounting Ethics,* 60.

42. Speake, *Dictionary of Proverbs.* The sixteenth- and seventeenth-century meaning of the proverb seems to echo more closely that of the Omani proverb.

43. 1897 UKPC 17, Sala Mohommed Jafferbhoy et al. v. Dame Janbai, Tharia Topan to Moosabhai Tharia, n.d. (August 22, 1891), and Tharia Topan to Moosabhai and Jafferbhai, August 10, 1890, pp. 178, 189; Aslanian, "Social Capital"; Maurer, "Anthropological and Accounting Knowledge"; Zaid, "Accounting Systems"; Udovitch, *Partnership and Profit,* 180.

44. Birla, *Stages of Capital,* 27, 49–51; Leonard, "Family Firms in Hyderabad"; Rudner, "Banker's Trust."

45. See Udovitch, *Partnership and Profit,* 223, 246.

46. 1924 UKPC 72, Ahmed Najoo Khan v. Ali Ibrahim Noor, pp. 12, 16, 22, Judgment.

47. ZNA: HC7/719, Cash Book of Tipoo Tip, 1893.

48. NAUK: CO852/1245/2, European Customs Union Study Group, Customs Valuation Report, July 6, 1951, 38; NAI: DCI/CT11–23, September 1905, File 19, Report of H. W. Maclean, July 22, 1904; NAI: DCI/CBR-1469-Cus.I 1939, Customs House, Calcutta, to K. G. Jacob, CBR, March 27, 1940.

49. ZNA: AA5/18, Mulji Nanji to Mr. Halliday, Zanzibar, February 16, 1889; NAI: DCI/CT11–23, 9/1905, File 19, Report of H. W. Maclean, July 22, 1904.

50. For a broader examination of the long history of debt and the generative fiction of cash transactions, see Graeber, *Debt.*

51. For example, see public tenders in *Al-Arab* (Arabic newspaper published in Baghdad by British administration), no. 145 (1919)—Announcements.

52. See Guyer, *Marginal Gains,* 15–16.

53. Randeraad, "International Statistical Congress." See also Tooze, *Statistics;* Porter, *Rise of Statistical Thinking;* Desrosières, *Politics of Large Numbers.*

54. International Statistical Congress, *Report of the Delegates,* 4–55; International Statistical Congress, *Report of the Proceedings,* 321–43, 493–95.

55. NAUK: T1/11646, Convention Establishing an International Bureau of Commercial Statistics, December 21, 1913; NAUK: DO35/853/3, International Convention for the Publication of Customs Tariffs, July 5, 1890; Royal Statistical Society, *Jubilee Volume.*

56. IOR: V/26/660/3, Report on Indian Trade Statistics, 1906; ZNA: AB43/1, Memo of East African Production and Supply Council, December 13, 1943; ZNA: AB43/1, Customs Management Decree, January 24, 1948; NAUK: FO881/7269X, Zanzibar Customs Regulations, 1899; NAUK: RG47/23, Report of the British Empire Statistical Conference, 1920.

57. IOR: V/24/454, Review of Customs Administration in India, 1925–26.

58. ZNA: BF17/9, Annual Report of the East African Statistical Department, 1949; ZNA: AB43/5, Langdon Renwick, Comptroller Customs, Zanzibar, to Chief Secretary, April 26, 1952; NAUK: CO852/569/8, Colonial Economic Advisory Council, 1945; NAUK: CUST49/3341, "Report of an Enquiry into Mechanizing Routine Operations in the Valuation Branch," by F. S. Varley, April 1950.

59. ZNA: BF17/9, Annual Report of the East African Statistical Department, 1949.

60. Sweeney, "Game Warden's Permit," 116.

61. ZNA: BA50/1, "Audit Department Report, 1932," by F. W. P. Kingdom, October 16, 1933; ZNA: BA 35/5, Customs Office Order, 1937. Regarding the concept of parallel documentary circulation, see Çalışkan, *Market Threads,* chap. 2.

62. IOR: V/27/322/71, Bombay Sea Customs Manual, Corrected up to December 1921, 236.

63. IOR: V/26/660/3, Report of the Committee on Indian Trade Statistics, 1906; IOR: V/27/322/7, Indian Sea Customs Manual, Corrected up to March 1928; IOR: V/27/322/17, Indian Sea Customs Manual, Corrected up to December 31, 1952; IOR: V/27/332/20, Indian Customs Tariff Guide, Corrected up to December 31, 1930; IOR: V/27/322/28, Manual of Customs Audit, Corrected up to March 31, 1938; IOR: V/27/322/63 Rules and Notifications under the Sea Customs Act, 1878; etc.

64. NAUK: CUST155/29, Theory and History of Ad Valorem and Specific Duties, June 15, 1921.

65. NAUK: CO533/529/19, Customs Fraud Commission Report, Mombasa, 1940.

66. For similar anxieties and subversions in South Asia, see Raman, *Document Raj;* Hull, *Government of Paper.*

67. NAUK: CO533/529/19, Customs Fraud Commission Report, Mombasa, 1940, pp. 73–75; Sweeney, "Game Warden's Permit," 318.

68. NAUK: CO533/529/19, Customs Fraud Commission Report, Mombasa, 1940, p. 80.

69. IOR: V/27/322/87, Bombay Customs Appraisers' Manual, First Edition, January 1922.

70. IOR: V/27/322/71, Bombay Sea Customs Manual, December 1921, especially pp. 236–50.

71. IOR: V/26/660/3, Report of the Committee on Indian Statistics, 1906, p. 19.

72. IOR: V/27/322/71, Bombay Sea Customs Manual, 1921, pp. 138–41.

73. IOR: V/26/660/3, Report of the Committee on Indian Statistics, 1906, pp. 6, 18–19.

74. ZNA: AB15/76, Secretary Economic Control Board to Chief Secretary, April 12, 1943.

75. IOR: V/27/322/28, Manual of Customs Audit, March 31, 1938.

76. NAI: DCI/ST1–12(A), 10/1915, Charles Armstrong, Bombay Chamber of Commerce, to GoI, January 27, 1914; IOR: V/27/322/87, Bombay Customs Appraisers Manual, 1922.

77. NAUK: CO885/6/1, Report on Import and Export Statistics in the Colonies, 1892; CO852/569/3, SSC to East African Governors Conference, June 15/1944.

78. NAI: DCI/CT11–23, 9/1905, File 19, Report of H. W. Maclean, July 22, 1904; NAUK: CO535/86/2, Somaliland Blue Book 1927; NAUK: CO 852/1330/2, Colonial Economic Survey of Aden, 1949. Regarding similar efforts encountered in eighteenth-century Europe, see the classic work Kula, *Measures and Men*.

79. IOR: V/27/322/71, Bombay Sea Customs Manual 1921, p. 121.

80. NAUK: FO 881/6526, Strickland, Collector Customs, to L. Matthews, First Minister, Zanzibar Govt., January 31, 1894; NAUK: CO 817/29, Aden Colony Trade and Navigation Report, 1949–50.

81. IOR: V/24/454, Review of the Customs Administration in India, 1925–26 and 1926–27.

82. IOR: V/24/454, Review of the Customs Administration in India, 1925–26 and 1926–27.

83. NAI: DCI/CT11–23, 9/1905, File 19, Report of H. W. Maclean, July 22, 1904; IOR: L/PJ/6/1746, Legislative Assembly Debate, February 22, 1921; IOR: L/E/9/749, E. G. S. Apedaile to Under-Secretary of State Burma, December 2, 1940.

84. IOR: R/20/B1310, Controller of Civil Supplies, to Acting Chief Secretary, Govt. of Aden, April 11, 1940.

85. IOR: V/27/322/87, Bombay Customs Appraisers Manual, January 1922, pp. 25–31; IOR: V/27/322/71, Bombay Sea Customs Manual, December 1921, pp. 132–40; IOR: V/27/322/28, Manual of Customs Audit 31/March 1938, pp. 29–33.

86. ZNA: AB43/19, Zanzibar Chamber of Commerce to Financial Secretary GoZ, April 17, 1955; IOR: V/27/322/87, Bombay Customs Appraisers Manual, January 1922, p. 15.

87. ZNA: AB43/19, Note by H. L. Renwick, Comptroller of Customs, Zanzibar, July 8, 1945.

88. IOR: R/15/2/1324, De Grenier, Director Customs, to PA Bahrain, December 5, 1934; IOR: R/15/2/1324, Customs House Notification, September 5, 1934; IOR: V/27/322/71, Bombay Sea Customs Manual, December 1921, p. 336.

89. NAUK: CO885/6/1, Report on Import and Export Statistics in the Colonies, 1892; regarding the work of grading commodities, see Cronon, *Nature's Metropolis*, 116–18, 133–36.

90. NAI: DCI/SC2529–2532(B), 12/1894, Collector Customs, Calcutta, to CBR, October 18, 1894; IOR: R/20/B3561, Aide Memoire on the Economy of the Yemen, June 1950; IOR: V/27/322/71, Bombay Sea Customs Manual, 1921, p. 136; NAUK: CO726/18, Tanganyika Trade and Information Local Advisory Committee Reports for July 1933 and for September 1934.

91. NAI: DCI/ST1–12(A), 10/1915, Southern Indian Chamber of Commerce to Chief Secretary Government of Madras, October 2, 1914; NAI: CBR1123-Cus-I/1936, Note by AMR, August 7, 1936; IOR: R/20/B/34, Aden Excise Ordinance, November 26, 1937; NAUK: CO535/86/1, British American Tobacco Co. to Under-SSC, December 14, 1928.

92. ZNA: AB77/4, Minutes of Second Meeting of the Controls Advisory Committee, December 19, 1943; ZNA: AB43/19, A. Bishop, Zanzibar Comptroller of Customs, to Chief Secretary, January 7, 1954.

93. IOR: R/20/B34, Aden Excise Ordinance, November 26, 1937; IOR: V/27/322/88, List of Articles Ordinarily Assessed on Real Value, Revised August 31, 1931, February 1, 1934, and August 1, 1938.

94. NAUK: CAB32/116, Minutes of Meeting Committee on Customs Administration, Imperial Economic Conference, July 28, 1932.

95. Gordon, *Fabricating Consumers;* Wickramasinghe, *Dressing the Colonised Body,* 55–57; Godley, "Selling the Sewing Machine"; R. Davies, *Peacefully Working.*

96. 1931 UKPC 46, Vacuum Oil Co. v. Secretary of State for India, p. 3.

97. NAUK: CO690/1–35, Zanzibar Blue Books, 1913–47; NAUK: CO817/1–29, Report on the Trade and Navigation of Aden, 1927–50; NAUK: CO852/98/5, G. L. M. Clauson to Reilly, Governor of Aden, May 26, 1938; NAUK: CO852/98/5, Note by Henlen, May 10, 1938; IOR: V/24/461, Report of the Customs Administration of Bombay, 1863–78; IOR: V/24/454, Report of the Customs Administration of India, 1925–26 to 1930–31; IOR: R/20/B603, Milner, SSC, to Officer Administering the Government of [All Colonies], November 19, 1920.

98. IOR: V/24/454, Review of Customs Administration of India, 1925–26 to 1930–31.

99. 1936 UKPC 114, Ford Motor Company of India v. Secretary of State for India, p. 17, Deposition of Gordon Edward Corey, January 16, 1935.

100. NAUK: CO726/18, Tanganyika Trade and Information Local Advisory Committee Report for January 1934.

101. IOR: R/1/1/4781, C. Latimer, Resident States of Western India, to Governor General, March 12, 1934; IOR: V/27/322/63, Rules and Notifications under the Sea Customs Act, 1878, 168; NAUK: CAB32/116, Minutes of Committee on Customs Valuation, Imperial Economic Conference, August 8, 1932.

102. IOR: R/1/1/4781, Note by P. Caddell, n.d. (1935); IOR: R/1/1/4781, Note by V. T. Krishnamachari, Diwan of Baroda, April 4, 1935; IOR: R/1/1/4781, Note by K. V. Gohel, June 8, 1935; IOR: R/2/639/319, Note by P. R. Caddell, Diwan Junagadh, February 18, 1934; Sweeney, "Game Warden's Permit."

103. NAUK: CO852/215/15, W.H. Ingrams, Resident Mukalla, to Sultan Salih (Qu'aiti), April 2, 1939.

104. IOR: L/PS/10/1053/2, Persian Council of Ministers Statement on Exemptions to Customs Duty, 20 Semboleh 1303; IOR: V/27/322/71, Bombay Sea Customs Manual, 1921, pp. 137–41.

105. IOR: V/26/660/3, Report of the Committee on Indian Trade Statistics, 1906, p. 18.

106. IOR: V/27/322/28, Manual of Customs Audit March 31, 1938, p. 34.

107. IOR: V/27/322/71, Bombay Sea Customs Manual, 1921, p. 122.

108. NAI: DCI/SC42–61(A), 1/1905, Note by J.A. Robertson, December 13, 1904; NAI: DCI/SC42–61(A), 1/1905, Note by L.B.B., December 29, 1904; NAUK: CO323/903, Note by G. Grindle, January 16, 1923; IOR: V/24/454, Review of Customs Administration in India, 1930–31.

109. NAUK: CUST 117/67, Customs Valuation Instructions 1935; IOR: V/27/322/28, Manual of Customs Audit, March 31, 1938, p. 41; IOR: V/27/322/87, Bombay Customs Appraisers Manual, January 1922, p. 37; IOR: R/2/641/333, Karbhari, Maliya State, to PA Western Kathiawar, April 12, 1936.

110. NAI: DCI/CS1–15(A), 9/1905, Extracts from the Report of the Committee on Indian Trade Statistics.

111. NAI: DCI/ST1–12(A), October 1915, W.J. Keith, Officiating Revenue Secretary, to GoI, DCI, August 4, 1914.

112. IOR: V/27/322/71, Bombay Sea Customs Manual, December 1921, p. 123.

113. NAUK: CO607/1–38, Somaliland Blue Books; NAUK: CO543/1–36, Kenya Blue Books; NAUK: CO690/1–35, Zanzibar Blue Books; NAUK: CO726/1–30, Tanganyika Blue Books; IOR: R/20/B602, Procedures for Compiling Blue Books, 1936; IOR: R/20/B603, Procedures for Compiling Blue Books, 1938; IOR: R/20/B604, Procedures for Compiling Blue Books, 1941.

114. NAUK: CO817/1–29, Reports on the Trade and Navigation of Aden; MSA: Political Annual Reports of the Seaborne Trade and Navigation of the Bombay Presidency and Sind; MSA: Reports of the Trade and Administration of the Persian Gulf.

115. IOR: L/PS/12/3434, F.A.G. Gray, Commercial Secretary, Tehran, to SSFA, Overseas Trade, April 8, 1933.

116. IOR: R.2.640/331, Agreement between H.M.G. and Rulers of Morvi, Porbandar, and Junagadh, 1935; IOR: R.2.640/331, Secretary to Crown Representative to States of Western India, December 15, 1937; IOR: R.2.640/331, Dewan Porbandar to Secretary to Resident States of Western India, July 14, 1938.

117. NAUK: CO852/569/8, Note by G.E. Wood, October 26, 1945; NAUK: CO1034/2, Report of Colonial Statisticians, 1950. Regarding the unreliability of public market information and the continued use of correspondence after its availability, see Trivellato, *Familiarity of Strangers,* 170–74.

118. ZNA: AB77/28, "Some Aspects of National Income Calculations in Colonial Conditions," enclosed in A. Creech Jones to Resident Zanzibar, July 25, 1949; ZNA: AB77/4, Indian National Association to Chief Secretary GoZ, May 4, 1943.

119. NAUK: CO726/18, Tanganyika Trade and Information Committee Report, June 1933; NAUK: CO535/121/9, Governor Aden to H. R. Cowell, CO, July 28, 1937; IOR: R/2/629/173a, Note by R. S. D., April 7, 1931.

120. Sweeney, "Game Warden's Permit," 116.

121. IOR: R/2/639/319, Note by P. R. Caddell, Diwan Junagadh, January 18, 1934.

122. IOR: R/2/641/333, Kabhari, Maliya State, to PA Western Kathiawar, December 4, 1936.

123. Regarding the usefulness of ignorance, see, for example, McGoey, "Strategic Unknowns"; for a similar notion of ambiguity, see Best, *Limits of Transparency,* chap. 1; Best, "Bureaucratic Ambiguity."

CONCLUSION

1. "Reluctant Don"; Zaidi, "Reluctant Mafioso."

2. See Zaidi, *Dongri to Dubai,* chaps. 2–3.

3. Zaidi, "Reluctant Mafioso"; Zaidi, *Dongri to Dubai,* chap. 3; Adhia, "Role of Ideas," 51–52, 63.

4. Singh, "Films Being Used"; Srivastava, "Bollywood and the Mafia"; Zaidi, "Reluctant Mafioso."

5. Karras, *Smuggling;* Friman and Andreas, *Illicit Global Economy;* Tagliacozzo, *Secret Trades.*

6. North and Thomas, *Rise of the Western World;* Greif, *Institutions;* Kuran, *Long Divergence;* Acemoglu and Robinson, *Why Nations Fail.*

7. See also Haynes, *Small Town Capitalism.*

BIBLIOGRAPHY

INTERVIEWS

Rajiv Ahuja (manager in Khimji Ramdas firm)
Interviewed by author, June 25, 2008—Muscat, Oman
Mohan Jashanmal (descendant and manager in Jashanmal firm)
Interviewed by author, June 18, 2008—Abu Dhabi, United Arab Emirates
Umesh Khimji (descendent of Khimji Ramdas)
Interviewed by author, December 9, 2009—Muscat, Oman
Usha Khimji (descendant of Ratansi Purshottam, married into Khimji Ramdas family)
Interviewed by author, January 12, 2010—Muscat, Oman
Vimal Purecha (descendant of Ratansi Purshottam)
Interviewed by author, June 22, 2008, and January 10, 2009—Muscat, Oman
Interviewed by author, May 29, 2008—Waltham, Massachusetts
Shawqi Sultan (descendant of Mohammed Fadhl)
Interviewed by author, December 8, 2009, and January 17, 2010—Muscat, Oman

PRIVATE PAPERS

Abdullah al-Ṭābūr Archive [AT], Jumʿa al-Mājid Library—Dubai, UAE
Faculty of Middle East and Asian Studies, Cambridge University
Papers of Bertram S. Thomas [BT]
Kings College Archives Centre, Cambridge University
J. M. Keynes Papers
Middle East Centre Archive, St. Anthony's College, Oxford University
Papers of Percy Z. Cox
Papers of William Rupert Hay
Ratansi Purshottam Archive [RP], in possession of Vimal Purecha—Muscat, Oman

BUSINESS RECORDS

Caird Library, National Maritime Museum [NMM]—Greenwich, UK
    British India Steam Navigation Company Records [BIS]
    Cayzer, Irvine & Company Records [CAY]
    Frank Strick & Company Records [SRI]
    Peninsular & Oriental Steam Navigation Company Records [P&O]
Guildhall Library [GL]—(Held at London Metropolitan Archives) London
    Eastern Bank Records [EB]
    Inchcape Group Records [ICG], including:
        Papers of Gray, Dawes & Company
        Papers of Gray, Mackenzie & Company
        Papers of Mackinnon, Mackenzie & Company
        Papers of Smith, Mackenzie & Company
Hongkong and Shanghai Banking Corporation Archive [HSBC]—London
    British Bank of the Middle East/Imperial Bank of Persia Records [BBME]
    Mercantile Bank of India Records [MBI]

LEGAL RECORDS

Bombay High Court Reporter, 1874, vol. 11: Regina v. Ba'pu Ya'dav and Ra'ma' Tulsira'm
League of Nations Treaty Series 45, 112 LNTS 371
Proceedings of Cases before the Judicial Committee of the Privy Council (British Empire)
    897 UKPC 17: Sala Mohommed Jafferbhoy et al. v. Dame Janbai
    923 UKPC 72: Ahmed Najoo Khan v. Ali Ibrahim Noor and Haji Ibrahim Noor
    929 UKPC 87 and 88: Julio Fernandes et al. v. Mercantile Bank of India
    931 UKPC 46: Vacuum Oil Company v. Secretary of State for India
    936 UKPC 114: Ford Motor Company of India v. Secretary of State for India

STATE ARCHIVES

India Office Records [IOR], British Library—London
    Aden Residency Records (R/20)
    Bahrain Agency Records (R/15/2)
    Bahrain Consular Court Records (R/15/3)
    Economic Files (L/E)
    Kathiawar Agency Records (R/2)
    Kuwait Agency Records (R/15/5)

Muscat Agency Records (R/15/6)
Persian Gulf Residency Records (R/15/1)
Political and Judicial Files (L/P&J)
Political and Secret Files (L/P&S)
Maharashtra State Archives [MSA]—Mumbai, India
Financial Department Records [F]
Judicial Department Records [J]
Marine Department Records [M]
Political Department Records [P]
Revenue Department Records [R]
National Archives of India [NAI]—New Delhi, India
Department of Commerce and Industry Records [DCI]
Central Board of Revenue [CBR]
Commerce and Trade [CT]
Customs [CS]
Merchant Shipping [MS]
Revenue, Agriculture & Commerce [RA&C]
Statistics [ST]
Statistics and Commerce [SC]
Foreign and Political Department Records [FP]
Foreign Department Records [F]
National Archives of the United Kingdom [NAUK]—Kew, UK
Admiralty Records [ADM]
Board of Trade Records [BT]
Cabinet Office Records [CAB]
Colonial Office Records [CO]
Customs Department [CUST]
Dominions Office Records [DO]
Foreign Office Records [FO]
High Court of the Admiralty Records [HCA]
Ministry of Transport Records [MT]
Treasury Records [T]
War Office Records [WO]
Zanzibar National Archives [ZNA]
High Court Records [HC]
Arabic Records [AA, AL, and AM]

PUBLISHED SOURCES

Abal, Shakir. *Al-hawā ʿalā niyyatnā* [The winds are fair, the same as our intentions].
   2012. Video. www.youtube.com/watch?v=E4CY2pRVwXM.
Abdullah, Thabit. *Merchants, Mamluks, and Murder: The Political Economy of
   Trade in Eighteenth-Century Basra*. Albany: SUNY Press, 2001.

Acemoglu, Daron, and James A. Robinson. *Why Nations Fail: The Origins of Power, Prosperity, and Poverty.* New York: Random House, 2013.

Adhia, Nimish. "The Role of Ideas in India's Economic Reforms." PhD, diss., University of Illinois, Chicago, 2010.

Agius, Dionisius. *In the Wake of the Dhow: The Arabian Gulf and Oman.* Reading, UK: Garnet and Ithaca Press, 2002.

Aitchison, Charles U., and Government of India. *A Collection of Treaties, Engagements, and Sanads Relating to India and Neighbouring Countries: Persia and the Persian Gulf.* Vol. 10. Calcutta: G. A. Savielle and P. M. Cranenburgh, Bengal Printing, 1892.

Akerlof, George A. "The Market for 'Lemons': Quality Uncertainty and the Market Mechanism." *Quarterly Journal of Economics* 84, no. 3 (1970): 488–500.

Alchian, Armen A., and Harold Demsetz. "The Property Right Paradigm." *Journal of Economic History* 33, no. 1 (March 1973): 16–27.

Allen, Calvin H. "Sayyids, Shets and Sultans: Politics and Trade in Muscat under the Al Bu Sa'id, 1785–1914." PhD diss., University of Washington, 1978.

Allen, Richard Blair. *Slaves, Freedmen, and Indentured Laborers in Colonial Mauritius.* Cambridge: Cambridge University Press, 1999.

Alpers, Edward A. *Ivory and Slaves: Changing Pattern of International Trade in East Central Africa to the Later Nineteenth Century.* Berkeley: University of California Press, 1975.

———. "The Story of Swema: Female Vulnerability in Nineteenth-Century East Africa." In *Women and Slavery in Africa*, edited by Claire C. Robertson and Martin A. Klein, chap. 11. Madison: University of Wisconsin Press, 1983.

Alpers, Edward A., Gwyn Campbell, and Michael Salman, eds. *Slavery and Resistance in Africa and Asia.* London: Routledge, 2005.

Ambedkar, Bhimrao Ramji. *History of Indian Currency and Banking.* Bombay: Thacker, 1947.

———. *The Problem of the Rupee: Its Origin and Its Solution.* London: P. S. King and Son, 1923.

Anderson, Clare. *Convicts in the Indian Ocean: Transportation from South Asia to Mauritius, 1815–53.* New York: St. Martin's Press, 2000.

Aslanian, Sebouh. *From the Indian Ocean to the Mediterranean: The Global Trade Networks of Armenian Merchants from New Julfa.* Berkeley: University of California Press, 2011.

———. "'The Salt in a Merchant's Letter': The Culture of Julfan Correspondence in the Indian Ocean and the Mediterranean." *Journal of World History* 19, no. 2 (June 2008): 127–88.

———. "Social Capital and the Role of Networks in Julfan Trade: Informal and Semi-Formal Institutions at Work." *Journal of Global History* 1, no. 3 (2006): 383–402.

Austen, Ralph A. "The 19th Century Islamic Slave Trade from East Africa (Swahili and Red Sea Coasts): A Tentative Census." In *The Economics of the Indian Ocean Slave Trade in the Nineteenth Century*, edited by William Gervase Clarence-Smith, 21–44. London: Frank Cass, 1989.

Avery, Peter, William Bayne Fisher, Gavin Hambly, and Charles Melville. *The Cambridge History of Iran: From Nadir Shah to the Islamic Republic*. Vol. 7. Cambridge: Cambridge University Press, 1991.

Bagchi, Amiya Kumar. *The Presidency Banks and the Indian Economy, 1876–1914*. Calcutta: Oxford University Press, 1989.

Bahadur, Gaiutra. *Coolie Woman: The Odyssey of Indenture*. Chicago: University of Chicago Press, 2013.

Ballard, Roger. "Coalitions of Reciprocity and the Maintenance of Financial Integrity within Informal Value Transmission Systems: The Operational Dynamics of Contemporary Hawala Networks." *Journal of Banking Regulation* 6, no. 4 (2005): 319–52.

Barendse, R. J. *Arabian Seas, 1700–1763*. 4 vols. Leiden: Brill, 2009.

———. "Trade and State in the Arabian Seas: A Survey from the Fifteenth to the Eighteenth Century." *Journal of World History* 11, no. 2 (October 2000): 173–225.

Bayly, C. A. *Rulers, Townsmen and Bazaars: North Indian Society in the Age of British Expansion, 1770–1870*. Cambridge: Cambridge University Press, 1983.

Benton, Lauren. "Colonial Law and Cultural Difference: Jurisdictional Politics and the Formation of the Colonial State." *Comparative Studies in Society and History* 41, no. 3 (July 1999): 563–88.

———. *Law and Colonial Cultures: Legal Regimes in World History, 1400–1900*. Cambridge: Cambridge University Press, 2001.

———. "Legal Spaces of Empire: Piracy and the Origins of Ocean Regionalism." *Comparative Studies in Society and History* 47, no. 4 (October 2005): 700–724.

Best, Jacqueline. "Bureaucratic Ambiguity." *Economy and Society* 41, no. 1 (2012): 84–106.

———. *The Limits of Transparency: Ambiguity and the History of International Finance*. Ithaca, NY: Cornell University Press, 2005.

Beunza, Daniel, Iain Hardie, and Donald MacKenzie. "A Price Is a Social Thing: Towards a Material Sociology of Arbitrage." *Organization Studies* 27, no. 5 (May 2006): 721–45.

Bhagwati, Jagdish, and Bent Hansen. "A Theoretical Analysis of Smuggling." *Quarterly Journal of Economics* 87, no. 2 (May 1973): 172–87.

Birla, Ritu. *Stages of Capital: Law, Culture, and Market Governance in Late Colonial India*. Durham, NC: Duke University Press, 2009.

Bishara, Fahad. "A Sea of Debt: Histories of Commerce and Obligation in the Indian Ocean, c. 1850–1940." PhD diss., Duke University, 2012.

Blake, George. *B. I. Centenary, 1856–1956*. London: Collins, 1956.

"Bombay Cricket: Saturday's Results." *Times of India,* October 20, 1924, 14.

Boxberger, Linda. "Avoiding Ribā: Credit and Custodianship in Nineteenth- and Early-Twentieth Century Ḥaḍramawt." *Islamic Law and Society* 5, no. 2 (January 1, 1998): 196–213.

Braudel, Fernand. *The Mediterranean and the Mediterranean World in the Age of Philip II*. Berkeley: University of California Press, 1995.

Brunschvig, R. "'Abd." In *The Encyclopaedia of Islam*, edited by H. A. R. Gibb, 1:24–40. Leiden: E. J. Brill, 1986.

Butler, Judith. *Gender Trouble: Feminism and the Subversion of Identity*. New York: Routledge, 2006.

———. "Performative Agency." *Journal of Cultural Economy* 3, no. 2 (July 1, 2010): 147–61.

Cain, P. J, and A. G. Hopkins. *British Imperialism, 1688–2000*. Harlow, UK: Longman, 2002.

———. "Gentlemanly Capitalism and British Expansion Overseas II: New Imperialism, 1850–1945." *Economic History Review* 40, no. 1 (February 1987): 1–26.

Çalışkan, Koray. *Market Threads: How Cotton Farmers and Traders Create a Global Commodity*. Princeton, NJ: Princeton University Press, 2010.

Callon, Michel. "An Essay on Framing and Overflowing: Economic Externalities Revisited by Sociology." In *The Laws of the Markets*, edited by Michel Callon. Oxford: Blackwell Publishers/ Sociological Review, 1998.

———, ed. *The Laws of the Markets*. Oxford: Blackwell / Sociological Review, 1998.

Campbell, Donald T. "Assessing the Impact of Planned Social Change." Dartmouth Public Affairs Center, Occasional Paper 8, December 1976. http://portals.wi.wur.nl/files/docs/ppme/Assessing_impact_of_planned_social_change.pdf.

Campbell, Gwyn, ed. *Abolition and Its Aftermath in Indian Ocean Africa and Asia*. London: Routledge, 2005.

———. Introduction to *The Structure of Slavery in Indian Ocean Africa and Asia*, edited by Gwyn Campbell, vii–xxxi. London: Frank Cass, 2004.

———. "Madagascar and the Slave Trade, 1810–1895." *Journal of African History* 22, no. 2 (January 1981): 203–27.

———, ed. *The Structure of Slavery in Indian Ocean Africa and Asia*. London: Frank Cass, 2004.

Campbell, Gwyn, and Edward A. Alpers. "Introduction: Slavery, Forced Labour and Resistance in the Indian Ocean, Africa and Asia." *Slavery and Abolition* 25, no. 2 (August 1, 2004): ix–xxvii.

Carter, Marina. *Servants, Sirdars, and Settlers: Indians in Mauritius, 1834–1874*. Oxford: Oxford University Press, 1995.

Carter, Marina, and Hubert Gerbeau. "Covert Slaves and Coveted Coolies in the Early 19th Century Mascareignes." In *The Economics of the Indian Ocean Slave Trade in the Nineteenth Century*, edited by William Gervase Clarence-Smith, 194–208. London: Frank Cass, 1989.

Cassanelli, Lee V. *The Shaping of Somali Society: Reconstructing the History of a Pastoral People, 1600–1900*. Philadelphia: University of Pennsylvania Press, 1982.

Catlin-Jairazbhoy, Amy, and Edward A. Alpers, eds. *Sidis and Scholars: Essays on African Indians*. Noida, India: Rainbow, 2004.

Chakrabarty, Dipesh. *Provincializing Europe: Postcolonial Thought and Historical Difference*. Princeton, NJ: Princeton University Press, 2009.

Chandavarkar, A. G. "The Nature and Effects of Gold Hoarding in Underdeveloped Economies." *Oxford Economic Papers* 13, no. 2 (June 1, 1961): 137–48.

Chatterjee, Indrani. "Abolition by Denial: The South Asian Example." In *Abolition and Its Aftermath in Indian Ocean Africa and Asia*, edited by Gwyn Campbell, 150–68. London: Routledge, 2005.

———. *Gender, Slavery, and Law in Colonial India*. Oxford: Oxford University Press, 1999.

———. "Slavery, Semantics, and the Sound of Silence." In *Slavery and South Asian History*, edited by Indrani Chatterjee and Richard Maxwell Eaton, 287–316. Bloomington: Indiana University Press, 2006.

Chatterjee, Indrani, and Richard Maxwell Eaton, eds. *Slavery and South Asian History*. Bloomington: Indiana University Press, 2006.

Chaudhuri, K. N. *Asia before Europe: Economy and Civilisation of the Indian Ocean from the Rise of Islam to 1750*. Cambridge: Cambridge University Press, 1990.

———. *Trade and Civilisation in the Indian Ocean: An Economic History from the Rise of Islam to 1750*. Cambridge: Cambridge University Press, 1985.

Chew, Emrys. *Arming the Periphery: The Arms Trade in the Indian Ocean during the Age of Global Empire*. Basingstoke, Hampshire: Palgrave Macmillan, 2012.

Churchill, Winston. *The Story of the Malakand Field Force: An Episode of Frontier War*. London: Thomas Nelson and Sons, 1916.

Clarence-Smith, W. G. *The Economics of the Indian Ocean Slave Trade in the Nineteenth Century*. London: Frank Cass, 1989.

———. "The Economics of the Indian Ocean Slave Trade in the Nineteenth Century: An Overview." In *The Economics of the Indian Ocean Slave Trade in the Nineteenth Century*, 1–20. London: Frank Cass, 1989.

Cohen, Arthur, Sir Alfred Edmund Bateman, and Sir David Miller Barbour. *Report of the Royal Commission on Shipping Rings: With Minutes of Evidence and Appendices*. London: H. M. Stationery Office, 1909.

Colomb, P. H. *Slave-Catching in the Indian Ocean. A Record of Naval Experiences*. London: Longmans, Green, 1873.

Cooper, Frederick. *From Slaves to Squatters: Plantation Labor and Agriculture in Zanzibar and Coastal Kenya, 1890–1925*. New Haven, CT: Yale University Press, 1980.

———. *Plantation Slavery on the East Coast of Africa*. Portsmouth, NH: Heinemann, 1997.

Crews, Robert. "Trafficking in Evil? The Global Arms Trade and the Politics of Disorder." In *Global Muslims in the Age of Steam and Print, 1850–1930*, edited by Nile Green and James L. Gelvin. Berkeley: University of California Press, 2014.

Daniell, Clarmont John. *The Gold Treasure of India*. London: K. Paul, Trench, 1884.

Davies, Charles E. *The Blood-Red Arab Flag: An Investigation into Qasimi Piracy, 1797–1820*. Exeter: University of Exeter Press, 1997.

Davies, Robert Bruce. *Peacefully Working to Conquer the World: Singer Sewing Machines in Foreign Markets, 1854–1920*. New York: Arno Press, 1976.

"Death." *Times of India*, September 27, 1927, 3.

de Certeau, Michel. *The Practice of Everyday Life*. Translated by Steven Rendall. Berkeley: University of California Press, 1984.

Desrosières, Alain. *The Politics of Large Numbers: A History of Statistical Reasoning.* Cambridge, MA: Harvard University Press, 2002.

Dua, Jatin. "A Sea of Trade and a Sea of Fish: Piracy and Protection in the Western Indian Ocean." *Journal of Eastern African Studies* 7, no. 2 (2013): 353–70.

Dutt, Romesh Chunder. *The Economic History of India under Early British Rule: From the Rise of the British Power in 1757 to the Accession of Queen Victoria in 1837.* London: Routledge, 1950.

Elias, Ney, ed. *Precis of Papers Regarding Aden, 1838–1872.* Simla, India: Government Central Branch Press, 1876.

Elyachar, Julia. *Markets of Dispossession: NGOs, Economic Development, and the State in Cairo.* Durham, NC: Duke University Press, 2005.

Erdem, Y. Hakan. *Slavery in the Ottoman Empire and Its Demise, 1800–1909.* London: Macmillan, 1996.

Ewald, Janet. "Bondsmen, Freedmen, and Maritime Industrial Transportation, c.1840–1900." *Slavery and Abolition* 31, no. 3 (2010): 451–66.

Fisher, Irving. *The Purchasing Power of Money: Its Determination and Relation to Credit, Interest and Crises.* New York: Macmillan, 1920.

Floor, Willem. "The Marketpolice in Qājār Persia: The Office of Dārūgha-Yi Bāzār and Muḥtasib." *Die Welt des Islams* 13, no. 3/4 (January 1, 1971): 212–29.

———. "The Office of Muhtasib in Iran." *Iranian Studies* 18, no. 1 (January 1, 1985): 53–74.

Foucault, Michel. *The Birth of Biopolitics: Lectures at the Collège de France, 1978–1979.* Edited by Michel Senellart. Translated by Graham Burchell. New York: Picador, 2010.

———. *Power/Knowledge: Selected Interviews and Other Writings, 1972–1977.* Edited by Colin Gordon. New York: Random House, 1988.

———. *Security, Territory, Population: Lectures at the Collège de France 1977–1978.* Edited by Michel Senellart. Translated by Graham Burchell. New York: Picador, 2007.

Friedman, Milton. *Essays in Positive Economics.* Chicago: University of Chicago Press, 1953.

Friman, H. Richard, and Peter Andreas, eds. *The Illicit Global Economy and State Power.* Lanham, MD: Rowman and Littlefield, 1999.

Furuseth, Andrew. *Safety of Life at Sea: Analysis and Explanatory Notes of the London Convention on Safety of Life at Sea in Relation to the American Merchant Marine.* Washington, DC: US Government Printing Office, 1914.

Gallagher, John, and Ronald Robinson. "The Imperialism of Free Trade." *Economic History Review,* n.s., 6, no. 1 (January 1, 1953): 1–15.

Gambling, Trevor, and Rifaat Ahmed Abdel Karim. *Business and Accounting Ethics in Islam.* London: Mansell, 1991.

Garretson, Peter P. "The Naggadras, Trade, and Selected Towns in Nineteenth and Early Twentieth Century Ethiopia." *International Journal of African Historical Studies* 12, no. 3 (January 1, 1979): 416–39.

Geertz, Clifford. "The Bazaar Economy: Information and Search in Peasant Marketing." *American Economic Review* 68, no. 2 (May 1, 1978): 28–32.

———. *Peddlers and Princes: Social Change and Economic Modernization in Two Indonesian Towns*. Chicago: University of Chicago Press, 1963.

Gibson-Graham, J. K. *The End of Capitalism (As We Knew It): A Feminist Critique of Political Economy*. Minneapolis: University of Minnesota Press, 2006.

Gilbert, Erik. *Dhows and the Colonial Economy of Zanzibar, 1860–1970*. Oxford: James Currey, 2004.

Godley, Andrew. "Selling the Sewing Machine around the World: Singer's International Marketing Strategies, 1850–1920." *Enterprise and Society* 7, no. 2 (2006): 266–314.

Goffman, Erving. *Frame Analysis: An Essay on the Organization of Experience*. Cambridge, MA: Harvard University Press, 1974.

Goitein, Shelomo Dov. *Mediterranean Society: The Jewish Communities of the Arab World as Portrayed in the Documents of the Cairo Geniza*. Berkeley: University of California Press, 1967.

Goldberg, Jessica. "Choosing and Enforcing Business Relationships in the Eleventh-Century Mediterranean: Reassessing the 'Maghribī Traders.'" *Past and Present* 216, no. 1 (August 1, 2012): 3–40.

———. *Trade and Institutions in the Medieval Mediterranean: The Geniza Merchants and Their Business World*. Cambridge: Cambridge University Press, 2012.

Goodhart, Charles. "Problems of Monetary Management: The U.K. Experience." In *Inflation, Depression, and Economic Policy in the West,* edited by Anthony Courakis, 111–46. Totowa, NJ: Rowman and Littlefield, 1981.

Gordon, Andrew. *Fabricating Consumers: The Sewing Machine in Modern Japan*. Berkeley: University of California Press, 2012.

Goswami, Manu. *Producing India: From Colonial Economy to National Space*. Chicago: University of Chicago Press, 2004.

Government of Great Britain. *Muscat Dhows Arbitration in the Permanent Court of Arbitration at The Hague: Grant of the French Flag to Muscat Dhows, the Case on Behalf of the Government of His Britannic Majesty and His Highness the Sultan of Muscat*. London: Harrison and Sons for the Foreign Office, 1905.

Government of India. *The Indian Arms Act, 1878: As Modified up to the 1st July, 1892*. Calcutta: Government Central Printing Office, 1892.

———. *The Indian Penal Code (Act XLV of 1860): With Notes*. Calcutta: G. C. Hay, 1861.

———. *Report of a Commission to Enquire into the Operation of Act XIX of 1861 Being an Act "To Provide for a Government Paper Currency."* Calcutta: Office of Superintendent, Government Printing, 1867.

———. *Reports of Currency Committees*. Calcutta: Government Central Branch Press, 1928.

Graeber, David. *Debt: The First 5,000 Years*. Updated ed. Brooklyn, NY: Melville House, 2014.

Grant, Jonathan A. *Rulers, Guns, and Money: The Global Arms Trade in the Age of Imperialism.* Cambridge, MA: Harvard University Press, 2007.

Green, Nile. *Bombay Islam: The Religious Economy of the West Indian Ocean, 1840–1915.* Cambridge: Cambridge University Press, 2011.

Greif, Avner. "Contract Enforceability and Economic Institutions in Early Trade: The Maghribi Traders' Coalition." *American Economic Review* 83, no. 3 (June 1, 1993): 525–48.

———. *Institutions and the Path to the Modern Economy: Lessons from Medieval Trade.* Cambridge: Cambridge University Press, 2006.

———. "Reputation and Coalitions in Medieval Trade: Evidence on the Maghribi Traders." *Journal of Economic History* 49, no. 4 (December 1, 1989): 857–82.

Grossman, Sanford J., and Joseph E. Stiglitz. "On the Impossibility of Informationally Efficient Markets." *American Economic Review* 70, no. 3 (June 1, 1980): 393–408.

Guyer, Jane I. *Marginal Gains: Monetary Transactions in Atlantic Africa.* Chicago: University of Chicago Press, 2004.

———. "Niches, Margins and Profits: Persisting with Heterogeneity." *African Economic History,* no. 32 (January 1, 2004): 173–91.

Hacking, Ian. "The Looping Effect of Human Kinds." In *Causal Cognition: A Multidisciplinary Debate,* edited by Dan Sperber, David Premack, and Ann J. Premack, 351–83. Oxford: Clarendon Press, 1995.

Haider, Najaf. "Precious Metal Flows and Currency Circulation in the Mughal Empire." *Journal of the Economic and Social History of the Orient* 39, no. 3 (January 1, 1996): 298–364.

Harms, Robert W., Bernard K. Freamon, and David W. Blight, eds. *Indian Ocean Slavery in the Age of Abolition.* New Haven, CT: Yale University Press, 2013.

Harvey, David. *The Enigma of Capital and the Crises of Capitalism.* London: Profile Books, 2011.

———. *The Limits to Capital.* Chicago: University of Chicago Press, 1982.

Haynes, Douglas E. *Small Town Capitalism in Western India: Artisans, Merchants and the Making of the Informal Economy, 1870–1960.* Cambridge: Cambridge University Press, 2012.

"Hoarding." *New York Times,* November 27, 1873.

Hopkins, A. G., ed. *Globalization in World History.* New York: Norton, 2002.

Hopper, Matthew. "The African Presence in Arabia: Slavery, the World Economy and the African Diaspora in Eastern Arabia, 1840–1940." PhD diss., University of California, Los Angeles, 2006.

———. "Imperialism and the Dilemma of Slavery in Eastern Arabia and the Gulf." *Itinerario* 30, no. 3 (2006): 78–94.

———. *Slaves of One Master: Globalization and Slavery in Arabia in the Age of Empire.* New Haven, CT: Yale University Press, 2015.

Horden, Peregrine, and Nicholas Purcell. *The Corrupting Sea: A Study of Mediterranean History.* Oxford: Blackwell, 2000.

Horii, Satoe. "Reconsideration of Legal Devices (Ḥiyal) in Islamic Jurisprudence: The Ḥanafīs and Their 'Exits' (Makhārij)." *Islamic Law and Society* 9, no. 3 (January 1, 2002): 312–57.

Hughes, Julie E. *Animal Kingdoms: Hunting, the Environment, and Power in the Indian Princely States.* Cambridge, MA: Harvard University Press, 2013.

Hull, Matthew Stuart. *Government of Paper: The Materiality of Bureaucracy in Urban Pakistan.* Berkeley: University of California Press, 2012.

Hunter, F. Robert. *Egypt under the Khedives, 1805–1879: From Household Government to Modern Bureaucracy.* Pittsburgh: University of Pittsburgh Press, 1984.

Ibn 'Abdūn, Muḥammad ibn Aḥmad al-Tujībī. *Risālah fī al-qaḍā' wa-al-Ḥisbah.* Edited by Fāṭimah Idrīsī. Beirut: Dār Ibn Ḥazm lil-Ṭibā'ah wa-al-Nashr wa-al-Tawzī', 2009.

Ibn Ruzaiq, Salil. *History of the Imams and Sayyids of Oman, from A.D. 661–1856.* Translated by George Percy Badger. Hakluyt Society, First Series, 44. Farnham, UK: Ashgate, 2010.

International Statistical Congress. *Report of the Delegates to the International Statistical Congress Held at St. Petersburg in August 1872.* Washington, DC: US Government Printing Office, 1875.

———. *Report of the Proceedings of the Fourth Session of the International Statistical Congress.* London: H. M. Stationery Office, 1861.

Jardine, Douglas James. *The Mad Mullah of Somaliland.* London: H. Jenkins, 1923.

Jayakar, Atmaran Sadashiva Grandin. *Omani Proverbs.* Cambridge: Oleander Press, 1987.

Jayasuriya, Shihan de Silva, and Jean-Pierre Angenot. *Uncovering the History of Africans in Asia.* Leiden: Brill, 2008.

Jones, Geoffrey, Frances Bostock, Grigori Gerenstein, Judith Nichol, and Alfred D. Chandler. *The History of the British Bank of the Middle East.* London: Cambridge University Press, 1986.

Jones, Lowri M. Review of the exhibition "Bombay Africans 1850–1910." *History Workshop Journal* 65 (2008): 271–74.

Kalpagam, U. "Colonial Governmentality and the 'Economy.'" *Economy and Society* 29, no. 3 (January 1, 2000): 418–38.

Karras, Alan L. *Smuggling: Contraband and Corruption in World History.* Lanham, MD: Rowman and Littlefield, 2010.

Keynes, John Maynard. *Indian Currency and Finance.* London: Macmillan, 1913.

Kirman, Alan P., and Nicolaas J. Vriend. "Learning to Be Loyal: A Study of the Marseille Fish Market." In *Interaction and Market Structure,* edited by Domenico Delli Gatti, Mauro Gallegati, and Alan P. Kirman, 33–56. Berlin: Springer, 2000.

Kolsky, Elizabeth. *Colonial Justice in British India.* Cambridge: Cambridge University Press, 2010.

Kula, Witold. *Measures and Men.* 2nd ed. Princeton, NJ: Princeton University Press, 2014.

Kuran, Timur. *The Long Divergence: How Islamic Law Held Back the Middle East.* Princeton, NJ: Princeton University Press, 2012.

Kuroda, Akinobu. "The Maria Theresa Dollar in the Early Twentieth-Century Red Sea Region: A Complementary Interface between Multiple Markets." *Financial History Review* 14, no. 1 (2007): 89–110.

Lane, Frederick C. *Profits from Power: Readings in Protection Rent and Violence-Controlling Enterprises.* Albany: SUNY Press, 1979.

"Law and Police: The Charge of Cheating the Chartered Mercantile Bank." *Times of India,* February 10, 1891, 3.

Layton, Simon. "The 'Moghul's Admiral': Angrian 'Piracy' and the Rise of British Bombay." *Journal of Early Modern History* 17, no. 1 (January 2013): 75–93.

Leonard, Karen Isaksen. "Family Firms in Hyderabad: Gujarati, Goswami, and Marwari Patterns of Adoption, Marriage, and Inheritance." *Comparative Studies in Society and History* 53, no. 4 (October 2011): 827–54.

Leur, J. C. Van. *Indonesian Trade and Society: Essays in Asian Social and Economic History.* The Hague: W. Van Hoeve, 1955.

Lewis, I. M. *A Modern History of the Somali: Nation and State in the Horn of Africa.* 4th ed. Athens: Ohio University Press, 2003.

Lydon, Ghislaine. *On Trans-Saharan Trails: Islamic Law, Trade Networks and Cross-Cultural Exchange in Nineteenth-Century West Africa.* New York: Cambridge University Press, 2009.

Machado, Pedro. *Ocean of Trade: South Asian Merchants, Africa and the Indian Ocean, c.1750–1850.* Cambridge: Cambridge University Press, 2014.

MacKenzie, Donald A. *An Engine, Not a Camera: How Financial Models Shape Markets.* Cambridge, MA: MIT Press, 2006.

MacKenzie, Donald A., Fabian Muniesa, and Lucia Siu, eds. *Do Economists Make Markets? On the Performativity of Economics.* Princeton, NJ: Princeton University Press, 2007.

Mankabady, Samir. "Insurance and Islamic Law: The Islamic Insurance Company." *Arab Law Quarterly* 4, no. 3 (August 1, 1989): 199–205.

Markovits, Claude. *The Global World of Indian Merchants, 1750–1947: Traders of Sind from Bukhara to Panama.* Cambridge: Cambridge University Press, 2000.

Marx, Karl. *Capital: A Critique of Political Economy.* Edited by Friedrich Engels and Ernest Mandel. Translated by David Fernbach. Harmondsworth, UK: Penguin Books, 1978.

———. *Grundrisse: Foundation of the Critique of Political Economy (Rough Draft).* Translated by Martin Nicolaus. 2nd ed. London: Penguin, 1993.

Masud, Muhammad Khalid, Brinkley Morris Messick, and David Stephan Powers, eds. *Islamic Legal Interpretation: Muftis and Their Fatwas.* Cambridge, MA: Harvard University Press, 1996.

Mathew, Johan. "Moral Economies of Violence across the Arabian Sea Littoral." In *Trading Circuits, Mobile Cultures: Port Cities and Littoral Societies of the Indian Ocean.* Mumbai: K. R. Cama Institute, forthcoming.

———. "Trafficking Labour: Abolition and the Exchange of Labor across the Arabian Sea, 1861–1947." *Slavery and Abolition: A Journal of Slave and Post-Slave Studies* 33, no. 1 (2012): 139–56.

Maurer, Bill. "Anthropological and Accounting Knowledge in Islamic Banking and Finance: Rethinking Critical Accounts." *Journal of the Royal Anthropological Institute* 8, no. 4 (December 2002): 645–67.

McCloskey, Deirdre N. *The Rhetoric of Economics.* 2nd ed. Madison: University of Wisconsin Press, 1998.

McDonald, Hamish. *The Polyester Prince: The Rise of Dhirubhai Ambani.* St. Leonards, Australia: Allen and Unwin, 1999.

McDow, Thomas. "Deeds of Free Slaves." In *Indian Ocean Slavery in the Age of Abolition,* edited by Robert W. Harms, Bernard K. Freamon, and David W. Blight, 160–82. New Haven, CT: Yale University Press, 2013.

McGoey, Linsey. "Strategic Unknowns: Towards a Sociology of Ignorance." *Economy and Society* 41, no. 1 (2012): 1–16.

McGuire, John. "Exchange Banks, India and the World Economy: 1850–1914." *Asian Studies Review* 29, no. 2 (June 2005): 143–63.

Mehta, Asoka. *Indian Shipping: A Case Study of the Working of Imperialism.* Bombay: N.T. Shroff, 1940.

Meilink-Roelofsz, M. A. P. *Asian Trade and European Influence in the Indonesian Archipelago between 1500 and about 1630.* The Hague: M. Nijhoff, 1962.

Metcalf, Thomas R. *Imperial Connections: India in the Indian Ocean Arena, 1860–1920.* Berkeley: University of California Press, 2008.

Midura, Edward. "Flags of the Arab World." *Saudi Aramco World* 29, no. 2 (April 1978): 4–9.

Miers, Suzanne. *Britain and the Ending of the Slave Trade.* New York: Africana Publishing, 1975.

———. "Slave Resistance and Rebellion in the Aden Protectorate in the Mid-Twentieth Century." In *Slavery and Resistance in Africa and Asia,* edited by Edward A. Alpers, Gwyn Campbell, and Michael Salman, 99–108. London: Routledge, 2005.

Mitchell, Timothy. *Colonising Egypt.* Berkeley: University of California Press, 1988.

———. "Economentality: How the Future Entered Government." *Critical Inquiry* 40, no. 4 (June 1, 2014): 479–507.

———. "Fixing the Economy." *Cultural Studies* 12, no. 1 (January 1, 1998): 82–101.

———. "The Limits of the State: Beyond Statist Approaches and Their Critics." *American Political Science Review* 85, no. 1 (March 1, 1991): 77–96.

———. "The Properties of Markets." In *Do Economists Make Markets? On the Performativity of Economics.* Princeton, NJ: Princeton University Press, 2007.

———. *Rule of Experts: Egypt, Techno-Politics, Modernity.* Berkeley: University of California Press, 2002.

Monfreid, Henry de. *Pearls, Arms and Hashish: Pages from the Life of a Red Sea Navigator.* Translated by Ida Treat. New York: Coward-McCann, 1930.

———. *Secrets of the Red Sea.* Translated by Helen Buchanan Bell. London: Faber and Faber, 1934.

Morris, Errol, dir. *The Unknown Known.* Prod. History Films, 2014.

Munro, J. Forbes. *Maritime Enterprise and Empire: Sir William Mackinnon and His Business Network, 1823–93.* Woodbridge, UK: Boydell Press, 2003.

Mwangi, Wambui. "Of Coins and Conquest: The East African Currency Board, the Rupee Crisis, and the Problem of Colonialism in the East African Protectorate." *Comparative Studies in Society and History* 43, no. 4 (October 2001): 763–87.

———. "The Order of Money: Colonialism and the East African Currency Board." PhD diss., University of Pennsylvania, 2003.

Naoroji, Dadabhai. *Poverty and Un-British Rule in India.* 1901. Reprint, Ulan Press, 2012.

———. *Poverty of India, Papers and Statistics.* 1888. Reprint, Forgotten Books, 2012.

North, Douglass C., and Robert Paul Thomas. *The Rise of the Western World: A New Economic History.* Cambridge: Cambridge University Press, 1973.

Nwulia, Moses D. *Britain and Slavery in East Africa.* Washington, DC: Three Continents Press, 1975.

Officer, Lawrence. "Gold Standard." Edited by Robert Whaples. *EH.Net Encyclopedia,* March 26, 2008. http://eh.net/encyclopedia/article/officer.gold.standard.

Onley, James. *The Arabian Frontier of the British Raj: Merchants, Rulers, and the British in the Nineteenth-Century Gulf.* Oxford: Oxford University Press, 2007.

Pamuk, Şevket. *A Monetary History of the Ottoman Empire.* Cambridge: Cambridge University Press, 2000.

Pankhurst, Richard. "The Ethiopian Slave Trade in the Nineteenth and Early Twentieth Centuries: A Statistical Inquiry." *Journal of Semitic Studies* 9, no. 1 (1964): 220–28.

———. "The Perpetuation of the Maria Theresa Dollar and Currency Problems in Italian-Occupied Ethiopia, 1936–41." *Journal of Ethiopian Studies* 8, no. 2 (July 1970): 89–117.

Parthasarathi, Prasannan. "Was There Capitalism in Early Modern India?" In *Rethinking a Millennium: Perspectives on Indian History from the Eighth to the Eighteenth Century,* edited by Rajat Datta, 342–60. New Delhi: Aakar Books, 2008.

Patel, Zarina. *Alibhai Mulla Jeevanjee.* Makers of Kenya's History 11. Nairobi: East African Educational Publishers, 2002.

———. *Challenge to Colonialism: The Struggle of Alibhai Mulla Jeevanjee for Equal Rights in Kenya.* Nairobi: African Books Collective, 1997.

Patinkin, Don, and Otto Steiger. "In Search of the 'Veil of Money' and the 'Neutrality of Money': A Note on the Origin of Terms." *Scandinavian Journal of Economics* 91, no. 1 (March 1989): 131–46.

Pearson, M. N. *The Indian Ocean.* London: Routledge, 2003.

———. "Littoral Society: The Concept and the Problems." *Journal of World History* 17, no. 4 (2006): 353–73.

Phillips-Birt, Douglas. *Fore and Aft Sailing Craft and the Development of the Modern Yacht.* London: Seeley, 1962.

Podolny, Joel M., and Fiona M. Scott Morton. "Social Status, Entry and Predation: The Case of British Shipping Cartels, 1879–1929." *Journal of Industrial Economics* 47, no. 1 (March 1999): 41–67.

Polanyi, Karl. *The Great Transformation.* Boston: Beacon Press, 1957.

A Popular Introduction to Rifled Ordnance, by an Artilleryman: For the Use of Learners of the Art of Gunnery. Woolwich, UK: Boddy, 1871.

Porter, Theodore M. *The Rise of Statistical Thinking, 1820–1900.* Princeton, NJ: Princeton University Press, 1986.

Powell, Avril A. "Indian Muslim Modernists and the Issue of Slavery in Islam." In *Slavery and South Asian History,* edited by Indrani Chatterjee and Richard Maxwell Eaton, 262–86. Bloomington: Indiana University Press, 2006.

Powell, Eve Troutt. *A Different Shade of Colonialism: Egypt, Great Britain, and the Mastery of the Sudan.* Berkeley: University of California Press, 2003.

Prakash, Gyan. *Bonded Histories: Genealogies of Labor Servitude in Colonial India.* Cambridge: Cambridge University Press, 1990.

Prange, Sebastian R. "The Contested Sea: Regimes of Maritime Violence in the Pre-modern Indian Ocean." *Journal of Early Modern History* 17, no. 1 (January 2013): 9–33.

———. "A Trade of No Dishonor: Piracy, Commerce, and Community in the Western Indian Ocean, Twelfth to Sixteenth Century." *American Historical Review* 116, no. 5 (December 2011): 1269–93.

Prestholdt, Jeremy. *Domesticating the World: African Consumerism and the Genealogies of Globalization.* Berkeley: University of California Press, 2008.

al-Qasimi, Sultan Muhammad. *The Myth of Arab Piracy in the Gulf.* London: Croom Helm, 1986.

Raman, Bhavani. *Document Raj: Writing and Scribes in Early Colonial South India.* Chicago: University of Chicago Press, 2012.

Randeraad, Nico. "The International Statistical Congress (1853–1876): Knowledge Transfers and Their Limits." *European History Quarterly* 41, no. 1 (January 2011): 50–65.

Ray, Rajat Kanta. "Asian Capital in the Age of European Domination: The Rise of the Bazaar, 1800–1914." *Modern Asian Studies* 29, no. 3 (July 1995): 449–554.

"The Reluctant Don." *Times of India,* April 11, 1993, 13.

Ricks, Thomas M. "Slaves and Slave Traders in the Persian Gulf, 18th and 19th Centuries: An Assessment." In *The Economics of the Indian Ocean Slave Trade in the Nineteenth Century,* edited by William Gervase Clarence-Smith, 60–70. London: Frank Cass, 1989.

Rispler-Chaim, Vardit. "Insurance and Semi-insurance Transactions in Islamic History until the 19th Century." *Journal of the Economic and Social History of the Orient* 34, no. 3 (January 1991): 142–58.

Robertson, Claire C., and Martin A. Klein. *Women and Slavery in Africa.* Madison: University of Wisconsin Press, 1983.

Roitman, Janet. *Fiscal Disobedience: An Anthropology of Economic Regulation in Central Africa.* Princeton, NJ: Princeton University Press, 2005.

Roy, Tirthankar. "Sardars, Jobbers, Kanganies: The Labour Contractor and Indian Economic History." *Modern Asian Studies* 42, no. 5 (September 2008): 971–98.

Royal Statistical Society. *Jubilee Volume of the Statistical Society, June 22–24, 1885.* London: Edward Stanford, 1885.

Rudner, David West. "Banker's Trust and the Culture of Banking among the Nattukottai Chettiars of Colonial South India." *Modern Asian Studies* 23, no. 3 (January 1989): 417–58.

———. *Caste and Capitalism in Colonial India: The Nattukottai Chettiars*. Berkeley: University of California Press, 1994.

Sālimī, 'Abd Allāh ibn Ḥumayyid. *Jawābāt al-Imām al-Sālimī*. Edited by 'Abd al-Sattār Abū Ghuddah. 6 vols. Muscat: Maktabat al-Imām al-Sālimī, 2010.

Schabas, Margaret. "The Temporal Dimension in Hume's Monetary Theory." In *David Hume's Political Economy*, edited by Margaret Schabas and Carl Wennerlind. London: Routledge, 2008.

Schabas, Margaret, and Carl Wennerlind. *David Hume's Political Economy*. London: Routledge, 2008.

———. "Retrospectives: Hume on Money, Commerce, and the Science of Economics." *Journal of Economic Perspectives* 25, no. 3 (August 2011): 217–30.

Schacht, Joseph. "Problems of Modern Islamic Legislation." *Studia Islamica,* no. 12 (January 1960): 99–129.

Schaefer, Charles. "'Selling at a Wash': Competition and the Indian Merchant Community in Aden Crown Colony." *Comparative Studies of South Asia, Africa and the Middle East* 19, no. 2 (1999): 16–23.

Schwartzberg, Joseph. "Nautical Maps." In *The History of Cartography*, edited by J. B. Harley and David Woodward, vol. 2. Chicago: University of Chicago Press, 1992.

Scott, James. *Seeing Like a State: How Certain Schemes to Improve the Human Condition Have Failed*. New Haven, CT: Yale University Press, 1998.

Seccombe, I. J., and R. I. Lawless. "Foreign Worker Dependence in the Gulf, and the International Oil Companies: 1910–50." *International Migration Review* 20, no. 3 (October 1986): 548–74.

Seshadri, R. K. *From Crisis to Convertability: The External Value of the Rupee.* Madras: Orient Blackswan, 1993.

Shayzarī, 'Abd al-Raḥmān ibn Naṣr. *Nihāyat al-rutba fī ṭalab al-Ḥisba* [The utmost authority in the pursuit of Ḥisba]. Translated by Ronald Paul Buckley. Oxford: Oxford University Press, 1999.

Sheikh, Munir A. "A Theory of Risk, Smuggling and Welfare." *World Development* 17, no. 12 (December 1989): 1931–44.

Sheikh, Samira. "A Gujarati Map and Pilot Book of the Indian Ocean, c.1750." *Imago Mundi* 61, no. 1 (January 2009): 67–83.

Sheriff, Abdul. *Afro-Arab Interaction in the Indian Ocean: Social Consequences of the Dhow Trade.* Cape Town, South Africa: Centre for Advanced Studies of African Society, 2001.

———. *Dhow Cultures and the Indian Ocean: Cosmopolitanism, Commerce, and Islam.* New York: Columbia University Press, 2010.

———. *Slaves, Spices, and Ivory in Zanzibar: Integration of an East African Commercial Empire into the World Economy, 1770–1873.* London: J. Currey, 1987.

———. "Social Mobility in Indian Ocean Slavery." In *Indian Ocean Slavery in the Age of Abolition*, edited by Robert W. Harms, Bernard K. Freamon, and David W. Blight, 143–59. New Haven, CT: Yale University Press, 2013.

Simpson, Edward. *Muslim Society and the Western Indian Ocean: The Seafarers of Kachchh*. London: Routledge, 2007.

Singh, Anil. "Films Being Used as Convenient Laundromat by Dubious Players." *Times of India,* January 14, 2001, 5.

Smith, Adam. *An Inquiry into the Nature and Causes of the Wealth of Nations*. Edited by Edwin Cannan. London: Methuen, 1904.

Sood, Gagan D. S. "'Correspondence Is Equal to Half a Meeting': The Composition and Comprehension of Letters in Eighteenth-Century Islamic Eurasia." *Journal of the Economic and Social History of the Orient* 50, no. 2 (June 1, 2007): 172–211.

———. "The Informational Fabric of Eighteenth-Century India and the Middle East: Couriers, Intermediaries and Postal Communication." *Modern Asian Studies* 43, no. 5 (2009): 1085–1116.

Soucek, Priscilla. "Coinage of the Qajars: A System in Continual Transition." *Iranian Studies* 34, no. 1/4 (January 2001): 51–87.

Speake, Jennifer. *A Dictionary of Proverbs*. Oxford: Oxford University Press, 2008.

Spivak, Gayatri Chakravorty. "Can the Subaltern Speak?" In *Marxism and the Interpretation of Culture,* edited by Cary Nelson and Lawrence Grossberg, 66–111. Urbana: University of Illinois Press, 1988.

Srivastava, Sanjeev. "Bollywood and the Mafia." *BBC News, South Asia,* October 1, 2003. http://news.bbc.co.uk/2/hi/south_asia/3152662.stm.

Stanziani, Alessandro. "Beyond Colonialism: Servants, Wage Earners and Indentured Migrants in Rural France and on Reunion Island (c. 1750–1900)." *Labor History* 54, no. 1 (February 2013): 64–87.

Steensgaard, Niels. *Carracks, Caravans and Companies: The Structural Crisis in the European-Asian Trade in the Early 17th Century*. Lund, Denmark: Studentlitteratur, 1973.

Stigler, George J. "The Economics of Information." *Journal of Political Economy* 69, no. 3 (June 1, 1961): 213–25.

Subrahmanyam, Sanjay, and C. A. Bayly. "Portfolio Capitalists and the Political Economy of Early Modern India." *Indian Economic and Social History Review* 25, no. 4 (December 1988): 401–24.

Subramanian, Lakshmi. "Of Pirates and Potentates: Maritime Jurisdiction and the Construction of Piracy in the Indian Ocean." *UTS Review: Cultural Studies and New Writing* 6, no. 2 (November 2000): 14–23.

Sweeney, Patrick B. "A Game Warden's Permit for a Corpse: The Life and Times of a Customs Officer." Self-published MS in British Library, n.d.

Tagliacozzo, Eric. *Secret Trades, Porous Borders: Smuggling and States along a Southeast Asian Frontier, 1865–1915*. New Haven, CT: Yale University Press, 2005.

Thompson, Virginia, and Richard Adloff. *Djibouti and the Horn of Africa*. Stanford, CA: Stanford University Press, 1968.

"The 3 1/2 per Cent. Loan of 1900–1." *Times of India,* July 5, 1900, 5.

"The 3 per Cent. Loan." *Times of India,* August 15, 1901, 3.

Thurston, Edgar. *History of the Coinage of the Territories of the East India Company in the Indian Peninsula and Catalogue of the Coins in the Madras Museum.* New Delhi: Asian Educational Services, 1992.

Tinker, Hugh. *A New System of Slavery: The Export of Indian Labour Overseas 1830–1920.* London: Hansib, 1993.

Toledano, Ehud R. *As If Silent and Absent: Bonds of Enslavement in the Islamic Middle East.* New Haven, CT: Yale University Press, 2007.

Tooze, J. Adam. *Statistics and the German State, 1900–1945: The Making of Modern Economic Knowledge.* Cambridge: Cambridge University Press, 2001.

Trivellato, Francesca. *The Familiarity of Strangers: The Sephardic Diaspora, Livorno, and Cross-Cultural Trade in the Early Modern Period.* New Haven, CT: Yale University Press, 2012.

———. "From Livorno to Goa and Back: Merchant Networks and the Coral-Diamond Trade in the Early-Eighteenth Century." *Portuguese Studies* 16 (January 2000): 193–217.

Tsing, Anna Lowenhaupt. *Friction: An Ethnography of Global Connection.* Princeton, NJ: Princeton University Press, 2004.

Udovitch, Abraham L. *Partnership and Profit in Medieval Islam.* Princeton, NJ: Princeton University Press, 1970.

Vianello, Alessandra, and Mohamed M. Kassim. *Servants of the Sharia: The Civil Register of the Qadis' Court of Brava, 1893–1900.* Leiden: Brill, 2006.

Villiers, Alan. "Some Aspects of the Arab Dhow Trade." *Middle East Journal* 2, no. 4 (October 1948): 399–416.

———. *Sons of Sinbad: An Account of Sailing with the Arabs in Their Dhows.* New York: Charles Scribner and Sons, 1940.

Vink, Markus. "'The World's Oldest Trade': Dutch Slavery and Slave Trade in the Indian Ocean in the Seventeenth Century." *Journal of World History* 14, no. 2 (2003): 131–77.

Wallerstein, Immanuel. *The Modern World-System: Capitalist Agriculture and the Origins of the European World-Economy in the Sixteenth Century.* Vol. 1. Berkeley: University of California Press, 2011.

———. *World-Systems Analysis: An Introduction.* Durham, NC: Duke University Press, 2004.

White, Harrison C. *Markets from Networks: Socioeconomic Models of Production.* Princeton, NJ: Princeton University Press, 2002.

Wickramasinghe, Nira. *Dressing the Colonised Body: Politics, Clothing, and Identity in Sri Lanka.* New Delhi: Orient Blackswan, 2003.

Willis, John M. *Unmaking North and South: Cartographies of the Yemeni Past, 1857–1934.* New York: Columbia University Press, 2012.

Winichakul, Thongchai. *Siam Mapped: A History of the Geo-Body of a Nation.* Honolulu: University of Hawaii Press, 1997.

Zaid, Omar Abdullah. "Accounting Systems and Recording Procedures in the Early Islamic State." *Accounting Historians Journal* 31, no. 2 (December 2004): 149–70.

Zaidi, S. Hussain. *Dongri to Dubai: Six Decades of the Mumbai Mafia.* New Delhi: Roli Books, 2012.

———. "The Reluctant Mafioso." *Livemint.com,* July 9, 2010. www.livemint.com/2010/07/09191326/The-reluctant-Mafioso.html.

INDEX

accounting practices, 153, *154,* 155

Aden, 13, 46, 166; British authorities in, 25; as coal depot, 39; dhow owners in port of, 29; emancipated slaves in, 74–75; Indian rupee as currency of, 124; market in Maria Theresa thalers, 134; piracy and conquest of, 88

adoption, slavery appearing as, 53, 69–70, 80

advertising, 164

Afghanistan, 89, *92,* 93–94, 103

Ahmednagar Mission School, 77

Ambani, Dhirubhai, 134–35

Amina (enslaved woman from Georgia), 78

Arab Gulf states, 37, 55, 124

Arabia/Arabian Peninsula, 63, 65, 78, 90; arms trade in, 91, 95; British colonial rule in, 90; currencies used in, 114, 120, 141; customs revenues in, 108; manumission and re-enslavement in, 74; slavery and slave trade in, 55, 57, 59, 62; women legally imported into, 71; World War II and Arab Revolt in, 110

Arabian Sea trade, 2, 8, 31; anti-slave patrols in, 67; Arabian Sea as liminal space, 174; arms trade, 104; British Empire dominance of, 13; coal depots and, 38–39; currency and specie flows, 124, *125;* dangers of, 23; laws structuring, 12; marginal utility in, 19–20; property rights and, 92; ships and, 18; slaves as integral part of, 58, 59; space and time of, 3–5

Arabic language, 16, 68, 72, 78, 103

arbitrage, 13, 14, 16, 20, 30–31, 176; commercial intelligence and, 144–45, 152; in currency, 135, 151, 179

arms (firearms, weapons) trade, 6, 19, 82–83; colonial regulations concerning, 92–104; commodity/contraband distinction and, 98–104; major distributions paths (map), *92;* private property and, 84–86; state monopoly on violence and, 86–92; state/society distinction and, 104–11; visibility of, 93, 97, 99; *wilayati* cartridges, 103, 202n79

Bab al-Mandeb, 25, 27–29, *28–29*

badli transactions, 139–140

Bagamoyo, 61, 66

Bahrain, 42, 70, 82, 131; arms trade in, 99, 107; British control of shipping services, 123

Baluchistan, 55, *55,* 59, 66

Baluchistan, SS, 81, 93, 97, 111

Bandar Abbas, 78, 96

bandars, 39–40

banias (Hindu merchants), 86, 104, 107, 125, 137

banks and bankers, 116–17, 123, 135–141, 142; documentation and, 160; exchange banks, 141, 178. See also *specific banks*

Bartle Frere, Henry, 61

Benaresi, Mahomed Reza, 73

Besse, Antonin, 134, 151

black market, 103

blockades, 40–41, 42, 43

"Blue Books," 169, 170

Bollywood film industry, 174

Bombay, 38, 41, 42, 56, 148; arms trade in, 94, 95, 97, 103, 105–106, 108; banks in, 137; brokers for registration of vessels in, 30; as coal depot, 39; colonial monetary policy in, 119; counterfeiting in, 127–28; freed slaves in, 77–79, 81; Haji Mastan network in, 173–74; Sidi community, 78–79

Bombay Steam Navigation Company, 46

bond system (shipping), 41, 42

borders, 6, 18, 130, 141; arms trade and, 85, 90; blurred, 12; closing of, 37, 51, 90–92; counterfeiting and, 127, 128; flows of money across, 113, 116; as frontiers for expansion, 1; maps and, 24; maritime borders of legal trade, *55;* security of private property and, 19

Borneo, 75

bribery, 43, 66

British Empire, 5, 13, 23, 30, 94, 110, 174; abolition of slave trade and, 54, 59; arms trade and, 103–104; banks and monetary authority of, 136; century of dominance in the Arabian Sea, 178; control over legitimate trade, 41; dhow traffic and, 23; French tensions with, 35–36; Great Game with Imperial Russia, 89; labor of freed slaves and, 79, 80; Maria Theresa thaler and, 133–34; monopoly on maritime violence, 87–90; protectionism versus free trade in, 166–67; racial dynamics of colonialism, 105; scientific cartography and, 28; standardized imperial weights, 162; steamship lines and, 44–45; technologies standardized throughout, 33; transactions sanctioned by, 14. *See also* Royal Navy

British India Steam Navigation Company, 33, 50; BISN, 46–47

Brussels Conference (re: slave trade), 25, 26, 35, 36–37, 38, 91

Bunce, Commander (Royal Navy), 61

bureaucracies, 4, 17, 161, 172, 173; attempts to disarm the population, 95; banking and, 136; capitalist markets defined by, 12–13; customs, 20, 43; free markets and, 8, 9; global monetary flows and, 114; invoices and, 143; market prices and, 146, 147; regulation of the market and, 85; transportation organized by, 33

al Bu-Saʿīdī dynasty, 96; Sayyid Saʿīd, 54, 60, 67; Sayyid Thuwainī ibn Saʿīd, 70; Sayyid Turkī ibn Saʿīd, 70

al-Bustan, Naz, 70–71, 72

Callon, Michel, 7, 9

capitalism, 3, 49, 83, 111–12, 136, 172; anachronisms integrated into, 11; *badli* transactions and, 140; capital as basic factor of production, 6; constant reframing of, 178; contrivance and arbitrage in history of, 14; dhows in infrastructure of, 51; documentation in history of, 179; expulsion of trades and, 8; framing out of the market and, 175; imperial patronage and, 16; interest-bearing capital, 7; limits and, 1, 2, 183n1; Marxist analyses of, 179; money and, 115; multivalence of, 10; performativity of, 11, 178–79, 180; private property and, 84; slave trade and, 65. *See also* commodities; political economy

"cash price," 169

Caucasus, slaves from, 59, 70

censorship, 17

Central Asia, 127, 128

Certeau, Michel de, 12, 184n20

Ceylon Steam Navigation Company, 46

Chapparband tribe, 126–27

charity, 19, 69, 132, 133

China, 3

Chindwara, SS, 50

Churchill, Winston, 89, 99

Church Missionary Society, 75

Circassians, 70

coal, shipping and, 38–39

coins, 7, 19, 114, 115; counterfeiting of, 118, 121, 206n29; gold, 117, 122, 131, 178; minted by East India Company, 119; monetary theory and, 117; Mughal coinage, 118, 119–120; *shroff* markings, 121–23; silver, 120–21, 205n26; smuggling of, 131; as speculative commodity, 116. *See also* Maria Theresa thaler; rupee, British-Indian; Qajar *kran*

Cold War, 5

colonial regimes, 8–9, 11, 12; abolition of slave trade and, 54; dhows neglected by, 22, 23, 51; freed slaves and, 76; limits of territorial power, 18; maps and, 23, 28, 38; monetary policy of, 116; shipping regulations, 31–32, 34; slave trade and, 52–53, 68; standards implemented by, 158; statistics and, 170–71

commodities, 2, 4, 85, 162; ambiguous relation to contraband, 86, 112; coins as speculative commodities, 116; contraband in same spaces as, 8, 84, 98–104; as intermediaries, 7; tariff rebates on, 167

Comoros Islands, 36

compliance, contrived, 12, 20

contraband, 8, 85, 132, 173; ambiguous relation to the commodity, 86, 98–104, 112; confiscation of, 9; firearms as, 84; human bodies as, 19

contracts, 17, 45, 74, 168; enforcement of, 144, 150; extension of, 153; government, 16; marriage, 71, 72

contrivance, 12, 14, 20, 26

"coolies," 76–77

cosmopolitanism, 4

counterfeits/counterfeiting, 7, 114, 118; cheating distinguished from, 121; concealment (invisibility) of, 125–132; difficulty of distinguishing from the genuine, 8; of gold and silver coins, 127–28

Cowasjee Dinshaw and Brothers, 32, 46

cowry shells, as currency, 118, 119, 123

credit, 31, 115, 137, 156; "cash price" and, 169; exchange banks as providers of, 139; market prices and, 152

customs, 6, 8, 10, 51, 163; arms trade and, 95, 98, 99, 100, 102, 107–108; of British India, 91; deceptive documentation and, 159–161; expanding bureaucracy of, 43; firearms as threat to property rights, 93; gold smuggling and, 130, 131; of Gulf sheikhdoms, 42; marginalist economics and, 146; merchant networks and, 20;

money flows across international borders and, 113–14; of Muscat sultanate, 83; standardized market transactions and, 11, 158; time of importation and, 168; value and, 161; wartime restrictions and, 41

Dar-es-Salaam, 61

Da Silva, Angelo, 159

debt bondage, 56, 57

Deccan Industrial School, 77

Dee, HMS, 61

deeds, 17, 52, 80

Dhamanmal Isardas (firm), 125

Dhofar, 70

dhows (littoral sailing vessels), 18, 31, 51, 178; advantages of, 31–32; as category of ships, 21–22; convoys of, 27; evasion of British naval patrols by, 30; flags and jurisdiction of, 34–38; names of, 26–27; nostalgia and romanticism associated with, 21; ports and nodes for, 38–44; pricing of cargo and passages, 47, 51; registration of vessels, 29–30; slave trade and, 56, 58, 59–60, 62, 65, 69; steamships compared with, 22–23; traffics and, 25–34. *See also nākhudās* (dhow captains)

diasporas/diasporic networks, 4, 116, 117, 146, 150–51, 152; Haji Mastan and, 174; reformatted as interstate trade, 157; renegotiation of value in, 153; subversion of regulations by, 160, 178

discounts, trade, 163–64

Djibouti, 13, 35, 42, 92, 96, 102

documentation, 13, 30, 42, 172, 175; altered through bribery, 43; courts and, 16; deceptive, 159–161; forged, 82; history of capitalism and, 179; silences and slippages in, 15, 17, 18, 175; surveillance and, 158; *waraqa* deed, 80; during World War I, 40

double-entry bookkeeping, 153, 155

Dubai, 37, 42, 174, 179

"dumps," as currency, 118

East Africa: abolition of slave trade in, 63–64; currencies used in, 114, 141;

East Africa *(continued)*
  manumission and re-enslavement in,
  74; shilling currency of, 124, 141; slavery
  and slave trade in, 55, *55;* 57, 58, 60;
  Sterling Area monetary system and, 124
Eastern Bank, in Bahrain, 135–36, 140
Eastern Exchange Banks Association, 136
East India Company, British, 6, 87–88, 90,
  118, 119
economics, 9–10, 145; Keynesian, 173;
  marginalist, 11, 19, 145, 146, 159; neoclassical, 84, 146; performativity of, 9
economies of scale, 22, 24, 31, 41; arms trade
  and, 93, 95; gold smuggling and, 132;
  steamship lines and, 43, 51
engagé system, 76
English language, 77
Erythraean Sea. *See* Red Sea
Ethiopia, 5, 13, 59, 79, 102; Italian conquest
  of, 110, 133–34; *näggadras* merchants, 108
exchange, 2, 4, 7, 144, 172, 175; boundaries
  between market and nonmarket, 19;
  constraints on, 6; diasporic, 14; gift, 19;
  monetized, 10; money and, 115; networks
  of, 6; organized outside the market, 178;
  ritual, 19; stabilization of, 116; statistical
  measurement and, 11–12; trafficking as,
  5; use-value and exchange-value, 145

Fiji, 75
firearms. *See* arms (firearms, weapons) trade
Fisher, Irving, 141
flags, maritime jurisdiction and, 34–38
Foucault, Michel, 9
Fracis Times and Company, 107
framing, 9, 12, 29, 177; of common currency, 117–124; of human bodies, 81; of
  security of property relations, 112; slave
  trade and, 53
framing out, 11, 12, 147, 174–75; defined, 8,
  9; dhows versus steamship lines, 23, 24;
  silences of colonial archive and, 16; of
  slavery, 54, 84; of violence from markets, 84, 86
France and French colonies, 13, 35–36, 44;
  flag and jurisdiction of, 35–36, 50, 51, 67;
  national shipping lines, 45; plantations
  in Indian Ocean, 76. *See also* Djibouti

Frank C. Strick and Company, 46, *48*
fraud, 19, 138, 161, 169; deterrence and
  policing of, 116, 136; misstated geographic origins, 166; in Mombasa
  customs house, 160; ubiquity of, 179
free markets, 24, 116, 147, 159, 177; as arbiters of value, 145; arms trade and, 82, 83,
  95; in labor, 53, 56, 73, 77, 80; racialized
  discourse and, 89–90; trafficking networks and, 172; transportation prices
  and, 23, 49; violence and, 83, 84, 112
free trade: gunboat diplomacy and, 6;
  imperial expansion and, 83; low tariffs
  associated with, 166; smuggling as, 1;
  statistical standards and, 157–59; steamship lines and, 18, 46

General Treaty of Peace (1820, Gulf), 88
geography, 3, 18, 164, 166–67, 177
Georgia, 78
Germany: colonies of, 44; national shipping lines, 45
al-Ghalib, Mohammed, 173, 174
Giorgis, Haile, 108
Goa, 13, 43
Goan Christians, 109–10
Goguyer et Cie., 107
gold, 6, 113–14, 115, 173, 178; circulation of,
  125; hoarding of, 117, 118, 122; international gold standard, 7, 19, 120, 136, 141,
  205n26; Mughal *mohur* coins, 119–120;
  smuggling of, 117, 124, 130–31, 132, 135;
  wartime surge in price of, 113
Great Depression, 166
Gujarat, 86, 132–33; Gujarati language, 16,
  160; merchants of, 123, 148
Gulf of Aden, 27, 32, 89
Gwadar, port of, 42, 43

Haleema (child slave), 67–68
al-Hāshimī, Sharif Hussein, 111
ḥawāla (bill of exchange), 129, 153
Hindi language, 77
hinterland markets, 43
ḥisba (Islamic market regulation), 114, 116,
  153, 155
ḥiyal (ruses or maneuvers), 12
hoarding, 117, 118, 122, 142

Ricardo, David, 10, 157
Rigby, Colonel C.P., 64
Royal Commission on Shipping Rings, 46
Royal Navy, 78, 95, 174; arms trade policed
by, 82; as guardian of property rights,
87; incidents with Iranian Navy, 37;
limited resources of, 65–66; monopoly
on maritime violence, 88; slave trade
and, 34–35, 54, 60, 62, 65–66
rupee, British-Indian, 120, 132, 141; circulation of, 122, 123–24, *125;* counterfeiting
of, 128; demonetization of, 120, 124;
East India Company minting of, 118,
119; economic debates and, 141;
exchange rates and, 132, 136

al-Sabah, Mubarak, 109
Safavid Empire, 5
sailors, 16, 37, 43, 175; in the arms trade,
108, 109–10; dhow crews, 21, 27; flags of
jurisdiction and, 34; mitigation of risk
by, 31; silences in documentation and,
18; slaves as, 57, 76; smuggling and, 65
Salalah, port of, 42
Saleha (enslaved Ethiopian girl), 72
al-Sālimi, Abdullah, 14–15
Salman, Ahmed bin, 89
Sassoon, David, 138
Saud, Abdul Aziz ibn, 110–11, 131
Saudi Arabia, 66, 71, 72, 130
Sayyid Ibrahim, 72
Schwarte & Hammer, 93
Scindia Line, 46
*serang*s (labor recruiters), 79
Seychelles, 75
shahi discount, 164
Shah Line, 47
Sharia (Islamic law), 12, 15, 66
Shatt al-Arab, 89, 167
sheikhs/sheikhdoms (Gulf), 5, 37, 136; arms
trade and, 107, 109; customs bureaucra-
cies of, 42; maritime truce imposed on
Gulf sheikhs (1820), 34, 88; piracy and,
88, 89 ·
Sheriff, Abbas Ali, 73
Shihr, port of, 42
*shroff*s [*sarraf*s] (merchant bankers), 121–23,
127, 137, 138–39, 206n28; currency *shroff*

marks, 121–22; exchange banks and,
141, 178
Sidi community, 78–79
silver, 19, 117, 120–21, 127–132, 141, 205n26
slaves/slavery, 2, 6, 53, 175, 178; agricultural
labor and, 68; as bonded laborers, 60;
British officials and perpetuation of, 54;
children, 56–57, 67–68, *68,* 195n67;
documentation of freed slaves, 80;
domestic, 68; lands of origin for slaves,
59; liberated slaves, 73–79; manumission, 53, 69, 73–74; racial distinctions
and, 53; self-interested enslavement, 52
slave trade, 9, 56; Atlantic "middle passage"
compared with, 56–59; barracoons,
60–61; continuation after abolition
treaties, 55; dhows and, 25; French flag
as protection for, 67; intelligence network of slave traders, 66; maritime
borders of legal trade, 54, *55;* overland
routes, 60, 66, 67; Portuguese slave
traders, 61; as transactions in kin,
67–73; visibility of, 53, 68–69; in West
Africa, 60
slave trade, abolition of, 53, 55–56, 59–63;
blockade as weapon against, 40; British
Indians and, 63–64; brokers ignored by
abolitionists, 80; effects of manumission, 73–74; evaded in plain sight of
British authorities, 68–69; kidnapping
("man-stealing") and, 64–65; Royal
Navy actions, 34–35, 65–66
Smith, Adam, 1, 2, 6, 10, 76, 145
smugglers/smuggling, 16, 25, 37, 160; Cold
War and, 5; of highly taxed commodities, 41; "smuggler's cove," 40; statistics
and, 169–172; as ultimate form of free
trade, 1
Socotra, island of, 65
soldiers, in the arms trade, 108–11
Somalia/Somaliland, 13, 40, 66, 75, 102,
103; arms trade and, 83, 99; Indian
rupee as currency of, 124; "Mad
Mullah" in, 89
Soviet Union, 173
Spain, slave trade and, 34–35
statistics, trade, 10, 11, 40, 157–59, 161, 162,
180; arbitrage and, 13; colonial economic

THE CALIFORNIA WORLD HISTORY LIBRARY

*Edited by Edmund Burke III, Kenneth Pomeranz,
and Patricia Seed*

Made in United States
North Haven, CT
23 February 2022

16424758R00159